Journey Around My Flat

Anthony Rudolf's publications include

Poetry
The Same River Twice
After the Dream
Mandorla (illustrated by Julia Farrer)
Broccoli (illustrated by Paul Coldwell)
Zigzag: Five Verse/Prose Sequences
European Hours: Collected Poems

Art
The Jew etc. (on Kitaj)
In the Picture: Office Hours at the Studio of Paula Rego (in progress)
Correspondence with Kitaj (in progress)

Memoirs
The Arithmetic of Memory
Silent Conversations: A Reader's Life
A Vanished Hand: My Autograph Album

Fiction
Kafka's Doll
Pedraterra (forthcoming)
The Mermaid from the Azores (forthcoming)

Literary (etc) Criticism
Byron's 'Darkness'
At an Uncertain Hour: Primo Levi's War against Oblivion
Wine from Two Glasses (Adam Lecture, Kings College London)
Jerzyk: Diaries, Texts and Testimonies
Engraved in Flesh: Piotr Rawicz and his Novel, Blood from the Sky
Rescue Work: Memory and Text
Menard Press Keepsake Catalogue
Isaac Rosenberg (forthcoming)

Edited

MPT (French issue)

MPT (Bonnefoy issue)

Poems for Shakespeare IV

Voices within the Ark: 20th Century Jewish Poets (co-edited with Howard Schwartz)

Sage Eye: the Aesthetic Passion of Jonathan Griffin

Collected Poems and Selected Translations of A.C. Jacobs (co-edited with John Rety)

Nameless Country: Selected poems of A.C.Jacobs (co-edited with Merle Bachman)

The Wedding-Guest: Selected poems of Keith Bosley (co-edited with Owen Lowery)

Yves Bonnefoy Poetry (co-edited with John Naughton and Stephen Romer)

Yves Bonnefoy Prose (co-edited with Stephen Romer and John Naughton)

Paul Claudel: Break of Noon (co-edited with John Naughton)

Book Translations

French Poetry: Yves Bonnefoy (5), Edmond Jabès, Claude Vigée (2)

Russian Poetry: Alexander Tvardovsky, Evgeny Vinokurov

Other Languages: Ifigenija Simonovic, Miriam Neiger-Fleischmann

French Drama and Fiction etc: Ana Novac, Honoré de Balzac, Jean Clair

Verse Play co-translated from Hungarian with the author, Eugene Heimler: The Storm

Journey Around My Flat

An Essay of Informal Inventory

Anthony Rudolf

Shearsman Books

First published in the United Kingdom in 2021 by
Shearsman Books Ltd
PO Box 4239
Swindon
SN3 9FN

Shearsman Books Ltd Registered Office
30–31 St. James Place, Mangotsfield, Bristol BS16 9JB
(this address not for correspondence)

www.shearsman.com

ISBN 978-1-84861-769-8

Typeset by The Book Typesetters
thebooktypesetters.com
us@thebooktypesetters.com
07422 598 168

Acknowledgements

I am grateful to my next-door neighbours Lynn and Una for balcony drinks and help with photography and support during lockdown. Also to Michèle Roberts for regular postal replenishments of herbs from her garden and equally flavoursome email dialogue, following our stroll round Hampstead Garden Suburb on 21 February 2020. Bonne continuation, as she would say.

Thanks to Rosemary Gray for her vital copy-editing *à l'ancienne* and to Susan Saffer for valuable thoughts on a late draft of the book. Thanks to Ron Denny for preparing floor plans. Thanks to Nat and Rachael Ravenlock, as always, for help with design expertise and patience. Thanks, as always, to Tony Frazer for all his qualities, including flexibility.

Thanks to Clive Wilmer and August Kleinzahler for permission to use the postcard from Thom Gunn. © Estate of Thom Gunn.

Thanks to Caroline and Stephanie in the Arnold House School office, to Christine Stephens in the Shrewbury School office, to the three Ks at City of London School, and to Stuart Martell. Also to Frankie Shrapnel, Michael Pennington, Robert MacLeod and James Loudon.

For Paula, who loves (a drink on) the balcony

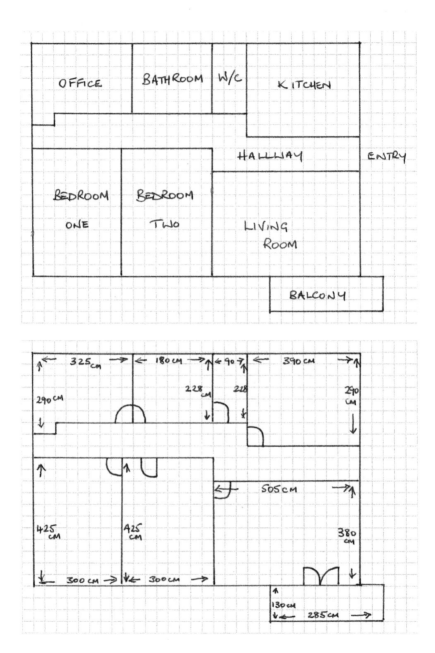

OFFICE   BATHROOM   W/C   KITCHEN

HALLWAY   ENTRY

BEDROOM   BEDROOM   LIVING
ONE   TWO   ROOM

                           BALCONY

325 CM   180 CM   90   390 CM

290 CM   228 CM   228   290 CM

425 CM   425 CM   505 CM

          300 CM   300 CM   380 CM

                                     130 CM   285 CM

Author's Note

The book is largely as written between 2004 and 2009. The main revision took place during lockdown in 2020. With the benefit of hindsight (2020 vision, ha ha), bestowed by the lengthy gap between date of publication and original composition of the manuscript, I have made various changes and updates. Where they are not explicit, I hope they are seamless and for the best.

Not everything in the flat has remained unchanged visually over the years but I have left most of the descriptions of objects and possessions as they were at the time of the 2004–2009 manuscript. I did not make any changes or even look at the text again until 2015/2016, that is to say after the writing and (in 2013) publication of my memoir *Silent Conversations*, a lengthy account of my books. *Silent Conversations* was originally intended to be a chapter in the present work, but the tail (tale) wagged the dog.

To reduce clutter in the main body of the text, I have end-noted published texts of mine that go into greater detail on the subject in question. (Why can't I reduce clutter in the flat itself? Answering that question might involve men in white coats.) Any readers that this book finds will have no problem deploying Google for details of significant third-party books quoted from or mentioned. Many pictures, etc. that I refer to can be Googled.

As for objects, do they begin or end in the imagination? A question for Wallace Stevens, who supplies my three epigraphs; a question for all of us.

– Anthony Rudolf, Woodside Park, 2020

Contents

Oh! blessed rage for order
  WALLACE STEVENS, *'The Idea of Order at Key West'*

A great disorder is an order
  WALLACE STEVENS, *'Connoisseur of Chaos'*

After the leaves have fallen, we return
To a plain sense of things. It is as if
We had come to an end of the imagination.
  WALLACE STEVENS, *'The Plain Sense of Things'*

SECTION ONE

Introduction

I want to explore – in this journey around my flat – aspects of my life as an adult, what I like to think of as my *arrière-pays*, to deploy the neologistic English-language title of Yves Bonnefoy's book, translated by Stephen Romer. Kafka's phrase, 'world history of my soul', comes to mind or, less grandly, certain continuities of feeling and thought that can be discerned in the impasto pentimentos of memory conjured up before my person is discontinued, whether from natural causes, terminal illness, human failings, terrorism or nuclear war. Another possibility is that my paper-laden flat will be destroyed in a fire, and, along with it, those documents and possessions which chart the life of a person whose course, apart from his day jobs, has been mainly on the page, even if much of the time – with all the translating and editing – the page is the page of others. I am not a philosopher or a theologian, a neurologist or a biochemist, or even Ian Dury's ticket man at Fulham Broadway Station. I am a writer, a human being who writes things down, and the time has come to pay attention to the endotic or infra-ordinary landscape of my *arrière-pays*. My early old-timer friends – Jonathan and Kathleen Griffin, George Buchanan, Geoffrey and Joyce Bridson – are long dead, and people who were in their forties when I first knew them in my mid-twenties – including Michael Hamburger and Hyam Maccoby – have joined the original old-timers. Now I am about to join the ranks of the old-timers or am already among them. [*Later: some of my contemporaries, younger and older than me, have died (I have written memorial notices elsewhere), and some have serious cancers; a few have dementia.*]

In an earlier memoir,[1] the rule of the game was to generate memories without reference to documentation or objects or the diaries I would keep for two or three weeks before abandoning them. This time I intend to use my possessions – apart from my books which are discussed in a second earlier memoir[2] – to generate memory and story. I don't often leave this flat, and now that I have a cross trainer exercise machine, I have fewer reasons to go out: thus, no more runs in the park, with cheery hellos to and from the woman with the two collies, no more pebbles picked up and aimed at passing bins and trees, no more fantasies about that couple's sex life, this dog-walking pipe smoker's day job; no more trips to Finchley Lido swimming pool where my races against myself would involve complicated combinations of strokes and lengths to stave off boredom – and no more Lido bonuses: athlete's foot and irritated bladder. Here in this flat, during the self-employed years following the end of my day jobs, I spend/save my life, except for time spent with my lady friend: sitting for her in the studio, taking her to the Barbican Cinema and the adjacent Côte Brasserie, drinking together in the Freemasons Arms, attending private views… and visiting my granddaughter Leah in East Finchley… and Skype time with grandsons Charlie and Jamie in New Zealand: as I said, here in this flat…

What does the future hold? Mental or physical infirmity? I know, we all know, or – along a broader spectrum – know *of*, people who have endured Alzheimer's, with its concomitant physical and mental distress, as I witnessed when visiting my comrade, Daniel Weissbort, who has since died. Later, Lucy Bonnefoy near Paris, in the same condition, has finally left the conversation, in the phrase of her husband Yves about another friend. My San Francisco friend, George Oppen, before being struck down by this terrible affliction, used to say quite beautifully of old age: 'What a strange thing to happen to a little boy.' He chose his epithet to qualify the word 'thing' with the unerring accuracy characteristic of a great poet, which is what he was. Oppen used this phrase (a variant of earlier versions) in a telephone conversation with Paul Auster. So struck was Auster by its power that he in turn phoned me from America, and we marvelled at it together, before agreeing that I should publish it on a MenCard, a Menard Press postcard [*fig. 1*],[3] which I did: twice. On one occasion, according to Donald Davie, Hugh Kenner tried to console George by saying that his poems were out there in the world. 'I would swap places with them any day,' said the afflicted poet. Around the same time I tried to get a translation for the MenCard series from Thom Gunn but failed [*fig. 2*].

The old man and the little boy are not the same person and yet 'at the same time' they are the same person. 'Old man, or lad's love', wrote Edward Thomas: two names for the same flower. I heard Maxim Vengerov on Radio Three explaining that his violin, the Kreisler Stradivarius, was once played in Beethoven's presence. For Vengerov and for this listener too, the association brought out what he called 'goose bumps'. Yes, I know, *the way* Vengerov plays the Kreutzer Sonata would have meant more to Beethoven than the fact it is played on that particular violin, but all the same, these accidental continuities matter, and why they matter shall emerge on this journey, with any luck.

Other Abodes

I have lived in this Woodside Park flat in London N12 since my marriage ended in 1981. Before moving to a top-floor flat at 1 Primrose Gardens off Englands Lane in Belsize Park, I lived for a year in a small flat in Granville Park, a road which leads from Lewisham to Blackheath, and before that in a room at 2 Powis Square, Notting Hill. I lived in Primrose Gardens from 1968 till 1974. In October 1974, my wife Brenda and I, with our infant son Nathaniel, moved to a house in what used to be known as Upper Holloway. It had an Anderson Shelter in the garden. Nathaniel had been born during the famous or infamous 'three-day week' of February 1974, brought about by the confrontation between the government of Edward Heath and the miners. (I wrote a one-line poem for the birth announcement, calligraphed by Janet Berg of Oxford and Jerusalem [*fig. 3*].

In stark contrast, our daughter Naomi was born in August 1976, a summer even hotter than the run of hot summers London has experienced in recent years. A few days before she was born, we visited London Zoo in the company of our friends Hans and Mira Sonderling from Los Angeles. A high point was the Penguin House, designed by the celebrated architect Berthold Lubetkin; I drove the party past another high point, Highpoint, a block of flats in Highgate, not far from Upper Holloway, a rare building by this fascinating radical who gave up architecture to become a farmer. Only once, around 1988, have I been inside Highpoint:

on the insistent recommendation of my then girl friend, the painter Audrey Jones, I went there for an Alexander Technique lesson with Peggy Williams, the last surviving practitioner trained by the founder of the eponymous movement. Peggy passed me on to a colleague of hers in Hampstead. I like the way Alexander practitioners describe the relationship as teacher/student rather than therapist/patient and note that friends of mine, distinguished musicians Naomi Gerecht and Carola Grindea, have used versions of it in combination with their own techniques for improving the breathing and posture of students.

I took over the Primrose Gardens flat from a university friend Nicholas Strauss (now a senior QC and part-time judge), with whom, towards the end of our three years, I used to play early-morning tennis on the Cambridge Backs every day before he went off to study efficiently for finals, unlike me. Primrose Gardens and Upper Holloway both hosted my early work as a writer, poetry translator and editor, while I subsidised these activities with a succession of day jobs which did not engage me.

I have always resisted describing myself as a poet although I may have written – against the grain of my mental inclinations as an abstractionist and conceptualiser – a few poems worthy of the name. Some were even written in direct reaction to recent events in my life, such as the birth of Nathaniel. One was triggered by the times I fed him bottled milk when Brenda went to her evening class in typography and design at the London School of Printing. Now that I have reinvented myself as a short-story writer and autobiographer, I hope that a large assortment of short texts will find publishers: verse and prose poems, literary and other essays, miscellaneous verse translations, interviews and obituaries; oh yes, and a Menard Press anthology. But before those books can even be considered, unpublished and published texts will have to be found or turn up in my chaos of a flat. The present journey to the heart of that chaos might enable me to garner them as a bonus or by-product of my primary concern in this manuscript, which is, as I have said, to generate memory and story from documentation and objects. But what if chaos – inner and outer – is a psychic given for some people, including yours truly? What if without it I would have done nothing at all? This question came up many years later in psychotherapy, four years ostensibly centred on sorting out my complex and complicated mid-life *folie à deux* relationship, the relationship being the theme the experienced therapist the late Deryck

OLD AGE

What a strange thing to happen to a little boy

George Oppen

(*in conversation with Paul Auster*)

MenCard 115A published by The Menard Press as part of its 21st birthday celebrations around 1990. The Menard Press, 8 The Oaks, Woodside Avenue, London N12 8AR. Tel: 01-446 5571

fig. 1

All good things must come to a beginning...
nathaniel david
rudolf
27 february 1974

fig. 3

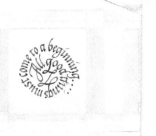

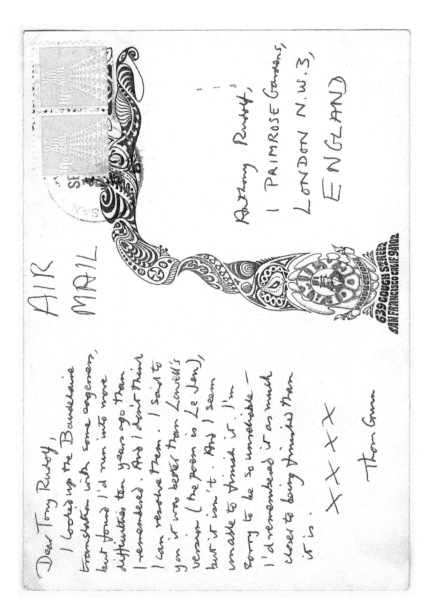

fig. 2

A special Pierre MenCard for our 25th anniversary
In memoriam Chris Skelton and Derek Maggs

THE FIVE LIVES OF

Pierre Menard

1 PIERRE MENARD
   (author of Don Quixote)
   information from the late J-L Borges

2 PIERRE MENARD
   (first Governor-General of Illinois)
   information from Menard author, Paul Auster

3 PIERRE MENARD
   (a late flowering iris)
   information from Menard author, the late Nicholas Moore

4 PIERRE MENARD
   (second violin, Vermeer String Quartet)
   information from Radio Times

5 PIERRE MENARD
   (Journals of)
   information from T. Rudolf and the late Peter Hoy

As some people know, the name of the Press, preceded by the Magazine (see no. 5), was inspired by the eponymous story of Borges (see no. 1), which can be read as a parable of translation. Nos 2, 3 and 4 turned up later.

If anyone wants to call their new baby Petra or Pierre Menard we would be very pleased to add the name to the list above, and eventually to sell the press to her or him, which would be a perfect conflation of life and art – at the very least an act of corporeal translation or trans-textuality.

Petra Menard is an anagram of Pen Dream Art. Pierre Menard is an anagram of Dreamer, Ripen: not bad mottoes as we hasten slowly towards our 30th anniversary in 1999/2000. Lear's 'ripeness is all' echoes with syntactic and alliterative appropriateness – as Yves Bonnefoy pointed out – Hamlet's 'readiness is all'. Not either/or but both/and.

fig. 4

fig. 5

fig. 6

Dyne used as a hook to hang other themes on. If I could decipher my notes written immediately after those sessions, I would learn a lot...

I know, and deeply regret, that I left behind at Primrose Gardens the pair of binoculars my uncle and aunt Isidore and Ethel Rudolf gave me on the occasion of my barmitzvah; it was suitably inscribed. One evening, I was looking through the bedroom window and trained my binoculars on the back of a house in Belsize Park Gardens – as you do – and to the left, quite by chance, saw a young woman in a second-floor bedroom in her underwear, brushing her hair. It was an intimate and intriguing experience. I have a poem[4] about a parallel experience at the Hayward Gallery during a Frank Auerbach exhibition, when I caught sight of a clothed woman reflected in the glass of a painting.

The True Inflections

1

I stand before an Auerbach picture.
She stands before an Auerbach picture.
She moves on to the space
in a partition where the door should be.
Behind her, through the window, realistic
buses cross the bridge.

2

She walks towards a picture;
she views it from some angles:
Participant observer, unaware,
in a voyeur's network of perception,
she is Auerbach's mirror,
reflected in his mind's eye.

HAYWARD GALLERY, London June 1978

I suspect that the intellectual erotics involved in these experiences tie in with my enduring fascination for paintings in which someone is seen reading. Indeed, some thirty years after the episode at the bedroom window, I proposed to Colin Wiggins of the National Gallery that I curate an exhibition of the Gallery's pictures on this theme, of which there are more than fifty; he politely turned down the idea on the grounds that it would be better realised in a book. While mentally plotting an essay on the pictures, I rationalised to myself that they absorb the viewer into their texture in a peculiar way, that they are centripetal inward-bound pictures par excellence. I experience a sense of intrusion when looking at them, which is the paradox of portrayed private reading. (I have written about readers in paintings in other books.)[5] In his forthcoming Covid diary, *One Hundred Days*, Gabriel Josipovici casts severe doubt on the usefulness or even existence of the mind's eye. My poem is unrepentant.

One of the greatest paintings in the world is Poussin's *The Ashes of Phocion Gathered by his Widow*, at the Walker Gallery in Liverpool. As its title makes plain, the widow is not reading, but is deeply engaged and indeed risking her life in an act of great courage, what Gillian Rose in her best book *Mourning Becomes the Law* – which uses this picture on its cover – calls 'a delegitimate act of tending the dead'. Like pictures of people reading, Poussin's is a study of inwardness, of love destroyed but surviving in an impersonal and hostile world, which has moved on: wherever a woman's place was, it was not *there*. The woman acting as the widow's lookout is in the picture to remind the painter and to tell the painting's readers that to look at the widow is at best a privilege we must live up to, at worst an invasion that shames us. And so, as with many of Poussin's pictures – *Landscape with Man Killed by a Snake*, in the National Gallery, is another example – we look away from the main focus. We have, in the modern cliché, intruded on private grief.

Primrose Gardens was a busy place. Paul Auster and three other New York poets, Judith Thurman, Michael O'Brien and Bill Zavatsky, turned up on the doorstep in 1968, via heaven knows which mediating friend(s). Mike remained a marvellous poet of the *lyric absolute*,[6] who belatedly received due attention, and sadly died in 2016. Judith became a biographer, Paul a novelist, Bill an educationist. Around 1970, Zavatsky produced a magazine called *Roy Rogers*, the One-Line Poems edition for which I gathered poems on this side of the pond, and which I also set as a *New Statesman* competition. Later, Paul Auster came to stay with us in Upper Holloway with a French girlfriend, after his marriage to Lydia Davis broke up. He read *The Adventures of Pinocchio* and one of Bernard

Stone's Mouse books to my children. Ten or twelve years later, my daughter, at secondary school, said: 'Hey, dad, didn't we know Paul Auster?' 'Yes,' I said, 'why?' 'All my friends are reading him,' she informed me. This was a perfect moment to influence Naomi, since children of literary parents often react against over-insistent recommendations. I told her that Paul was an old friend and that I was his first UK publisher. I then wrote to him in Brooklyn saying please send a card to insert in an Auster book I will give her. He sent a Danish translation of one of his books, remembering in the inscription 'a little girl with tomato soup all over her face'. Some years later he sent me yet another sighting of Pierre Menard, that multi-faceted personality who gave his name to my Menard Press. The various Pierre Menards ended up on a MenCard [*fig. 4*].

During the years I lived in Belsize Park and Upper Holloway, and until 1996, I had a parallel life of salaried or contract day jobs alongside a frenetically busy life of the mind, which was too widely cast to concentrate on the essential – supposedly the writing of poetry and then fiction – and involved too many editorial and other time-consuming matters to permit growth as a husband, which is a reason but not an excuse for what I now construe as selfishness. However, being a father was hugely important to me. I was present at the births of my two children – for years and years my daughter loved hearing how I knew she was a girl before her mother did – in University College Hospital where some years later I had two minor operations. (During the unforgettable night of Nao's birth I was reading Octavio Paz's *Alternating Current*.) Looking after children was something fathers ought to do, I knew that. What came as a surprise was that, some of the time at least, it was *interesting*. What's more, of all the forms of love we are privileged to experience, this one requires the greatest sensitivity to the responsibility of power, apart from decisions involving aged parents who cannot make their own any more.

In 1974, I participated in a research project of the now famous linguistician, David Crystal, then based at the University of Reading. We were required to record the early sounds of children. I lay on the floor, spool tape on, encouraging Nathaniel to talk. Recently, he and Naomi recalled that he was inspired to become a barrister after watching *LA Law* on television from around 1986. At Warwick University he was accepted for work experience at the Bar in Mike Mansfield's chambers. His excitement was palpable when he reported to me that Mansfield had got a man off the death penalty in the Court of Appeal for Jamaica heard in London and, from that moment, his professional ambition crystallised. Maybe he's good at talking because he participated in Crystal's researches. My father too wanted to be a barrister but, back then – from a poor background – it was impossible for financial reasons: you had to pay a premium. Sadly he did not live to see his grandson in action. [*17 Dec 2020: Nathaniel has been appointed QC.*]

'Life of the mind' is a grand phrase. As I said, it was a 'frenetically busy' mind, in an equally busy body, which rushed around afraid of the silence that was a pre-requisite for plucking the centripetals of the flowers of creative thinking. I was a literary and cultural boy scout, an attendant lord, editing and guest-editing magazines, co-founding and running a small press, discovering for myself and then translating French and Russian and other poets, involving myself in the activities of the Poetry Society, and in general trying to make sense of the arts, which along with politics and to a lesser extent religion, was what most preoccupied me. Outside the inner circle of family and friends of my own age, I looked for and found people to hero worship or try to impress or both – I salute parental figures or older sibling substitutes who put up with my neediness, such as Octavio Paz, George Oppen, Jonathan Griffin, Eugene Heimler, Donald Davie, Christopher Middleton, Kathleen Raine, Elaine Feinstein, Moris Farhi, Alberto de Lacerda, Yves Bonnefoy, Andrew Glaze, Claude Vigée, Peter Hoy, Edmond and Arlette Jabès, Miron Grindea, Felek Scharf, Albert and Evelyn Friedlander, Michael and Jacqueline Goulston, Lionel Blue and surely others who are sadly beyond awareness that I have omitted their names.

An aspect of associating with older people is that obituaries eventually enter into the loop. When Edmond Jabès died in 1990, my old friend David Gascoyne was asked by the *Independent* to write his obituary. He advised them that he was not up to the task and that I was the person to do it. I was fortunate in one sense: the kind of personalised essay I knew I wanted to write was what Jamie Fergusson at the paper's obituary desk (known as the gazette) wanted to publish. The one on Jabès was the first of about twenty obituaries, parting gifts to friends, which I wrote for Fergusson, a stellar editor who revolutionised broadsheet obituaries. Following the closure of the *Independent* in March 2016, he followed his star and is now one of the last writers of traditional, learned and entertaining book-dealer catalogues, a highly personal genre ripe for analysis in the style of Georges Perec.

Yes, being a boy scout was a way of avoiding the essential: as the Portuguese saying has it, the arse runs away from the syringe. But Michael Schmidt of Carcanet Press liked my work enough to publish books of poems in 1976, 2010 and 2017[7] and, say I defensively, I recently noticed on an old CV that Christopher Ricks had deemed a manuscript of mine good enough to put on the short list for the Leeds New Poetry award in 1970. I shall maintain a dignified silence about a much earlier pamphlet – which I buy from secondhand bookshops and websites and throw away – but the 1976 volume has its moments. This book received one very good review, by George Mackay Brown, which in black moods I would look at over the years, in order to rediscover that I did exist as a writer, perhaps even as a poet. Three years later, Howard Schwartz, in the USA, invited me to publish a volume at his press[8] and I made a new selection, mainly from the Carcanet book. I cut many of them down to the bone against the advice of a colleague of Michael Schmidt's, the poet Val Warner, a good friend and serious reader, who insisted that in all cases the longer versions were better than the shorter ones. But poetry was beginning to nourish me less than it had before. Correction: I was beginning to nourish poetry less than I had before. I was losing courage, I was lazy. And I took refuge more and more in translation, which had always been a temptation. [*While working on a final edit of this book in October 2020, I learned that Val, a troubled and lonely woman with a great heart, had died.*]

Back in 1968, the young Michael Schmidt had invited me to read my Bonnefoy translations at the Oxford Poetry Society he chaired as an undergraduate. In addition to my own poetry, he has also published my some of my books of translations. I can only envy the prodigious Michael whose level of activity, in the same areas as my own, reminds me that one could do so much more or so much better if one was more organised. The chaos in this flat and the equivalent in my mind which is always digressing have cost me at least an hour a day for thirty years. Tot that up over a lifetime, and you have several books and/or improved relationships. As a poetry translator I have worked directly from the French of many twentieth-century poets, four in particular: Bonnefoy (and all the poets in this paragraph),[9] Vigée, Jabès and Deguy – plus a few Russians, two in particular, Vinokurov and Tvardovsky. I have also translated from several languages in collaboration with the poet, such as Ifigenija Simonovic from the Slovenian and Miriam Neiger-Fleischmann from the Hebrew. Such collaborations, once done by fax, are natural beneficiaries of email.

My entire life, in the interstices of day jobs and family, has been a mental roller coaster swaying between the drive to write poetry and, later, fiction and autobiography, and the conflicting or complementary drive to be an editor and publisher, at the service of others. But the fulcrum of this seesaw, the synthesis of this process has, I now see, been literary criticism and criticism's most intense mutation, poetry translation. The latter sometimes brings both drives together in a fascinating, compelling and dangerously obsessive sidetrack, for me at least, a sidetrack where introvert and extrovert are at one, and therefore combine in an irresistible or, more modestly, immoveable force.[10] As a critic, I have tended to focus on writers and other creators I associate with World War II, such as Primo Levi, Piotr Rawicz, Bruno Schulz, Jakov Lind, Arnost Lustig, Jorge Semprun, Paul Celan, Claude Lanzmann, even R.B.Kitaj.

One of the best things about living in Upper Holloway was our proximity to Waterlow Park. I see them now: Naomi in her pram clutching some Fisher-Price toy, Nathaniel trotting along beside us. Unable to pronounce her brother's name, she would call him 'boy', and later 'Faniel'. We got to know Charlie the myna bird, who could speak his own name and, prompted by his audience of several parents with young children, say, 'Show us your knickers.' We would play hide and seek and cricket. Then we would walk up to Lauderdale House at the top of the park, where one is encouraged to reflect on the subject of time before the sundial in the garden, or the plaque on the wall to Andrew Marvell, who lived in a cottage on the estate. We also went to Kenwood, one of my favourite places in London [*fig. 5*], rephrase that: in the world. The children would run to the orangery to look at their favourite painting, Stubbs's *Whistlejacket*, now in the National Gallery after a sojourn at Gainsborough's House in Suffolk. Once a week my late mother and her friend Leonie Westbury would come round to take the children out for tea. Leonie – later lost to us through Alzheimer's – lived until 2015 in the same sheltered accommodation where my mother lived (and died in 2011), very close to this special treasure of suburban London.

At the 1981 Cambridge Poetry Festival (founded in 1975 by Richard

Berengarten), there was a glorious moment in a pub when Vasko Popa produced a short untitled poem in memory of his main translator the late Anne Pennington, which he had written very recently, perhaps even there and then. Weissbort, Peter Jay and I co-translated it on the spot.[11] In 1965 or 1966, I met Pablo Neruda at the house of Miron Grindea and was ticked off by Rosemary Tonks for daring to ask him if he intended to translate a second Shakespeare play. He himself had no objection to my question for, a couple of years later, in a green-ink letter he happily agreed ('Yes, dear Anthony, yes, yes') to translations by Jonathan Griffin being included in the magazine that was the forerunner of Menard Press,[12] *The Journals of Pierre Menard*. In the early 1980s, Rosemary Tonks appeared to have vanished: there were rumours that she was chilling out in India; John Horder claimed she was a nun in Eastbourne. Editors of anthologies were looking for her, to authorise reprints of poems. Finally Neil Astley tracked her down and persuaded her family to allow Bloodaxe to publish her collected poems. She was one of many people I met through Miron Grindea, who was the nuttiest and most infuriating of the mentors whose memory I cherish; I retain great affection and respect for him, wrote his obituary, and defend him when something hostile comes up in the press, such as the correspondence columns of the *Times Literary Supplement*.

In translation, the primary creative impetus is given: Elaine Feinstein's Tsvetayeva, Ifigenija Simonovic's Carol-Anne Duffy, Bonnefoy's Yeats, Weissbort's Zabolotsky, Hamburger's Hölderlin, Tarn's Neruda, Bosley's and Weinfield's and Coffey's Mallarmé, Griffin's Pessoa: how many such combos there are in the creative lives of friends residing in this particular room in the mansion of literature! A PhD student once asked me if I knew any cases where a translation was an improvement on the original. My reply was no, because improvement would only happen if you were translating a bad poem and why would you want to translate a bad poem? A good poem must be turned into, *listened* into a parallel good poem, as Pierre Leyris put it: that is the bottom line. A good poem has an aura, and that aura encompasses its translations and critiques.

In literary criticism and biography, a different kind of primary impetus is given, and I name only a few favourites by friends residing in another room of the mansion: Bonnefoy's Rimbaud, Prince's Milton, Vigée's Bible studies, Josipovici's Kafka, Hindus's Reznikoff, Kathi Diamant's Dora Diamant. John Felstiner's book on Celan, *Poet Survivor Jew*, is a rare perhaps unique example of a virtual merging of translation and criticism that has wrongly been criticised for self-centredness. I wrote a long letter to the editor of a magazine in protest against a harsh review of the book by David Constantine, a fine poet and translator. To his great credit, Constantine, editor for some years (with his wife Helen) of *Modern Poetry in Translation*, did not hold this against me.

Translators inhabit the paradoxical role, at once hubristic and humble, of *becoming* the poet in the time and space of the poem. How many poets have produced *only* translations? If Arthur Waley and Pierre Leyris (see the latter's Hopkins, Shakespeare and Eliot for examples of a great French poet at work) produced 'original' work of their own, I am not aware of it. Some of my poetry translation was plausible and effective work evasion, plausible and effective as evasion because it was patently worthwhile – always the most fatal technique of evasion. This was not work evasion through the booze, not work evasion through travel, not work evasion through sexual misdemeanours: this was work evasion through work, this was a good cause, *this was translation of poetry.* And yet Paula Rego, the most focused artist I have been privileged to know, always says that in the end you do what you *want* to do, and so maybe it was what I wanted to do, and that, as I suggested earlier, the alternative was not to write more and better stuff of my own, but to do nothing – if being a full time editor and publisher would have been doing nothing – and know my place in the scheme of things.

In 1970, I was appointed literary editor of the cultural magazine *European Judaism* and in 1972, managing editor. The three-year editorship of *European Judaism* ended in tears, after the mother of all rows. In charge for one more issue, I signed off with an editorial containing a phrase I was proud of: 'the ten lost diatribes of Israel', later quoted in the press. Twenty five years later, thanks to Rabbi Aviva Kipen, now back in her native Australia, I made peace with Albert Friedlander and *EJ* and more than forty years later wrote a memoir for the magazine's fiftieth-birthday issue, remembering its original publisher, the rich, gay, brilliant, hypochondriacal and deeply insecure Dutch bookshop-owner and classical scholar who had been at school with Anne Frank: Johan Polak.

In 1975, I found myself more involved with the *Jewish Quarterly* and its first editor the late Jacob Sonntag, a singular and single-minded personality who had much in common with his rival and my closer friend

Miron Grindea, equally single-minded and even more singular. Louis Littman, the wealthy backer of the *Quarterly*, took me to lunch at the Reform Club, and over the cheese told me that the club's dairy produce came from his farm. He asked if I would like to work with Sonntag and hinted I could be Jacob's successor, but the job on offer turned out to be reviews assistant, not what I had in mind after already editing a magazine. In any case, Sonntag, like Grindea, could not work with someone else, least of all a much younger person who would be a perpetual reminder of mortality. Sonntag's magazine, however, has survived his demise, unlike Grindea's his. [*Later: the fate of the* Jewish Quarterly *is not certain at the time of this revision.*] Although the *JQ* reflected Sonntag's personality it was not completely identified with it, as was Grindea's with *Adam*, so it could survive his passing. Jacob edited the *Jewish Quarterly* for more than thirty years. In the years since his death in 1984, there have been six editors.

The Journey Begins

Outside the Flat

If you were to walk up the single flight of stairs to my flat on the first floor – which is also the top floor – of this small block, you would pass, on your right, framed posters of artwork by John Swanson, and immediately ahead of you a Victoria and Albert Museum limited-edition poetry poster signed by Ted Hughes and the artist, Leonard Baskin. Nailed to my front door are a Portuguese tile with the flat's number on it, and another tile, from the Old City of Jerusalem, with my name in English, Hebrew and Farsi – a gift from Naomi Gerecht. Naomi, a mezzo-soprano (taught by Jenni Tourel), gave only a few public recitals before settling in Jerusalem, where she is a celebrated teacher of voice. I published a poem about one of these recitals, held at a City church, St Mary-at-Hill.[13] The recital was privately recorded, and until recently I had the only known cassette, given to me at a time when the voice's owner had her reasons. However, I recently decided to send her a copy in case my flat goes up in flames.

Blue-Tacked alongside the two tiles on the door are an old visiting card printed for me on his Adana press by the late Derek Maggs, and a fake coat of arms suggesting that I am from an aristocratic German family of Rudolfs. Aristocrats we were not. However, one of my ancestors was a bailiff on the estates of the eponymous Archduke (hence our name) and Rudolfs were among those Jews who moved to the easternmost province of Austria-Hungary, East Galicia, now West Ukraine, to work the fertile land in the bread basket of the empire. That branch of my family ended up in Stanisławów, now Ivano-Frankivsk; later, most of them would make the short train journey to Belzec death camp or the longer one to

Auschwitz. When I discovered that Paul Auster was related to Daniel Auster, the first mayor of Jerusalem, I told him that Daniel too came from Stanisławów and lived in a cottage on the property of the parents of my relative Bronka (née Vogel) Fliderbaum, a more affluent branch of the family than my grandfather's. *The Invention of Solitude*, Paul Auster's most singular book, quotes a letter from 'T. in London' (that is, me) as speculating that he and I might be distant cousins. When I visited our town in 1991, I met a psychologist who was a dead ringer for Paul, but my host, Rabbi Victor Kolesnik, told me that this gentleman was not a local person. Very recently I discovered that the database of Hamburg docks contains records of five Josef Rudolfs. My grandfather Josef told me he arrived here in 1903. The only one of the five who could possibly be my grandfather apparently arrived in 1905, having worked as a labourer in his last place of residence, Dembica, near Cracow. Josef never mentioned Dembica. However, his rail route would have taken him north to L'viv *aka* L'vov *aka* L'wow (which he knew as Lemberg) and then due west through Dembica, Cracow and Oswiecim (i.e. Auschwitz) and thence via Wroclaw and Berlin to Hamburg. Perhaps he stopped off in Dembica. An unintended irony: the only place on the route Josef[14] made specific mention of was Auschwitz – a hub like Crewe where you changed trains.

At the Front Door

Open the front door of the flat and you will see a long narrow hall. Along the right side are four rooms: kitchen, toilet, bathroom and bedroom; along the other side, overlooking the large garden shared by two blocks (fourteen flats), which my two children, Nathaniel and Naomi, virtually monopolised when young, are the lounge and two bedrooms. Two of the three bedrooms were inhabited by Nathaniel and Naomi, who lived with me half of each week after Brenda and I moved from Upper Holloway, in the wake of our separation and decision to co-parent, to two flats in Woodside Park. Naomi's quondam bedroom is now my chaotic office, where I am revising this book originally written in the lounge (see later); Nathaniel's is a storeroom, chock-a-block with unsorted papers, documents and folders. One day I will find the time and willpower to tidy up. Already the papers are spilling over into other rooms. The carpet in my son's room predates our arrival here, the only room where this is the case. [*fig. 6*]

Bedroom

Apart from the bed and the enormous scroll-front cabinet facing it, virtually nothing in this flat goes back to previous abodes, only books, discs, photographs, personal effects and a table that belonged to Claude Royet-Journoud before he returned to France. All my eleven addresses, (see Appendix 1), are written on the flyleaf of the smallest of my French dictionaries.[15] The latest address is in the handwriting of my son, then seven years old, who after dating it 1981 changed the figures to 1881.

The bed and mattress were bought from an Indian neighbour in Upper Holloway, whose child, Rebeccah, was at Ashmount Primary School, Hornsey Lane, with Nathaniel. The base, now raised, was very low and obviously home-made, wooden slats nailed together. I have twice or three times replaced the original mattress – a block of foam rubber – with a new one from a shop in Pentonville Road, where I also bought a mattress cover. I doubt that the first foam rubber, which did not have a cover, was all that hygienic. As well as being a dust trap and bug haven, it could have acquired its share of menstrual blood, sperm, snot, flaking skin, fartleberries and perhaps other bodily emanations over the years, not to mention coffee, whisky and breadcrumbs. In later years, thank goodness, I became more fastidious, at least by my standards.

The tour of my bedroom reveals a number of pictures. There are prints by Paul Coldwell and Aldous Eveleigh and reproductions on wood, bought in the Rijksmuseum, of two favourite paintings: Pieter de Hooch's *Country Cottage* and Rembrandt's *Jewish Bride*. But the works are mainly serigraphs and drypoints by the friend whose posters you encountered recently outside the front door, John August Swanson of Los Angeles, some given to me, some purchased. John arrived on the scene courtesy of the American poet Howard Schwartz, who submitted poetry and fiction when I was editing magazines. Later came Schwartz's beautiful Menard book *Midrashim* (with new illustrations by Swanson) and in 1980 our giant anthology[16] of twentieth century Jewish poets from all languages, with Swanson again on the cover. John Swanson, dryly funny, introspective, gentle, is a half-Swedish, half Mexican Catholic: classic American melting-pot cocktail. He is an example of that fruitful paradox, perhaps oxymoron, a sophisticated naïf. His serigraphs are editioned, genuinely original works, closely supervised by the artist. He writes: 'The serigraph that took the most colours was *The Procession*. It is based on a 1982 painting, now in the Vatican Museum of Modern Religious Art. I began the serigraph in September 2006. It took me twelve months to complete it. We printed 89 colors, each color required a complex and elaborate stencil.' Often his subject matter is Old Testament: the prints in the bedroom include Daniel in the lion's den, Joseph and the coat of many colours, Jacob's ladder, Ecclesiastes and Ruth. My favourite, *The Peaceable Kingdom*, is an account of the episode which rivals the best of the many versions by Edward Hicks, the Quaker artist much admired by the late Jon Silkin, one of whose early books has that title. Swanson's larger prints always contain a narrative sequence of images, as in medieval tapestries and books of hours. Russian, Mexican and Islamic art have surely influenced his work. [*fig. 7*]

On one wall is a suite of nine aquatinted etchings [*fig. 8*] called *City Wall* (one of which is on the cover of a book of mine),[17] as if the artist had modernised the structure of his narrative by separating out the story from one of his medieval-style large-scale multi-episode pictures. Swanson has said that the etchings were influenced by a composition of Charles Ives, and also by the paintings of Edward Hopper and Reginald Marsh (whose work Paula and I saw at the Whitney in New York), as well as by black-and-white detective movies. The presence of his father can be felt in the suite: Swanson *père*, who lived in hotels and worked in an LA wholesale market, reminds me of characters in novels by John Fante, the Los Angeles writer much admired by Bukowski and pressed upon me by James Hogan. Edward Hopper was a favourite of mine long before I discussed him with John Swanson and it feels good that my own Hopper poem was included in Gail Levin's Hopper anthology.[18]

Menard Excursus

Howard Schwartz's book *Midrashim* was one of fifty (nearly a third of the entire list over forty years) printed for Menard Press by Christopher Skelton, a nephew of Eric Gill; Skelton printed poetry books as a way of keeping sane amidst the jobbing work of letterheads and brochures, and (like my chartered-accountant father with his writer clients) never charged 'boss's time' when, in his case, visiting the small press customers whose literary world was his own. A father of nine, Christopher died only a few months after retiring from Skelton's Press in the mid-1980s. For some years I was fortunate to work with his former second in command, Alan Bultitude.[19]

I spent about five years publishing pamphlets on the nuclear issue. One day, in the summer of 1982, a roly-poly man wearing lederhosen, every inch the overgrown schoolboy, turned up on my doorstep. Within five minutes, while I busied myself with making tea, Oliver Postgate had seated my son on one knee and my daughter on the other, and went one better than Paul Auster by reading the children a story he had written himself. This was the fun part. The serious business involved two pamphlets: the title of the first one, *Thinking it through: the Plain Man's Guide to the Bomb*, offended a feminist bookshop in Edinburgh. The 'plain man' formula was a nod to his father Raymond Postgate, who had written a famous series of books labelled in that way. Oliver was famous as a writer of children's stories – his characters include Ivor the Engine, Noggin the Nog, Bagpuss, the Clangers – but came to Menard in his other capacity, a layman worrying about the Bomb. After Ronald Reagan was elected President, the children picked up on the anxieties floating around the flat. But there was a semblance of normality in the small-change of life, the routines unchanging. I did my best to persuade the children to practise the piano, go to Hebrew classes on Sunday mornings, eat sensible food, and not watch too much TV. They attended a local primary school, Moss Hall, coincidentally in the street where Postgate had grown up.

Following 9/11 and sixteen years after the original series ended, Menard returned to the political fray with a pamphlet by Dan Plesch, called *Sheriff and Outlaws in the Global Village*. Plesch has no doubt and nor do I that this country's slavish support for America is a direct result of the extraordinarily close links in defence and intelligence matters between the two countries, with Britain always in America's armpit so that we can continue with our so-called independent nuclear deterrent, or weapons of mass destruction as they ought to be called. Unlike that of France, Britain's policymaking in this area has been a deliberately smoke-screened deception, to enable us to remain (in fantasy) at the top table and break bread with America. The nuclear powers have not kept to their side of the bargain concerning non-proliferation, and now the genie is out of the bottle, including most recently in the issue of space. If the dangerous bluff of deterrence ever existed (see Oliver Postgate, Nick Humphrey, Sir Martin Ryle and other Menard pamphleteers),[20] which is doubtful except possibly between the USA and the Soviet Union during the cold war, I fear it no longer does. We are entering a phase where the bomb is more likely to be used and, by definition, without democratic sanction (Elaine Scarry, *Thermonuclear Monarchy*, 2016). If the bomb is used, climate change will have speeded up, pandemic will be normal and 9/11 will have been terrorism-lite. Recent British governments appear not even to pay lip service to what previous governments said in public, namely that there were no circumstances in which we would use nuclear weapons first and that deterrence resides in the uncertainty as to whether we would retaliate: see Peter Hennessy (*The Secret State*, 2010) on the first duty of new prime ministers: the secret letter of last resort addressed to the commanders of nuclear submarines. What with our deep involvement in Star Wars implied by the upgrading of American facilities here, we share responsibility for an extraordinarily irresponsible and counter-productive policy. The West is more compromised and dangerous in its self-righteousness and ignorance than the earlier alliance led by FDR and Churchill. I hope the American and Russian and, now, Chinese leaders are reading up about the Cuban Missile Crisis. [*Later: Trump never reads anything but Biden does. Any trade deal will be conditional upon security issues (and the vexed issue of Northern Ireland), and it will be one-sided in favour of America. Putin and China have been demonised and the Baltic States and Poland are making mischief. Ubu-Johnson at one point made a lazy and inappropriate reference to nuclear weapons. Andrew Corbett, a former Trident submarine commander, wrote in July 2020 that he does not trust this government's political/military attitude and would not serve under it. I am tempted to write to him and suggest a pamphlet. December 2020: all credit to Dominic Cummings for expressing concern about accidental nuclear war.]*

Menard was supposed to be a poetry publisher and although nothing was more important than poetry, I argued that poetry 'presupposes future, presupposes continuity'. Consequently there has to be a world for poetry to exist in: the world is held in trust by each generation for its children, like the Patek Philippe watch in the advertisement. I read an article about the novelist Maggie Gee in the *Guardian* in 1983 and wrote her a letter. Six months later she replied, and I had a new friend, equally obsessed by the bomb; her concern shows up in several of her books, in particular *The Burning Book*. At a time of apocalyptic anxiety that was and is soundly based in the world we inhabit, it was a comfort to have like-minded friends, among them Alex Kirby, quondam environment correspondent of the BBC, the late Robin Dilkes and Ronald Aronson. I recall a political meeting about the bomb held at the Art Workers' Guild in Queen Square, at which I met Raymond Briggs who, along with Maurice Sendak, Roald Dahl, Quentin Blake and Norton Juster (*The Phantom Tollbooth*), was a writer my children loved. Another favourite was the bookseller Bernard Stone, whose Mouse books I mentioned earlier; his sophisticated in-jokes amused the grown-ups without alienating the children.

The late Susannah York had been the partner of my old Cambridge friend Nicholas Humphrey, who was the only scientist in the circle editing *Granta*, then a student magazine. That year (1963–4), it centred on John Barrell's room next door to mine on E staircase in Angel Court, Trinity College. But the architecture of E is Great Court architecture and the staircase was incorporated into Angel Court and renamed when the court was built in the late 1950s. I invited Nick and Susannah and other people involved in the nuclear issue such as Edward Thompson, to Menard's fifteenth birthday party at Conway Hall in 1984. This was one crazy and well-lubricated event, with a film about Bessie Smith, songs from Leon

Rosselson, speeches by Richard Burns and others, and a reading by Susannah of Byron's 'Darkness', the subject of my own Menard series pamphlet, a poem which appears to predict nuclear winter. None of the party photographs came out.

Susannah (a version of whom appears as Daisy in Alan Wall's novel *China*) became a close friend and would regularly phone me up for a briefing about this or that topic. Like other friends of hers, I went to theatres all over the country to see her perform. Famously beautiful, she was a very committed and intelligent actor, deeply thoughtful about interpretation and ever worrying about detail and nuance. While an image may sometimes be hard won, beauty is a gift not a virtue. This she knew. Once upon a time, when her cocktail of qualities brought in lots of money, she could afford to own a fine Lucian Freud, but ultimately it had to be sold. The less said about her potboilers the better, but some of her films are exceptional, such as *Greengage Summer* and *They Shoot Horses, Don't They?* – my two favourites, and indeed her own. Later, she concentrated on theatre, mainly on the fringe. Her favourite twentieth century playwright (Paula's too, and, along with Beckett, mine) was Tennessee Williams: Susie's Blanche in *Streetcar* at the Bolton Octagon, for example, was remarkable. Nor shall I forget performances of Jean Cocteau's *La Voix humaine* in French and English, probably at the French Institute. I remember driving her back from Portsmouth after she had starred in *The Glass Menagerie* in a grand Edwardian theatre with superb acoustics. She appeared alongside Peter O'Toole in *The Applecart* in London's most beautiful theatre, the Haymarket, immediately after she starred there in *Fatal Attraction* [fig. 9]. *The Applecart* was a glorious opportunity to get O'Toole's rarely given autograph for my son. Susannah explained to me that she had to move out of dressing room number one, being number two in the pecking order on this occasion. Jonathan Griffin was deeply smitten with her, and never appeared to mind that she revised parts of *Break of Noon*, his translation of Claudel's *Partage de Midi*, on the transparently face-saving grounds that he had produced great poetry for the page but that she had to *speak* the words. It is fair to say that Jonathan made other translations that work very well on stage, such as his Kleist versions, and back in 1970 the Griffin fan club organised a charabanc to Ipswich to see *Partage* in Pierre Rouve's production, with the virtually unknown Ben Kingsley and Annie Firbank in the main parts, a production rubbished by Harold Hobson but praised by other critics. Susannah was always encouraging new dramatists by appearing in new plays on the fringe, and good work as director, writer and performer lay ahead of her, but she died of cancer in 2011; she delayed treatment, having refused to cancel a long tour of the USA. Twenty years earlier, I had visited Jonathan Griffin in the Royal Free while he lay in a coma. And now I visited Susannah after her son Orlando phoned me to come immediately to the Marsden or it would be too late to say goodbye. Old timers become 'experts in farewells', in the phrase of Osip Mandelstam.

Back to the Flat

The Menard excursus started with thoughts inspired by John Swanson's work. Having, as it were, bounced off the bed and off my pictures in the bedroom, what else is there in that room to explore – a room where I have spent more time than in any other room in my entire life, albeit mostly sleeping badly after late-night reading: current books, in case you're interested, are Max Sebald's *On the Natural History of Destruction* and a volume of Morton Feldman's essays – as I was saying, what else is there to explore before we move into the hall?

fig. 7

fig. 9

fig. 8

fig. 10

fig. 11

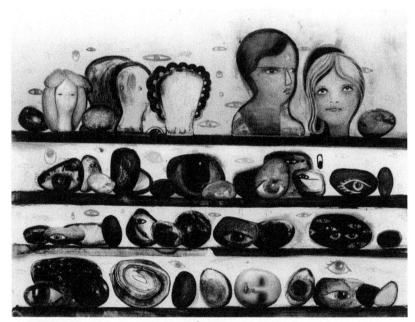

fig. 12

Bedroom Resumed

Perched by the scroll-down cabinet (discussed at length later) in the bedroom is a sculpture called *The Captain Hanged by the Feet Upside Down* – two long thin wooden planks of different lengths, one painted green the other red, which can be placed against each other at any angle – a wedding present from Michel Couturier which I was allotted when Brenda and I divided up our 'things' on separation. (Even the gift itself, theoretically, lends itself to division.). Michel, French poet and BBC broadcaster, told us at the time that the name of the sculptor was a secret. Later he claimed that the work was by an unknown English artist called Malcolm Casserley and finally confessed what I should have guessed from the initials, namely that he had made it himself [*fig. 10*]. Eventually I published English prose poems by Malcolm Casserley on a Menard Press gift sheet ('I am a fly, I married one, we are pleased to announce the birth of a fly'). In the best French tradition, Michel wrote serious essays on art. I arranged publication of his interview with Francis Bacon.

Brenda and I were independently close to Michel. Gay poets and artists (apart from Edouard Roditi) – Michel, Alberto de Lacerda, John Swanson, as well as Rabbi Lionel Blue, Johan Polak and others – got on very well with her, but the implications of such friendships can be over-dramatised. 'Fag hag' is an ugly phrase ('Queen's Moll' was used in the Colony Room), they weren't and aren't fags, and she wasn't a hag. Nor was it a question of the husband feeling unthreatened by a gay man, which always seems to mean that the only kind of threat is sexual; but although gay, Michel fancied Brenda and on one occasion at Chalk Farm Station told her he loved her, after kissing her on the lips at the other end of the platform from me. We had a lodger at one time, Sharon Nelson, a Canadian poet. My mother Esther, in her traditional way, wrongly thought Sharon was a threat to our marriage. Sharon later married my Cambridge contemporary, computer wizard and electronic composer, Peter Grogono. They settled in her native Montreal, where she died in 2016.

Brenda and Sharon got on well for the usual mixture of reasons involving give and take – never directly symmetrical or mirror-image, but ending up approximately equal – which account for why people like each other. On the subject of marriage: my mother spent twenty four years unmarried, forty eight years married, and twenty four years a widow. My father had a different symmetry: one third of his life unmarried, two thirds married.

I was introduced to Michel by his fellow poets Claude Royet-Journoud and Anne-Marie Albiach, then living in Hornsey Lane, whom I had met in turn through Anthony Barnett. Barnett, like me, was one of several junior members of Miron Grindea's circle. It was at a party in the Hornsey Lane flat that I first came into contact with Anthony Howell, Michael Hamburger, Eva Tucker and others, possibly including Alberto de Lacerda, who remained friends over the years. Michel, Claude and Anne-Marie ended up influencing the course of French poetry through their own writings – which include translations of Zukofsky (Anne-Marie), Oppen (Claude) and Ashbery (Michel) – and their magazine, *Siècle à mains*, its name a phrase from Rimbaud. Either they or Yves Bonnefoy introduced me to Rimbaud's house in Royal College Street, Camden Town, whose preservation I later became involved in, with Julian Barnes, Marina Warner and others. Michel lived alone in Chalcot Road off Primrose Hill and never once made himself a coffee there, let alone a meal. He went back to Paris after many years in London, but found it hard to make a living after having been a professional Frenchman in the UK, a stalwart of the French Section of the BBC World Service. He died a lonely death in 1985. I miss him. More than thirty years later, his collected works have finally been edited with devotion and care by the poet Marie de Quatrebarbes.

On one of my regular visits to Paris, Michel and I arranged to meet for a cassoulet, preceded by a drink in a bar on rue Jacob, near rue Bonaparte. I was early. Ensconced beside a big mirror, reading Barthes's autobiography and drinking a kir, I looked up from my book and happened to glance in the mirror: whom should I see but the suave, elegant and handsome Roland Barthes himself at a table, writing. This episode would have impressed André Breton, and rightly so, but a meditation on *Nadja*, one of my favourite books, must await another occasion. Surely the network of correspondences would have amused Barthes too. However, I was shy and left him alone, although he might have welcomed a chat. Michel came in rather late – 'Hello, Anthony, my dear' – and we left for our cassoulet. It must have been later that I met Barthes in London, perhaps at the French Institute, and we corresponded briefly. I admired Barthes for his acumen, methodology and writerly skills. He is as insightful a critic on his terrain as Jean Starobinski was on his, the highest praise I can bestow. Barthes's magnificently intelligent autobiography *Roland Barthes* is a truly pathfinding work, in a direct line from the first and best autobiography in the modern sense of the word, Stendhal's *La Vie de Henry Brulard*.

Had Barthes lived, he would surely have turned to fiction, as a work like his Stendhalian *Lover's Discourse* suggests to the reader. The point about obsession, the book suggests, is not that it makes you happy or unhappy but that it is *meaningful* down to the minutest detail. Friends divided equally about this book, especially those who, like Audrey, had no time for literary criticism. Indeed, she hated it. Fiction reader *par excellence*, she persuaded me to read long contemporary novels I would not otherwise have sought out, for example *Earthly Powers* by Anthony Burgess, alternating it, to Audrey's voluble disapproval on a beach in Crete, with an extraordinarily brilliant work dependent on theories galore, the poet and scholar Lewis Hyde's *The Gift*. [*Later: in 2020, I have read his book on forgetting, as well as Gabriel Josipovici's and David Rieff's books on the same subject.*]

A visit with Paula Rego to Paris in 1996 included dinner with three Paris friends – Anne Serre, Mark Hutchinson and Raymond Mason – at Chez Paul, a restaurant on the south-east corner of the 'sexe de Paris', Breton's name for Place Dauphine. Anne, who is now a famous novelist, talked about Barthes's posthumously published College de France course notes, and described them as a coded statement that he was a failed novelist. I had bought the book that very morning, and later noted that it ended with a section on Proust and photography. Anne thought that Barthes, in effect, chose to die as a result of literary disappointment. I recounted her speculation to Yves Bonnefoy the following evening. Yves disagreed with Anne, saying that Barthes had had some kind of official lunch with François

Mitterrand and was knocked down by a car when crossing the road after a heavy meal; there were no grounds for supposing Barthes wanted to die. During our dinner at Chez Paul, a magical and compelling child aged about five, Anton, kept running out of the restaurant on to the triangular square that so enchanted Breton. We engaged him in serious conversation, until he and we were sidetracked by the sight of a dog shitting on the square. For sure Anne will put Anton and the dog in a novel one day. [*2020: She has told me about* Intérieur, *a book by Thomas Clerc about his flat. I suspect his surname is onomastically relevant.*]

Cabinet and Wardrobe

Now it is time to move on to other aspects in my bedroom: let us begin with my huge and favourite piece of furniture in the entire flat, a former kitchen cabinet with a scroll-down cover, sole survivor of possessions from Primrose Gardens, where it had stood, certainly from the 1920s and perhaps earlier. [*fig. 11*] The cabinet itself is chock-a-block with papers and photographs – which we will come to – and bric-a-brac, such as an 1862 ha'penny, about the same size as a modern two-penny coin. One shelf contains my 'grandfather papers'. Grandfather Rudolf himself rests in Willesden Jewish Cemetery where, in his last years, he would clean the tombstone of my grandmother with a handkerchief during visits to her grave.

Bed, pictures, cabinet cornucopia: what else is there in the bedroom to use as a springboard? Not the books, which are in there on a temporary basis, queuing up to be read. This leaves my clothes: not much story there, given that I spend most of my time at home in a tracksuit and trainers. My brown boots 'remind me, distant now' (Thom Gunn), of walking and themed holidays with my children. From 1981 or 1982, for about seven years, we took our summer holidays in the UK: for three years we went to CHA centres (Countrywide Holidays Association, now defunct), one up from Youth Hostels, with hikes led by professionals. We went to Westward Ho! in Devon, to Barton in the New Forest and to Hope in Derbyshire. Every day we would put on our boots, pick up our packed lunch and go off. The first year was the best, the gifted leader, Arthur –

who swore by trainers rather than boots – organised and entertained the children and ensured that they were at the front, not lagging behind. I made no friends on these holidays but was grateful that the children enjoyed themselves. I took books, a notebook, and, in the teetotal CHA centres (a hangover from their Victorian temperance-movement origins), a bottle of whisky for the evenings, and would read in the bedroom I shared with the children, while other adults were Gay-Gordoning or Dashing-White-Sergeanting or playing charades. On the beach in Devon I invented a character called Pebble and attempted to tell stories about his life and times. Pebble has been resuscitated in order to entertain my grandchildren. These are spontaneous tales. But I have finally written a children's story, a fable, for grownups (or the other way round), inspired by the early oral versions, called *Pedraterra*. The fable quotes stone poems such as Christopher Middleton's 'Climbing a Pebble' and Auden's 'In Praise of Limestone'. I commissioned illustrations and a print from Cathie Pilkington[21] for the eventual book which I am revising yet again, thereby keeping a patient publisher waiting. [*fig. 12*]

For two years we went to the excellent summer school at Lancaster University, where we signed up for different sports and crafts courses. One evening, Naomi, always a late bird like me– Nathaniel, like his mother, has an opposite rhythm – insisted on staying up to watch *Amadeus*. The second year we were there, I did my back in on the first day during a sports session, and retired to bed for twenty-four hours, accompanied by a fluffy doll which Naomi, always attentive in this way, brought me for consolation. I remember that I was reading John Cheever's stories and journals, and Susan Cheever's painful book about her alcoholic father. I spent the rest of the week in the university library continuing my research on Balzac's *Le Chef d'oeuvre inconnu*, which I would later translate,[22] writing a long essay to accompany this fabulous story. The boots were next used a few years later when, in November 1993, I would spend a month at Hawthornden Castle, on a writing fellowship, along with the poet Harry Guest and the American playwright Peter Josyph. We walked to Rosslyn Chapel, happily not yet famous for Dan Brown.

On our final family holiday of this nature, we went to a place recommended by our friends the Rowan-Robinsons: Headland Hotel in Newquay, hard by a famous surfing beach. This was not a great success, partly because it rained a lot, partly because the children were neither young enough nor old enough to enjoy what the hotel had to offer. Nathaniel was reaching the age of departure and the next year he went in a youth group to Israel and then further afield, doing his own thing.

For three more years Naomi, joined by her cousin Amy, was happy or resigned enough to come with me, once to Israel and twice to Spain. Amy's willpower, courage, hard work, eloquence, intelligence and humour have since combined to enable the transformation of a circus jill-of-all-trades specialising in sword-swallowing into a considerable performing artist. By the time we rented an apartment near Malaga, the girls were proper teenagers, old enough and at the same time young enough to be 'trusted' out of my sight, in the fleshpots of Estepona, a tiny fishing village with karaoke and bars and fish and chips. It was understood that in the evening they would come home late but not too late and I knew that this village was backdrop to the transitional, liminal years at the end of childhood, just before adolescence proper would kick in with a vengeance, or at any rate with drama. One evening in Estepona I informed the girls we would be going to Africa the next day. They could not get their brains round this idea. Surely Africa was thousands of miles away, something you did in geography? We took the ferry from Algeciras, and saw the sights in Tangier. There I bought a djellaba, which years later I donated to Paula's studio after wearing it in her series based on Eça de Queiros's novel *La Reliquia*. [*Later: I wore it again in 2020, posing as Kubla Khan and* Shakespeare's *Cleopatra cross-dressed as Antony (Act 2 Scene V.)*] I preferred our inland trip to the hill city of Ronda, not least the pilgrimage to the Hotel Victoria, where Rilke's small room is now a museum.

The only items of clothing with significant underlying story are my ties, none of which I have thrown away. James Hogan and Musa Farhi aka the Turk, are mystified by my attachment to ties, or their attachment to me. Musa only wears them for funerals and similar occasions, as when we went together to see our friend Harry Levy (aka the Reverend Isaac Levy, notoriously the most tolerant and easygoing Orthodox rabbi in London, for whom we later penned a joint obituary in the *Independent*) when he was sitting *shiva* (the week of mourning after death) for his wife Toni. We went again to Levy's house to meet Judaea Pearl, the father of the journalist murdered in Pakistan, Daniel Pearl. Harry Levy was one of the army chaplains who were present at the liberation of the camps, and this may have contributed to his later ability to mingle not only with non-Jews but with non-Orthodox Jews, something some of his professional colleagues found hard to handle. I always liked ties: after all, you didn't have to dress like a Bohemian to be Eliot, Breton or Stravinsky. When young, I was struck by the public non-Bohemian image of these exemplary artists. What mattered, I knew, was what was going on inside your head, the outer garb was a matter of personal taste, perhaps a disguise to keep intruders at bay, a pose. The Turk, in his Turkish wisdom, seems to think it means one is uptight, a sergeant-major or hospital matron or *yekke* doctor with a corncob up the arse. These days, when ties are a style statement rather than a uniform, all the more reason to pick and choose, mix and match the outfits. There is even something to be said for putting on the style when working at home, but I do not stretch to that; I dress up when I go out. So, Turk, don't dress me down when I dress up, or you might end up with that corncob in your nose.[23]

James Joyce told a traditional man, who was about to paint his portrait and was wittering on about his intentions, 'never mind my soul, get the tie right.' Paula 'gets the tie right' in her 1995 Germaine Greer portrait, or in this case the Jean Muir dress, the non 'fuck-me' footwear, the power and the glory of the woman's intelligence and beauty are caught, thanks to a masterful capturing of surfaces with pastel paints: is this not the soul of Germaine? Well, it is an aspect of her psyche, which is the soul translated, caught on the wing, like a butterfly. It takes imagination and empathy to copy. 'In order to tell whether a picture is true or false, we must compare it with reality': Ludwig Wittgenstein. He was referring to (philosophical) propositions not to the pictures made by artists, but twenty years on, the picture *is* the reality of Germaine Greer when it was painted. Let's look at my ties before leaving the bedroom for the hall. Some of them came from my father's wardrobe after he died. Fastidiously or superstitiously, I wanted nothing else – his suits, etc. went to his youngest brother Leon. All this was a far cry from the days of my grandfather, visiting the houses of Jewish mourners in the East End with his pedlar's cart, to buy the clothes of the departed, and sell them on to other poor people; on one occasion he went to Sydney Street for this purpose, and found himself stuck there for a few hours as a result of the siege directed in person by the Home Secretary, Winston Churchill. Some of my favourite silk ties came from my father's wardrobe, including a very beautiful Stefano Ricci.

Inventory of silk ties: Aquascutum, Chester Barrie, Austin Reed (2), Marks and Spencer, Yves Saint-Laurent (3), Hardy Amies, Pierre Cardin, Metropolitan Museum of New York, Kenzo (2), Allander, Stefano Ricci.

My two black and white poetry ties [*fig. 13*] are unique creations by the Slovene potter, poet and fabric designer, Ifigenija Simonovic: their design includes words taken from poems of hers we translated together, words also found on various ceramics around the flat. When I revisited Chicago in 1986 after more than twenty years I absurdly bought myself a 'Here's Chicago!' tie as a souvenir. This great city still calls out to me in the night, no doubt because it was where I first lived independently. I remember being taken to a ball in the lion house of the zoo by a girl from our office who limped. I remember too a married secretary who hinted that she did not have long to live. We briefly kissed in front of the Art Institute.[24]

A beautiful tie from the Met in New York was given to me by my cousin Judy Rappaport who used to live at 1111 Park Avenue, a very smart address which mightily impressed a taxi driver – 'Did you say one one one one?' – as he drove me there, in 1986, from the Port Authority on Eighth Avenue, where I had returned on a Greyhound Bus after a visit to Rudolf cousins in New Jersey in 1986. Two Kenzo ties came from Paula as a reward for posing. Shopping with Paula is an education in fashion design. Three ties survive for sentimental reasons but have never been worn: my Old Citizens tie (the old-boy tie of City of London School), my Cambridge Union tie and my Trinity College Cambridge tie. These are narrow scrawny bits of cloth, reminders of institutional affiliation and, the latter two, of failure that my future life would rage against, perhaps redeem in part.

Cambridge Excursus

The Cambridge Union tie recalls my fantasy that I was a good debater, worthy of being put up against the Tories I knew and occasionally had a drink with: Michael Howard, Ken Clarke, John Selwyn Gummer, Norman Lamont and company. Years later, it was, shall I say, interesting to watch them do their wrong stuff as ministers in Thatcher and Major governments. I remember travelling with Lamont to villages where, *Question Time* or *Any Questions* style, a Union team of what surely looked like toffs answered the locals' questions on politics. The last time I saw Ken Clarke (until bumping into him in Covent Garden in the 1990s), we chatted on Trinity Parade before he and his future wife Gill rode away on bikes into his precocious future as a politician. Michael Howard had a pair of long suede boots and he was as smooth as his boots. His Welsh accent was stronger in those days than it is now. I think he came once to the Jewish Society on a Friday night, which I attended more regularly. I recall a slanging match I had with that small bundle of coiled energy, John Selwyn Gummer, across the Union floor, which I thought ended in a draw. But, as so often in my life, I willed the end and not the means; basically I was not committed enough to the political life to learn my rhetorical trade in the Union. Still, I volunteered to help restock the library's Russian and French books, and timidly dated girls like Caroline Waddington (future Mrs Nicholas Humphrey and later, as Lady Rees, châtelaine of Trinity College) and Diana Marquand, daughter of a former Labour cabinet minister, in the Union restaurant after a sherry at the bar.

The main impact Trinity College had on me derived from my proximity to and membership of John Barrell's circle, culminating in organising myself a room next door to his. With his brilliant mind and general demeanour, he affected the rest of my life more than any other male contemporary, and probably without knowing it. John was far more sophisticated in the ways of the world than me or Eagleton or anyone else in the circle, but Eagleton's brain power rivalled that of Barrell, which made up for the provincial manners and leather trousers he sported: 'they're all wearing them in London, sir,' the Manchester salesman had told him. [*Later: I have found the burlesque radical/philosophical text we co-wrote [fig. 14]*]. As a mentor, Barrell, by definition, needed me not at all. I don't think he despised me, but he may have felt sorry for me, and I'm fairly sure he liked me. He behaved quite well sometimes, not least on the occasion when he came into my room while I was out – to replace or borrow bread or sugar, who knows – and rewrote, without mocking it, an early poem of mine I had left on the piano we used to have singsongs around, with T. Eagleton on the penny whistle. Barrell was an experienced student poet, and had enviable experience of women. As his next-door neighbour I was a witness, perhaps even a connoisseur, of his life. He improved my poor text as much as it could be improved. This unnerved me, but it was a true gift that I would be grateful for later on. Barrell's action prefigured the larger scale reading Andrew Glaze would give my work a few years after I left Cambridge, described later. Perhaps inevitably, I later wrote a poem about what happened when John rewrote mine, but even after all these years it keeps changing its shape, as if the very memory or felt thought about the memory is unstable: it finally made the cut and ended up in my collected poems.[25] I remember one conversation with John Butt and John Barrell when, all three equally unlearned in this respect at least, we wondered what it would be like to make love to a woman who had had a baby. Surely it would not feel as good as… Barrell had what it took to attract the girls (one in particular), he was determined to get a first-class degree, he wrote poetry, edited *Granta*, and I, attendant lord ('deferential glad to be of use') with a ringside seat, watched and stored it all up.

Cambridge was a personal disaster area: if I can't be first, I'll be last, was in effect my defiant exhibitionistic bullshit, and I duly proceeded to get a non-honours degree, known as a pass or ordinary degree. I did not stay for the 1964 Senate House graduation ceremony (the same occasion parodied by Howard Jacobson in his first novel, *Coming from Behind*) but pissed off to New York. There I remember seeing *The Blue Angel* with my new friends Marion and Josef at the Thalia Cinema on the Upper West Side, near Marty Reisman's table-tennis club. Marty had been US champion, and I stopped to chat with him. I fancied myself as a table tennis player, and although I played Eton Fives for my school [*fig. 15*] and once for the university (against my school old boys' team, or was it the other way round?), it was table tennis I loved best and wrote about in a book about my autograph album.[26] I ended up as College freshman champion with a cup on the mantelpiece but, despite playing in trials, I never got a university-team place, unlike Howard Jacobson, ten days older than me. His table-tennis novel, *The Mighty Walzer*, is one of his two best books.

On the ground floor of the staircase where John and I had our rooms was the office of the college matron, Miss Lumley, whom Tom Lowenstein could imitate to perfection. She whistled all her esses. Tom went into a tobacconist once and asked for cigarettes in Miss Lumley's voice. The man replied: 'Yesss, sssir, what sssort?' Tom, a fine poet and later an authority on Inuit ethno-poetics, was tactful and kind to me on the roof of the Arts Theatre, where I showed him my early poems. He remains one of my benchmark contemporaries, the now auratic or talismanic people I met as a student or slightly later in the sixties, people whose existence still matters even after one has lost touch with (some of) them. Paula too has that feeling about her Slade contemporaries. There is another category of people, which overlaps with the benchmarkers, people of whom Paula says: 'He/She *knows.*' They are perceived to be privy to magical knowledge, which, on a level beneath conscious awareness, feeds into the work and self-understanding of those who make art. This magic is what Rothko was referring to when he quoted Martin Buber as saying that if you are looking for the fire, you will find it underneath the ashes.

Cabinet

Photographs

Among the contents of the cabinet in my bedroom are old photographs. Under the sign of Barthes, Breton and Sebald, warily but not wearily I tread a well-worn path; it is no less thrilling for that. The cabinet is one of the treasure troves in this flat, along with the rickety Chinese chest from my mother's house formerly in Nathaniel's old bedroom (and now chucked out), the metal filing cabinet in the kitchen, and Octavio Paz's cardboard filing box in my hall. In recent years, when I stopped keeping things reasonably tidy, my new photos were not (and still are not) filed away but left lying around, all over the place. But here, in the bedroom cabinet, are my *old* photos: the family remembrancer crosses the frontier, enters the event horizon of his past, where ancient signs and lost wonders proliferate. But first, let us look at the famous argument about photographs versus the painted portrait as a true representation of reality, albeit reality already shaped and posed, like a question; there is no contest: the answer lies (that is, speaks true) in the works of great artists, bio/graphers such as Van Dyck, Sargent and Raeburn. Visit the wondrous National Portrait Gallery (Oh, how boring I found it when I was a child!): study whichever commissions happen to be on display: Steven Conroy's Jonathan Miller, Paula's Germaine Greer and/or David Hare, Christopher Lebrun's George Steiner, Philip Oliver Hales's Thomas Adès, Victoria Russell's Fiona Shaw, Lucian Freud's Jacob Rothschild.

Freud's self-portraits, autobiographics indeed, ask to be read against those of Rembrandt. How can a photograph, even by a master such as Henri Cartier-Bresson or Walker Evans, compete? How can you introject such a sensual, diachronically composed eyeful from a photograph? The real life of a photograph is centrifugal. And yet photography has been interrogating painting ever since it entered into the spirit of our culture (and vice versa), and cannot not accompany us when we look at paintings of what has also been photographed. This is not the case of course with earlier work, such as Branwell Bronte's famous 1834 group portrait of his sisters and himself, in the National Portrait Gallery since 1914: he has

fig. 13

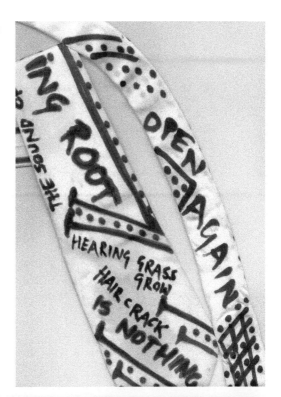

fig. 15

FOUR TYPES OF AMBIGUITY

The Alienated Self in Process of Self-Appropriation

    I   object

How can we Know the Coloniser from the Colonised?

    I   subject

Process or Praxis?

    I   project

The Crisis of Proletarian Self-Awareness as Political Liberation

    I   reject

Tony Rudolf & Terry Eagleton
Cambridge, 1963 or 1964

Personal note

The undated typescript of this previously unpublished text or poem turned up recently in a cupboard. It was written in Cambridge not before October 1963 and not later than April or May 1964. Internal evidence suggests that the ideological pre-text was furnished in Morleys or the Criterion. The final version would have been polished up there or in our temporary home, Angel Court in Trinity. Even though it builds self-mockery into the aporetic critique of its sub-textual procedures, the poem is perhaps a little pretentious but, as T. E. wrote to me in a letter agreeing to its belated publication, "Were we really as clued up as that in 1963? It's hard to believe but strangely gratifying." *Four Types of Ambiguity* is the tenth and final card published over the last few months to mark Menard's twenty-first birthday. It also serves the publisher (if no one else) as an affectionate and sentimental reminder of an old friendship ("Leather trousers? They're all wearing them in London, sir" — T. E. in October 1961 quoting the Salford shop assistant to explain the garment he wore on arrival in Cambridge. Ah, le bon vieux temps, quoi.)

A. R.

fig. 14

fig. 16

fig. 17

fig. 18

fig. 19

painted himself out, although the ghost shows through. Photography, however, was about to take off, indeed that very year Henry Fox Talbot created negative images for the first time. Only a few years later, Charlotte as a celebrity would be photographed. And in 2005, the 150th anniversary of Charlotte's death, yours truly appeared on the second-class postage stamp and the £1-12p stamp, disguised as Mr Rochester, thanks to Paula's skills.

The very process of painting is part of the image in a way that is not true of a photograph. 'Shudderings of images awakening,' writes Bresson in his *Notes on Cinematography* (translated by Jonathan Griffin, of whom more elsewhere). Written in light, the photograph that we ourselves have taken or that has been taken of ourselves – leave on one side Atget and Vishniac with their rescue of worlds they knew they must capture before it was too late, leave on one side the smiling pre-catastrophe photographs in Serge Klarsfeld's memorial book to the French deported children whose destiny our hindsight back-shadows – the photograph offers a 'magical interiority' in the phrase of Alan Wall, a sadness, a yearning, a *hantise*, that is not in the least self-indulgent. It represents, it presents rather, a trace of loss, a layer in the pentimento of our hidden faces, fleshes out the bones of our dead and gone. 'You were photographed, therefore you were'; 'You were painted, therefore you are.' Study Henri Cartier-Bresson's two iconographical portraits of Giacometti – the artist in his studio looking like one of his own sculptures and the one where he is crossing the street in the rain with his coat over his head, looking like one of his own portraits. Here the interactive ramifications between two ways of seeing, and indeed being, are endless.

Item: photo of myself as best man, reading out the telegrams at the wedding of one of my two oldest friends, Michael Pinto-Duschinsky, to Shelley Markham from Virginia. I remember at the reception where this was taken being mildly tipsy and saying a little too loudly to a bunch of young American visitors 'there are no virgins in Virginia;' a tall woman rushed over: 'Yes there are, while my daughter is still unmarried.' This and other photos reveal longer hair and sideburns (although tidier and not as long as now, while I am revising during the Covid lockdown). [*fig. 16*]

Item: a formal photo taken in the studio of Mr Iltis at the Archway end of Holloway Road: Josef, Henry, Anthony and Nathaniel Rudolf. I had been in there some years earlier with a family photograph from my grandfather's town Stanisławów for Mr Iltis to copy. Before I could name the place of origin, he glanced at the photo and to my total astonishment said the original had been taken by his father: he recognised the props. The four-generation photograph was prefigured by one taken in our Middleway garden. [*fig. 17*]

Item: photographs of a Menard Press launch party at Conway Hall, with Audrey's paintings on the wall (one of them can be seen in the photo), allowing them to breathe away from her house at least for one evening. Brian Coffey, Samuel Beckett's oldest friend, is reading from his volume of Mallarmé translations, published that day in 1990, Menard's hundredth book. Brian, as uncompromising a modernist as his exact contemporary Louis Zukofsky, lived in Southampton, halfway between his large London family and equally large Ireland family. Coffey's work was brought to my attention by his devotee, our mutual friend, James Hogan: I am proud I published the first trade editions of Brian's two major long poems, in addition to the Mallarmé.[27] Coffey was a better poet, in the strict sense of the word, than Beckett who, as we know, turned to fiction and drama for the fulfilment of his genius. According to Brian, when Deirdre Bair wanted to write the first biography of Sam, the writer said to his friends that he told her: 'I shall not help you and I shall not hinder you,' which they took to mean she was semi-authorised to ask questions and that they could speak to her provided they chose their words carefully and that he was keeping an eye (ear) open. Beckett trusted them to reveal some things but not everything. He was a wise and modest man. The wartime activities he covered up were greatly to his credit. He headed off the swine by casting pearls before the multitude of curious readers, of whom I am one. The life of Brian (no joke intended) in its own way represents an exemplary commitment to poetry. The son of the President of Trinity College Dublin, Coffey taught mathematics in London secondary schools for years, helped his English wife Bridget (a scion of the literary Farjeon family) raise their nine children, and 'did his thing', that is to say, wrote poetry, and virtually nothing but poetry. He did translate French and Spanish poetry occasionally, as almost all the

Pound-influenced writers did. Eliot published a few reviews by him in *The Criterion*, but what Coffey was, was a poet. If you were short of time to do your work, he told Augustus Young (although not perhaps on this occasion), you slept less, no problem. [*fig. 18*]

Item: 1973 photograph of Brenda in Nice, about three months pregnant with Nathaniel, pointing at a street sign of interest: Avenue Docteur Ménard, where the object of our visit, the Chagall Museum, is situated. [*fig. 19*] We were staying in Saint-Paul-de-Vence and had driven there after a twenty-four-hour visit to Donald and Doreen Davie, who were spending a year in Tours. Donald modestly saw himself as a literary critic who sometimes managed to write real poems 'against the grain of my tendency towards abstraction.' I understood this thought very well, identified it as reflecting my own situation, and aspired to his high level of achievement as a poet and critic. In 1974, we had a quarrel about the miners' strike, with the Barnsley-born Davie supporting Edward Heath; later he had a bash at me in *Poetry Nation Review*. A letter came through my door in the early nineties: I recognised the familiar handwriting on the envelope. I opened it expectantly, but found it contained a flyer for a recording he had made of his poems. He had not enclosed a personal letter. With hindsight, I wonder if it was an invitation to make contact rather than merely a sales pitch. I did nothing and now, in the concluding words of D.H. Lawrence's poem 'Snake', '…have something to expiate: / a pettiness' – a poem I have resumed reading to Paula after she retired it for a few months. I waited until Davie's memorial service in Cambridge in 1995 before making posthumous peace with this inspirational and profound albeit touchy and difficult man.[28]

In Saint-Paul-de-Vence we stayed at the house of Edward and Juliette Pollitzer. Edward ran the family firm, Beck and Pollitzer, with its distinctive fleet of removal lorries, the Harry Stobart of his day. Edward, who died too young, was a wealthy, cultivated and sweet-natured man, a generous patron of the arts (including backing Miron Grindea's *Adam* magazine), who once allowed me to drive his Rolls-Royce in Regent's Park after tea at the house of Mary B, the mistress of Lord Shackleton. Through me, Edward met his French wife Juliette, also known as Claude, later a 'Carl Rogers' psychotherapist in London.

Saint-Paul de Vence

Once more I name
　　　　　a city where the stone
inspired a life, a life inspired the stone.
It was a place whose 'moral shape… and moulds
of commonwealth' revealed themselves within
its walls of refuge, where a life was lived,
not happiness pursued, though peaceable
you died, assured of continuity.

Now it is thanks to commerce that the old
place survives, and thanks to commerce will
die tomorrow. Why complain of that,
since this reprieve is after-life? The ancient
city yields the time before a poem.

Our house is always open to the sun
Beating on a wall where, like my hand,
A lizard flees.

The embedded quote in my 'Saint-Paul-de-Vence'[29] is from an early poem by Donald Davie; this is a revised version of one of ten or twelve I sent Donald during the short but intense period when I elected him mentor, a role he fulfilled with tact and generosity.

I worked hard during that 1973 summer holiday, thinking about the books of James Baldwin,[30] preparing translations of Evgeny Vinokurov (whom Daniel Weissbort and I discovered later we were independently translating)[31] and writing my own poems in between trips to various places – the Matisse chapel and the Karolyi Foundation where we met by chance the poet Grace Schulman, not yet the girlfriend of our Jerusalem friend Carmi, at whose empty house in Abu Tor I stayed in 1969 on my first visit to Israel even before I met him, thanks to his kindness and the influence of a mutual friend, the poet Avraham Shlonsky. At the end of the holiday, we drove back to Paris and had dinner with Paul Auster, Lydia Davis, Claude Royet-Journoud and perhaps other friends. Grace and I are back in touch after decades, thanks to our mutual friend the painter, Julia Farrer.

S.

Term _Summer. 1953_

Name _Ian Anthony Rudolf_ Age _10·10_

ARNOLD HOUSE SCHOOL

Form _Upper IV_ Place by Term's Marks _4th Shin_

Number of Boys in Form _7_ Average Age _11·1_ Place by Examinations _1st_

READING WRITING SPELLING	Good. Usually neat. Accurate.	_yrs_
LITERATURE ESSAY VERSE SPEAKING	He has worked keenly and well and has a good knowledge for his age. His essays are well set out and his work has been satisfactory. He has learnt his verses well.	_yrs_
SCRIPTURE	Very good this term; he has worked well throughout.	_hmf._
HISTORY GEOGRAPHY	He has quite a good basic knowledge of the principal facts, but he has not really worked energetically. Satisfactory on the whole.	_hmf._
ARITHMETIC ALGEBRA GEOMETRY	It is mechanical work in Arithmetic is sound and promising but he often fails to give sufficient thought to problems especially in algebra and geometry	_HB_
FRENCH	He has done a good term's work. He is a keen and able pupil in this subject.	_On._
LATIN	He has achieved a good standard for his age: a successful term	_EG_
GREEK	English Grammar. A good term's work and progress.	_oys_
SCIENCE DRAWING	He can think out a pleasing and well-balanced design.	G.U.S
MUSICIANSHIP AND SINGING	He can sing a tune in the middle register, if it is played very slowly.	E.S
PHYSICAL WORK BOXING	He has worked very keenly & he is making good progress.	A.G.
GAMES	He can bowl a good ball, but at times rather erratic.	WHS
CONDUCT	He has worked soundly and successfully this term and has joined enthusiastically into all the school life. I wish him very well in the future	

George M. Smart.

Next Term begins on _Tuesday September 22nd_

fig. 21

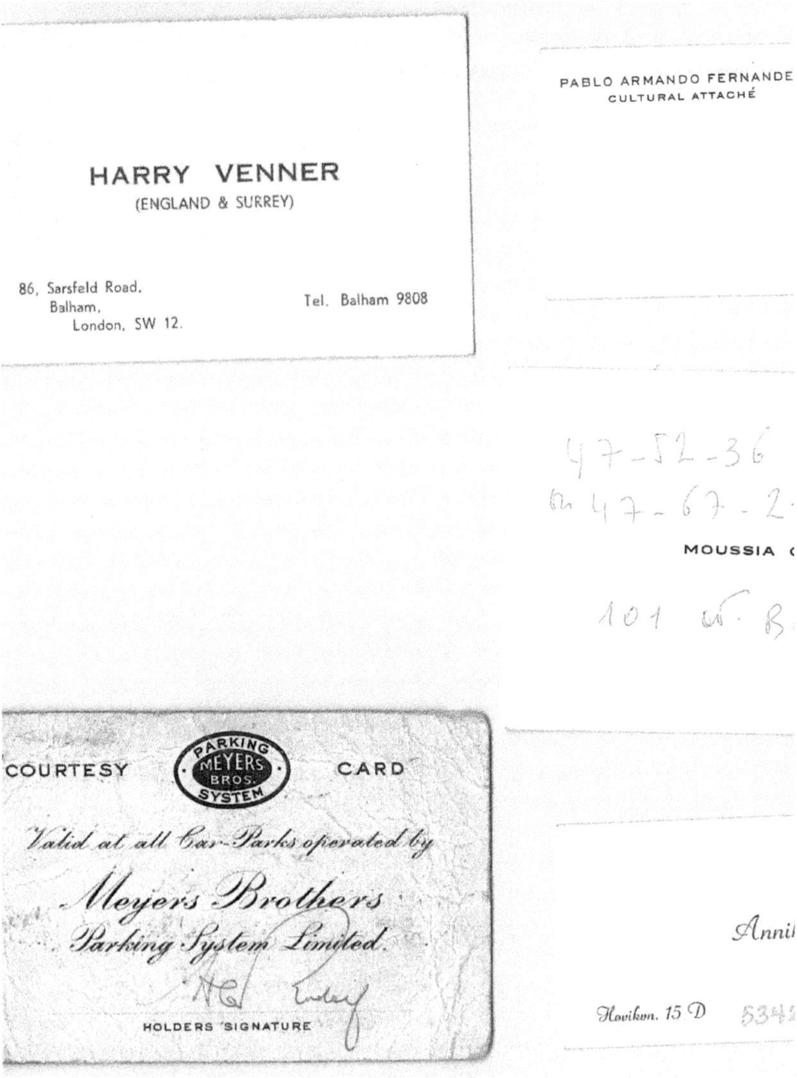

HARRY VENNER
(ENGLAND & SURREY)

86, Sarsfeld Road,
Balham,
London, SW 12.

Tel. Balham 9808

PABLO ARMANDO FERNANDE
CULTURAL ATTACHÉ

47-52-36
62 47-67-2·

MOUSSIA (

101 w· R·

COURTESY   MEYERS BROS. PARKING SYSTEM   CARD

Valid at all Car-Parks operated by

Meyers Brothers
Parking System Limited.

HOLDERS SIGNATURE

Anni

Høviken. 15 D   534

fig. 20

z

EMBASSY OF CUBA

CL 8-8681

SOL WINICK

Painter, Decorator and Paper Hanger

1727 OCEAN AVENUE   BROOKLYN 30, N. Y.

1

ЭOMS

RILLAT
SAVARIN

BRUXELLES 5

TELEPHONES MONARCH 2303/4/5/6

H. C. Rudolf & Co.,
CHARTERED ACCOUNTANTS.

Mr Henry C. Rudolf, F.C.A.

*Lee House,
London Wall,
London. E.C.2.*

Tel: MUSeum 1969, LANgham 8933

Vladimir Ph. Kasatkin
Representative for the United Kingdom

INTOURIST
314 Regent Street, London, W.1

ken Thue

3½5   Hevik

N 638

𝔒𝔵𝔣𝔬𝔯𝔡 𝔞𝔫𝔡 ℭ𝔞𝔪𝔟𝔯𝔦𝔡𝔤𝔢 𝔖𝔠𝔥𝔬𝔬𝔩𝔰 𝔈𝔵𝔞𝔪𝔦𝔫𝔞𝔱𝔦𝔬𝔫 𝔅𝔬𝔞𝔯𝔡

GENERAL CERTIFICATE EXAMINATION

Ordinary Level

ADDITIONAL MATHEMATICS II

FRIDAY, JULY 11TH, 1958. 2 HOURS

Answer questions from at least **two** *of the sections,* A, B, C.
Do not attempt more than **seven** *questions in all.*

SECTION A

1. (i) The value of k is such that one factor of $x^3 - 2x^2 - x + k$ is $x+1$. Find the other two factors.

(ii) The expression $x^7 - ax^3 + b$ is divisible by $x-1$ without remainder, and has a remainder 8 when divided by $x-2$. Find a and b, and find also the remainder when the expression is divided by $x+2$.

2. (i) The first term of an Arithmetic Progression is 3. Find the common difference if the sum of the first 8 terms is twice the sum of the first 5 terms.

(ii) An Arithmetic Progression and a Geometric Progression have the same third term, and both have 4 for the first term. Given that the eleventh term of the A.P. is equal to the square of the second term of the G.P., find the common difference of the A.P.

3. ABC is a triangle, with $BC = 8$ in., $CA = 5$ in., $AB = 7$ in.

(i) Calculate the angle ACB.

(ii) Calculate (a) the area of the triangle ABC in square inches to one place of decimals; (b) the length of BP, where P is a point on CA such that $CP = 3$ in. and $PA = 2$ in.

fig. 24

E 490

Oxford and Cambridge Schools Examination Board

GENERAL CERTIFICATE EXAMINATION

Ordinary Level

FRENCH

PAPER III. COMPOSITION AND STORY

MONDAY, JULY 14TH, 1958. 2 HOURS

1. Write a piece of "Free Composition," giving in FRENCH the story of which the following is an analysis:

> [*The Supervisor has a copy of the story, which must first be read to the Candidates.*]

ANALYSIS

> [*It is not intended that this analysis should be copied; it is only meant to give an outline of the story. Candidates are cautioned not to write too much, and to revise very carefully what they have written before giving it up.*]

Too clever by half

Fermier dans le Midi — souffre d'une bronchite chronique — l'essai de plusieurs remèdes en vain — veut aller consulter un médecin célèbre — découvre ce qu'il faudra payer — ruse du fermier avare — "Me voici de nouveau." — interrogation — conseil du médecin.

[*Turn over*

fig. 22

fig. 23

Theatre and Concert Programmes, Etc.

Next to the photographs in the cabinet are my many theatre and other programmes (including sports events) and a folder of about a hundred visiting cards [*fig. 20*], each of which tells a story, had I but world enough and time… Here we find eight, including my father's business card and his free permit for access to an American client's London carparks, which I was able to use; only one survives, under different management, in Brewer Street. Here is the card of a cousin's small business in Brooklyn, these two American capitalists balanced by the poet Pablo Armando Fernandez, then at the Cuban Embassy, and a Russian official from Intourist. Harry Venner's card bears witness to my life-long love of table tennis: I used to drive to his training club in Putney. Moussia Ooms is the late widow of a deceased Belgian poet and former government minister, Arthur Haulot. She is here for the euphonious name. Lastly, Anniken, my girlfriend when possible in the mid nineteen sixties, given she lived in Oslo.[32] So, visiting cards, but not cigarette cards: sadly I donated my collection to a Middleway neighbour when I was a teenager.

Here are Arnold House prep school reports [*fig. 21*] and two group photos of Arnold House Juniors dated July 1951, a couple of months before my ninth birthday, and some time in 1953. I recognise the faces of most of the boys and remember the names (*see Appendix Two*) of about two thirds, including an easily recognisable Michael Pennington, now a famous actor and a contemporary of mine at Cambridge. [*fig. 22 & 23*]. The women teachers were addressed as 'sir', a splendid example of unwoke nomenclature. I am fifth from the right in the back row in the first picture. Michael Pennington is in the front row, seated on the ground, third from the left. In the second photo I am on the extreme right in the third row down.

Here are my O' Level examination papers of 1958. I look at these with amazement. Perhaps the only one I could take again without preparation and with any certainty of passing would be French. Maths is now entirely beyond my ken. We were well taught this subject by Horace Brearley, father of Mike Brearley, with whom I am in email contact after a few years. Elementary and Additional Maths were among my eight 'O' levels, along with French, English Language, English Literature, Latin and

Greek, and the 'General Paper'. I failed geography. Not exactly a broad spectrum of subjects. [*fig. 24*]

When I was a boy my father wisely encouraged me to keep my theatre programmes as he himself had done: I dated each one and added the name of my companion(s). I saw plays with family or friends, concerts I attended alone or with friends, and there was the occasional ballet or opera. I kept and annotated my programmes until about 1996. My mother was an anti-hoarder: tidying up one day, she chucked out my father's collection; he would have liked to be a hoarder, but she ruled the roost at home and that was the deal. In terms of relating to people, I am more like my mother than my father (let us say periscopic rather than telescopic in interactive approach), but in the way I relate to things I am decidedly a hoarder, more like my father. I am not, however, a systematic hoarder (is there such a thing?) and it is a great shame I did not keep and annotate more of the post-1996 programmes. Nonetheless this cache is a cornucopia of documentary poetic significance Georges Perec would have appreciated, a thread à la Roubaud that can be traced, despite the gaps, amidst 'the claims of ruin', in John Clare's phrase. Many of the programmes contain advertisements and other time-bound material one could deconstruct in a dedicated book. One of the books I am too old to write.

I never kept a record of the films I've seen, although I knew someone who listed all the books he read over a lifetime. More than films or concerts, live theatre – a buzz-generating collective experience threatened now by pandemic protocols – for me requires a companion, and dinner afterwards, when you talk about the play.

London

Item: Long Day's Journey into Night, Globe Theatre, 27 November 1958 [*fig. 25*]

This was a school trip and not a fives trip and evidently the cast signed programmes, or at least my programme. It would have been a rush to go home after school, have dinner and rush out again, but I remember doing that at least once, when I saw a play with a schoolfriend Martin Lester. One did not go to a restaurant before or after a play in school circumstances.

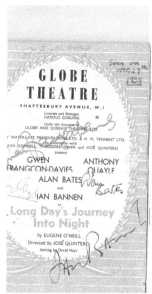

fig. 25

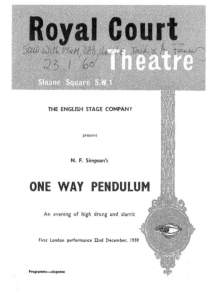

fig. 26

fig. 27

fig. 28

fig. 29   *fig. 30*

Item: Simple Spymen, Whitehall Theatre, 19 March 1959 [*fig. 25*]
The names on the programme include 'Taggy' Manning, a teacher of French at my school who also ran the Fives Club, and Mike Brearley, later known to the wider public for his cricketing exploits.

Item: One-Way Pendulum by N.F.Simpson, Royal Court Theatre
'Saw with Mum, Dad, Uncle Jack and Aunt Fanny, 23/1/60.' This was a famous play in its day, an early example of the Theatre of the Absurd outside France. [*fig. 26*]

Item: A Passage to India, E.M.Forster (adapted), Golders Green Hippodrome, 16 April 1960
'Saw with Mum, Dad, Ronny Hooberman and Martin Vegoda.' There were two schoolfriends. We would have wanted to see this because the novel was one of our English Literature A Level set books that year, which doubtless accounted for the production. [*Later: Except that I now recall the set book was* Howards End.] [*fig. 27*]

Item: Irma La Douce, Lyric Theatre, 5 June 1960
I saw this play with John Shrapnel, in my class at school (and, like Michael Pennington, my contemporary at Cambridge), who later became a distinguished theatre and television actor. I saw other plays when he was in the cast; he played the lead at the National Youth Theatre on at least one occasion. The director of Irma La Douce [*fig. 28*] was Peter Brook. John died in 2020, early during the lockdown.

Item: Wesker Trilogy, Royal Court, 1960
Wesker and Pinter and N.F. Simpson and others had a huge influence on people of my age. As you can see from the Wesker programme, I went to *Chicken Soup with Barley* on my own, to *Roots* with Ruth (my sister) and to *I'm Talking about Jerusalem* with Susan (probably Leveson). I don't know how I got a ticket for the dress rehearsal of the first one. I do know I thrilled to these voices, whether 'kitchen sink' (native) or 'Absurd' (French influence), who displaced the final years of the English poetic drama, Eliot, Fry and Jonathan Griffin, not to mention such playwrights as Terence Rattigan, now at last resurrected. I wrote a little note in the programme: 'the failure of their beliefs remains tinged with optimism and

pride.' I also saw *Roots* at the same theatre on 4 July 1959 with my parents and my French exchange friend, André Both. [*fig. 29 & 30*]

Item: The Cherry Orchard, Aldwych Theatre,
'Saw with Mum, 13.12.61': a very rare occurrence indeed, my mother attending a play without my father. Perhaps he had a filthy cold, and I stood in. It was a charity performance. To this day, Chekhov is one of my two or three favourite playwrights. The version was by John Gielgud who played opposite Peggy Ashcroft. Also in the cast were Judi Dench and Dorothy Tutin. An advertisement in the programme for Garners Restaurant in Wardour Street claims it is 'just across the road from this theatre'. Obviously this phrase was lifted unproofed from a programme for a Shaftesbury Avenue theatre. And the restaurant has gone the way of all the flesh it served up over the years. [*fig. 31*]

Item: The Crazy Gang, Victoria Palace [*fig. 32*] and others
I saw this (on 28 December 1960) and other shows with Paul Rochman. That may have been the last show I saw before leaving for my six months in Paris, a period of my life I discuss elsewhere in this book and in an earlier book.[33] While the majority of my outings were to plays and classical concerts, there were also jazz concerts and comedy shows and musicals.

Items: On 8 October 1960, I saw alone at the Garrick *Fings Ain't Wot They Used T'Be*
On 27 November 1965 I saw Dizzie Gillespie with Susie Schroter. No venue. But this was a souvenir brochure for sale at all venues.
I saw Charles Aznavour on 14 March 1967 with Terry and Rosemary Eagleton. The programme does not name the venue but a Google search reveals it was the Royal Albert Hall.
I saw Jacques Brel at the same venue on Friday 18 November 1966 with Sue Leveson: his final UK performance.
On 14 November 1959 I saw Les Frères Jacques at the Adelphi with Patricia Hammerson. The advertisement on the back of the programme indicates one of the ways you could go to Paris before Eurostar started in 1994. [*fig. 33*]

When it came to family outings, my parents would have chosen the show carefully, in order to accommodate four children, with me nine years older

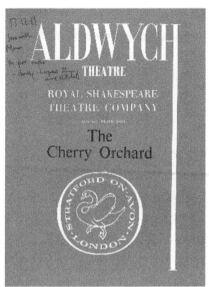

fig. 31   _fig. 32_

fig. 33

HER MAJESTY'S THEATRE
Haymarket, S.W.1.
Licensed by The Lord Chamberlain to Prince Littler

General Manager : FREDERICK CARTER
Manager for Her Majesty's Theatre : WALTER CLARK

Harold Holt Ltd.
(Managing Director : IAN HUNTER)

present

sine ira et studio *

TOM LEHRER

Sundays at 8 p.m.

June 7th and 14th, 1959

* *without rancour or partiality* — Tacitus - Annals. I.i.

Price 6d.

fig. 34

NEW THEATRE
ST. MARTIN'S LANE, W.C.2
Licensed by the Lord Chamberlain to SIR BRONSON ALBERY
Lessees: THE WYNDHAM THEATRES LTD.
Managing Directors: SIR BRONSON ALBERY and DONALD ALBERY

oliver!

A new musical
book, music and lyrics by
LIONEL BART

fig. 36

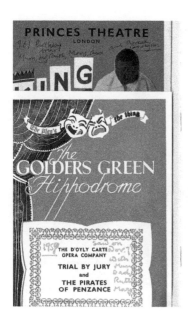

PRINCES THEATRE
LONDON

THE D'OYLY CARTE
OPERA COMPANY

TRIAL BY JURY
and
THE PIRATES
OF PENZANCE

fig. 35

Charles the Second

Theatre Royal
Drury Lane

My Fair Lady

This design is copied from the original Charter granted by King Charles II to Thomas Killigrew in 1663 the original document is still in existence.

than the youngest, Annie. My nineteenth birthday outing was after Paris and before I started at Cambridge. Musicals solved the problem.

Sundry items: Tom Lehrer, Haymarket Theatre, June 14 1959 [*fig. 34*]
Gilbert and Sullivan, Golders Green Hippodrome, 7 November 1959
My Fair Lady, Drury Lane, 26 December 1960
*King Kon*g on my nineteenth birthday, 6 September 1961
Oliver by Lionel Bart, New Theatre, 26 December 1961.
Oliver might well have been the last time we all went to a theatre together. [*fig. 35 & 36*]

Item: Gala concert at the Royal Festival Hall for Israel's twentieth anniversary, 28 May 1968
The concert was given by the Israel Philharmonic Orchestra, conducted by Zubin Mehta, with Artur Rubinstein playing Chopin's 2nd piano concerto. Among the advertisers were my father's clients, the property developers Lewis and Tucker. The programme states, perhaps for the benefit of the many listeners who would not have been regular concert-goers: 'During a recent test in the Hall, a note played *mezzoforte* on the horn measured approximately 65 decibels of sound. A single 'uncovered' cough gave the same reading. A handkerchief placed over the mouth when coughing assists in obtaining a *pianissimo*.' Or, as they say today, please switch off your mobile. There is no indication on this programme whether I went with someone or even that I went at all. It is possible the programme ended up in my collection accidentally.

Item: Beethoven concert at the Royal Albert Hall, 10/12/61
'Saw with Paul, John and David Griggs', I have written on the front. Paul was Paul Rochman. John was his younger brother. David was a school friend of Paul's. Needless to say, I could not care less about him nor he about me, but it would be possible and, for me, interesting, to explore all the names in old address books that no longer ring a loud bell in the clock tower of the mind, but the hands of that clock suggest to me that this is not a priority, unless I am granted years to pursue my Perec-style researches (see Pereciana in the two appendices). [*fig. 37*]

Paris

During my six/seven months in Paris in 1961 I went to plays and concerts every week. I attended many productions of the classical repertoire at the Comédie-Française, often alone, sitting in the cheapest seats. Usually accompanied by my friend Juliette, I saw several plays – including works of Ionesco and Beckett – at the Renaud-Barrault Company at the Odéon. I was a member of a student organisation, Jeunesses Musicales de France, which was imbued with the spirit of prommers. [*fig. 38*]

Item: Concert at Salle Pleyel
'Saw with Michael Harrison and Raphael Sommer, 15.1.61.' This was only a few days after I arrived in Paris for my six months of study at the Institut Britannique: clearly I was making friends early. I lived at the Jewish students' house, 9 rue Guy Patin, near the Gare du Nord. Raphael and Michael were cellists. Raphael, who survived Theresienstadt as a child, was later to become a famous teacher and international soloist and died in 2001, aged only sixty-four. The concert, conducted by Igor Markevitch, included the first French performance of Shostakovitch's cello concerto played, of course, by Mstislav Rostropovitch: so, a special occasion for my two companions. I shared a room at Guy Patin for a while with Rafi, who was up at the crack of dawn to practise and went to bed about eight o'clock, already the disciplined artist. The building – with its long communal history – survives, but it is no longer a students' house.

One of my friends at the hostel was Henri Béhar, born in Egypt. At one stage I shared a room with him. He was a film and theatre buff and wanted badly to come to England, if his board and lodging could be financed. I wrote to John Shrapnel to see if the National Youth Theatre, where he was a leading actor, could help. Today (13 August 2020), unprompted, John's widow, Francesca (daughter of Deborah Kerr), told me she had found my letter while going through John's papers but sadly it vanished again. Needless to say, the NYT did not have the funds. An Internet search reveals that Henri has had a stellar career as a sub-titler, including films of Tarantino and Woody Allen, not to mention films written by David Hare: *Plenty* and *The Hours*. David himself could not

ROYAL ALBERT HALL
Manager: G.R. Pope

BEETHOVEN CONCERT

Sunday, 10th December, 1961

Directors: Harold Holt Ltd

fig. 37

JEUNESSES MUSICALES DE FRANCE

THEATRE DES CHAMPS-ELYSEES

LE LIVRE D'OR
DE LA MUSIQUE SYMPHONIQUE

LORIN MAAZEL
MICHELE BOEGNER

BRAHMS

SCHUMANN

R. STRAUSS

ORCHESTRE DES CONCERTS LAMOUREUX

LORIN MAAZEL

fig. 38

Mᵐᵉ Andrée de CHAUVERON
(Photo Lipnitzki)

Mᵐᵉ Renée FAURE
(Photo G.-R. Aldo)

CRÉATION
L ' O N C L E   V A N I A
SCÈNES DE LA VIE DE CAMPAGNE, EN QUATRE ACTES, DE
ANTON TCHÉKHOV
TRADUCTION FRANÇAISE D'ELSA TRIOLET

ALEXANDRE VLADIMIROVITCH
SEREBRIAKOV . . . . MM. Jean MARCHAT
ILIA ILITCH TELEGUINE . . . . . François VIBERT
MIKHAIL LVOVITCH ASTROV . . René ARRIEU
IVAN PETROVITCH VOINITZKI Daniel IVERNEL
MARIA VASSILIEVNA
VOINITZKAIA . . . . Mᵐᵉˢ Berthe BOVY
MARINA . . . . Andrée DE CHAUVERON
SOPHIA ALEXANDROVNA . . . . Renée FAURE
(Sonia)
ELENA ANDREEVNA . . . . Yvonne GAUDEAU

ÉLÈVE DU CONSERVATOIRE :
M. Baudouin VANDERMEUSE, un Valet de ferme

M. Montana, au Veilleur de nuit
Mise en scène de M. Jacques MAUCLAIR
Décors et costumes de M. René ALLIO

Les décors et les costumes ont été exécutés dans les Ateliers de la Comédie-Française
Le tailleur de Mⁱˡˡᵉ Yvonne GAUDEAU a été exécuté par la Maison KARINSKA
Sa robe verte par Françoise DANGEL et Anne LE BOUTILLIER
Souliers de GOUDIN-BOR et de la GAVOTTE
Fontes de GENCEL
Tissus de LAJOINIE - DREYFUS - PEZÉ - DORMEUIL
Dentelles de Pierre BRIVET et de LA VILLE-DU-PUY

Soirée du Mercredi 22 Février 1961

fig. 39

THEATRE DE LUTECE

fig. 40

fig. 42

LES FARCEURS FRANÇAIS ET ITALIENS
A l'extrême gauche, Mondlus, dans le rôle d'Arnolphe de l'École des Femmes (Foyer des artistes)

La dernière modification du théâtre eut lieu en 1935. Elle porta plus sur la modernisation technique de l'éclairage, du chauffage, de la ventilation, et sur le rééquipement de la scène que sur la transformation de la salle de spectacle. L'architecte, M. Marrast, s'efforça, sans rien bouleverser, de créer une harmonie générale, au moyen de certaines corrections dans les lignes, la décoration et la couleur. Il fut procédé en outre à la remise en état du péristyle, du grand foyer, à la création d'un nouveau

fig. 41

help but a message to the French sub-titlers association (link sent to me by the UK equivalent) obtained an almost immediate email from Henri: almost sixty years after we last met.

Item: Uncle Vanya by Chekhov, La Comédie-Française
Saw alone '22.2.61.' One of the actors is Daniel Ivernel, also a film actor. Years later I met his son, the painter Thomas Ivernel, at the funeral of Yves Bonnefoy, whose portrait he has finely drawn. I remembered the surname from the old days and promised him a programme, if I found it, which I did. [*fig. 39*]

Item: The Caretaker by Harold Pinter,[34] Théâtre de Lutèce, 9 March 1061
I remember very well how empty the *salle* was: a handful of people. These were early days for Harold Pinter. The French adaptation was by Jacques Brunius, well known as a film actor: he is one of the young men in Renoir's *Partie de campagne*. The theatre was later pulled down, as I discovered when I went online to see if the phone number was still the same. [*fig. 40*]

Item: Ruy Blas by Victor Hugo, La Comédie-Française
'Saw alone, 21/5/61.' The programme tells me I was attending a Sunday matinee. I cannot resist checking out the advertisers on Google: Técla jewellers at 2 rue de la Paix are still there. Mercier frères, furniture makers, founded in 1828, are gone. We learn from the company's advertisement that 'The styles of the Gothic, Renaissance, Regence, Louis X1V, Louis XV and Louis XVI periods all re-emerge in the late 18th century. Leading manufacturers included Bastet, Krieger, Mercier Frères, and Sormani.' Schweppes Indian Tonic is described as 'Le drink des gens raffinés.' The pageboy was played by 'Le petit Henri Ascencio.' That Sunday afternoon, after the play, I would have walked to Palais Royal Metro station and gone back to Guy Patin. I would then have had dinner, quite likely at the first-floor cafeteria (ah, the bread and mustard while waiting for the food to arrive) opposite the station, alone or with one of my hostel friends. Not being a clairvoyant, I could not know that I would meet my college friends Barrell and Butt, Eagleton and Tyler in Cambridge a few months later, our mild exploits now recalled as if they took place yesterday. This is a blindingly obvious thought and yet, to me, mildly scary. And Henri

Ascencio, did he dream of becoming a famous classical actor? Life, in one reading, has three phases: 1) birth; 2) dreams; 3) death. The moral? Don't waste time. Transport the dreams to the other side of the mirror of reality, which is to say into a story, the dream of a dream. [*Later: Confession: Henri Ascenscio does not appear in this Comédie-Française programme but another one that has gone AWOL. When I wrote this paragraph in 2005, I evidently conflated two of my many programmes from the theatre. But stet. Little Henri no longer has the Google footprint I recall he had back in 2005*] [*fig. 41*]

Item: L'Annonce faite à Marie by Claudel, Théâtre de l'Oeuvre, 21 June 1961

I remember distinctly the diction and registers of Danielle Delorme and Loleh Belon in Claudel's poetic prose. 'Ne soyez pas triste, mère,' is a phrase that has never left me. [*fig. 42*]

Items: Lucia di Lammermoor, L'Opéra, Saturday 24 June 24 1961; *La Cantatrice chauve* and *La Leçon* by Ionesco, Théâtre de la Huchette, 20 June 1961; *Boris Godounov* by Moussorgski, Théâtre Sarah Bernhardt, 22 June 1961

I was wrong to infer from the name and address written by the person on a page in the Paris Opera programme, Birgitta Sjögren, that we met for the first time at this Saturday performance. Other programme evidence reveals that on the previous Tuesday I went with her and a Canadian acquaintance of mine Len Manko to the Ionesco plays at the tiny theatre in rue de la Huchette which have been running there even longer than *The Mousetrap* in London, and on the Thursday to *Boris Godounov*. Later she sent me a press cutting from Sweden. She was a television and film actress. Almost sixty years later, out of curiosity, I emailed someone with her name which I found online. The woman very kindly replied and explained by return that she was not her. At my request, she checked out the facts and found that 'my' Birgitta, now Birgitta Palme, had died in 2000, aged sixty. Somewhere in this *bordel* of a flat I have the cutting. The upside-down line in my handwriting on the programme reads: 'Rachmaninoff uses a melody from the second act. Dum de diddley dum.' Were Len Manko and I competing for her attention? I resolve to contact him but Google tells me that he died in 2012. [*fig. 43*]

fig. 43

fig. 45

fig. 44

Seminars and Lectures, Alphabetical by Speaker

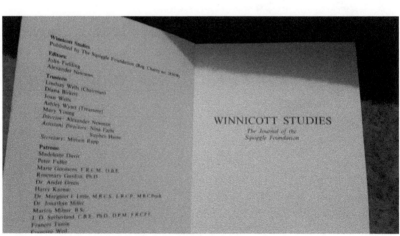

fig. 46

fig. 47

fig. 48

USA

Item: Thelonius Monk, 29 July 1964
I spent July 1964 at Camp Reinberg, Palatine, Illinois, a forest preserve with a work camp run by Quakers where Russian, USA and UK students were practising co-existence, building and labouring and engaging in discussions. A concert by Thelonius Monk I attended suggests I was more musically woke than I remember, unless we went as a group.[35] [*fig. 44*]

Item: Edward Albee, *The American Dream* / LeRoi Jones, *The Dutchman*, Cherry Lane Theatre, NY, 15 July 1964
I saw these two plays with Linda Goldfine, my painter friend. [*fig. 45*]

Miscellaneous

Item: English Open Table Tennis Championships programme, Wembley 28/29 March 1958 [*fig. 46*]

The advertisement for table-tennis balls features a hero of mine, Johnny Leach, the former world single champion, who is not named and does not need to be named in the circumstances of this publication. I have his autograph.[36] I filled in the scores of the games I saw. Once I saw Richard Bergmann play, a defensive genius, and one of many greats who lost six years of their professional lives, thanks to the War. Think: Len Hutton. An algorithm could tell us how many more runs he would have scored.

Item: Nina Farhi's contributions are extracted from a full list of lectures given at Squiggle Foundation, because the leaflet I had in my cabinet has vanished. [*fig. 47*]
The title of the lecture was 'In the Beginning there was Darkness: Images across the Void.' Nina Farhi, who died in 2009 and at whose funeral I spoke, was the wife of Musa Moris Farhi, my close friend and the older brother I never had. She was a dear friend in her own right. Nina nearly became a post-graduate student of Bill Fishman before she embarked on what was to become a distinguished career in psychotherapy. Whenever I think of Nina, I think of her communing with her belovèd orchids in the wee small hours of the morning, Conrad's 'secret sharer': here she was

free, here she was safe. Nothing speaks louder to an interpreter of words than the silence of flowers.

The late Professor William J. Fishman (self-styled BA Wapping, failed), whose accomplishments included teaching my delighted young son a verse about peeing on your neighbour's foot, entertained and instructed a generation with his legendary walks around the East End. The streets of Stepney and Whitechapel and Spitalfields are as haunted for him as the streets of Stanisławów are for Victor Kolesnik, the guardian of memory in my ancestral town, who took me down a passageway by an old synagogue in 1992 and invited me to enter, 'just for a moment,' the world of my paternal great grandparents.

Bill Fishman has been an inspiration to the likes of Iain Sinclair and Rachel Lichtenstein, thanks to his singular personality and scholarly work on the lost world of East End Jewish socialists and anarchists, notably Rudolf Rocker. In a book that helped shape them and me and many others, *East End Jewish Radicals 1875–1914*, Bill wrote that as a child and young man 'I breathed, ate, laughed and dreamed dreams with the immigrant poor. For better or for worse they were my people. As long as there is one cobbled alleyway, one undeserted tenement left, which recalls the voices and the dreams of the *chaverim*, I still walk with my father.' Here was a strong Jewish narrative that was neither religious nor Zionist nor Holocaust, and its implications warmed the heart while stretching the mind. Bill introduced me to surviving *chaverim* [comrades], including Rudolf Rocker's son the painter Fermin Rocker and Sam Dreen, a follower and indeed disciple of Rocker *père*, a magnificent German gentile who learned Yiddish in order to lead the Jewish workers in East End in their cultural and political activities and who, more than most, is entitled to be called 'man of action'. Sam Dreen taught the young Al ('Alfie') Alvarez Hebrew when working as a tailor in Al's dad's East End factory. When I phoned Al with the news that Sam (fellow guest was another Sam, Samuel Menashe) was at our place for dinner, Al, as he recalls in his memoirs, instantly got into his car and drove the short distance from Hampstead to Primrose Gardens in Belsize Park. The heroic movement led by Rudolf Rocker was something quite special and moves me even now.

Given that the variables are many and complex, counter-history can be self-indulgent: what if the bomb plot against Hitler had succeeded?

What if Yasser Arafat had tossed the ball back into Ehud Barak's court or Barak had made a better offer? But the variables are reduced in number when we talk about, say, an individual private soldier who died in World War I, for example a Bristol-born lad from Rocker's East End, namely Isaac Rosenberg. To put it in perspective, Rosenberg was ten years younger than my grandfather Josef Rudolf – who lived till 1980 – and the exact contemporary of an American poet I corresponded with, Charles Reznikoff. Rosenberg was born thirteen years before my friend Carl Rakosi, who died aged one hundred in June 2004. I had tea with Isaac's nephew Bernard Wynik a few years ago and met Rosenberg's brother David Burton around the time the three biographies of Isaac were published in the 1970s. So, one could have, would have met the poet, still radical, still an active writer, in London or on a kibbutz. Unlike Kafka, who also talked about emigrating to Palestine, Rosenberg might have fitted in there. His personal perspectives on Eliot and Pound would have been salutary. He is a poet with much to teach writers from all backgrounds. Like David Jones but unlike Owen and Sassoon and Graves, Rosenberg was not an officer. He wrote extraordinary poetry, with diction and rhythm quite unlike any of his contemporaries. It would be echoed later in the work of one of his best critics, Jon Silkin.

Back to the Farhis: if my marriage broke up without gang warfare, it was not only because my wife and I subscribed, as one should, to the view that cooperation is self-evidently a sine qua non for minimising damage to children caught in crossfire, but also because the state of affairs was contained by Moris and Nina Farhi, and that at a time when Nina was already chronically ill with lupus. She was a heroic person, continuing to work as a therapist until the end of her life, when her suffering was great. I met Musa back in 1978 thanks to the demands of an anthology of Jewish poets, *Voices within the Ark*, already mentioned. I needed advice on the Turkish section (Howard Schwartz and I wanted as many countries, or rather, languages as possible) and I phoned up the only Turkish-language poet I knew, Taner Baybars, an ex-Cypriot and the main translator of Nazim Hikmet. Taner, who died in 2010, said that I should speak to a certain Musa Moris Farhi, a Turkish Jewish poet living in London. I phoned Moris. He invited me to come round for lunch. I resisted, saying that I was very busy and could not meet new people, and please forgive me but could we conduct our business on the phone or by post. The mellifluous voice worked its seductively insistent magic (as it had on Nina a few years earlier and as it would have done in later years, on calls from women, during his Samaritans night shifts) and I capitulated, heading over to Hampstead Garden Suburb, to the beautiful house in Heathgate, where he fed me a wicked meal that was the mother of all cholesterol cocktails – today it would be out of order, off the radar – washed down with red wine, and ending with cups of strong Turkish coffee and cigarettes. And so began a friendship as close as those he describes between Gypsy blood brothers in his marvellous novel, *Children of the Rainbow*.

Musa, who died in 2019, was the world's best host and most giving friend. Such a man should have a weakness, and if our vices are intimately linked to our virtues, then it is appropriate that his forgivable and minor weakness was that outside his own house he was visibly uncomfortable, edgy because he was not in apparent control. The explanation is that he was a very shy patriarch and it may be that only when he was surrounded by his books and paintings (including prints by John Swanson and Paula Rego), serving up food to four or five friends, taking care of Nina and fielding phone calls from friends or family in Israel and France, was he able to relax. The Turk's only competition in the stakes to out-do Napoleon and Julius Caesar for simultaneous activities is Rubens, Pieter-Paul I mean, not Musa's friend Bernice, whose ex-husband the late Rudi Nassauer wrote books now as wrongly neglected as Eva Tucker's. Musa was an authority figure par excellence, as his stepdaughter Rachel will tell you; he was surely an ideal Samaritan night and day for all the many years – via the telephonic furrow – he ploughed that field of pain and loneliness. Musa and I knew each other's intimate secrets and if you know the secrets of others in addition to your own (not necessarily shameful ones, though I suspect one is sometimes in denial on that front), you know something else: you know one of the reasons why people write novels. Jenny Diski exaggerates when she says that 'memoirs lie, fiction tells the truth', but she is making a good point: if a writer writes fiction and autobiography you can sometimes suss out the factuality, if not the actuality, by reading one against the other. But why would you want to do that?

That lunchtime we sorted out the business quickly, and soon after joined each other's club: the tiny group of people permitted to read unpublished work in manuscript and with a licence to point the finger at rubbish, in other words to act as Hemingway's 'built-in shock-proof shit-detector' (precisely because one cannot always do it for oneself), just as Lucian Freud and Frank Auerbach called on each other's services when something was going wrong. Musa was a poet with a capital P, a rhetorical swashbuckler, who could generate paratactical verses and catalogue poems, metaphor-based networks rather than syntactically-imbricated meshes, at the drop of a whisky, the drop of a gallows, the drop of a knicker: Hikmet and Neruda rather than Oppen and Tomlinson; Whitman rather than Dickinson; raw rather than cooked; redskin rather than paleface. By bizarre coincidence, his hip operation took place on the same day as that of Paula's close friend the painter Natalie Dower,[37] both of them in the strong hands of the celebrated surgeon who is now a woman. The next day Paula and I turned up with two bottles of champagne, toasting Musa and Tilly with Francis Bacon's famous words: 'real pain for my sham friends, champagne for my real friends'. Musa's book *Young Turk* is a lovely account of his childhood, growing up in a Sephardi Jewish world far removed psychologically from the more puritanical and repressed Ashkenazi world centred on Norris Lea Synagogue in Hampstead Garden Suburb that was my experience, and indeed that of Nina Farhi, up the North Circular Road in Hendon. Nina and I are remotely related by the marriage of two distant cousins from Fournier Street – one of whom apparently did a runner – but the Rudolfs cannot compete with her mother's family, the seven Klinghoffer sisters from Cannon Street Road, one of whom, Clara, became a well known painter and another the mother of Michael Podro, the art historian. [*fig. 48*]

Records: 78s, 45s, 33⅓s

I am old enough to own three kinds of gramophone records: Seventy Eights (78s); Extended Play (EPs or 45s); Long Playing, known as LPs (33⅓s), the figures standing for revolutions per minute, or rpms. My earliest memories of records, told elsewhere,[38] are of the collection in my childhood home. When my parents started buying records, some time between their marriage in 1938 and their move to 41 Middleway NW11 shortly before I was born in 1942, EPs and LPs did not yet exist. I made my first purchases of records in 1957 or 8 when I was fifteen/sixteen. I would go to HMV in Oxford Street – the fascia is still there – and listen to records, classical and popular, in the little booths, before not buying most of my choices. 78s were still available: pop songs were issued on 78 and on 45. According to my expert John Whiting, there were already commercially recorded reel-to-reel tapes, but I never saw one. Cassettes were not on the market until the early 1970s. Many of my surviving 78s are fast-track boosters to the old days, in other words to my younger days, as are my 45s. Some of the 78s – Guy Mitchell, Sparky's Magic Piano and others – suggest a crossover between the period when I listened every Saturday to *Children's Favourites* on the BBC Light Programme (presented by 'Uncle Mac' of Children's Hour) before going to Sabbath morning service at the synagogue, and my very mild pop music phase, since classical music was beginning to impact on my time. I bought a few secondhand 78s later on, when they were already history and surviving like steam trains, because I rightly suspected that one day I would experience nostalgia for them. I remember that popular tips on recycling waste material included heating up 78s until they could be shaped into a flowerpot, complete with readymade hole in the middle. Not that I ever did, any more than I used the thingy on my penknife to remove nails from horses' hooves.

My 78s

Note: by excluding three 'classical' 78s (an incomplete set of Chopin's sonata in B minor played by Brailowsky and a bizarre vocal arrangement of the composer's mazurka in A minor), I find (in 2005) I have seventy-eight 78s, a nice accident. A popular song, lasting three minutes (cause or effect?), fitted nicely on to one side of a 78. These records are fragile. I have been careless and cracked two I had been hoping to replay on my old Bush Monarch.

The Portuguese Washerwomen
This one is not from the old days. I bought it in a local sale in 2002, because I thought it would interest Paula. The MGM label has the familiar lion. Immediately I encounter a problem that did not exist, when I wrote

the earlier book:[39] the main rule of that particular game was to download memories from my brain without consulting any documentation whatsoever. In the present work, by contrast, I am confining my research to personal documentation – thus for example these 78s – otherwise, and this is the problem, I will spend too much time surfing the Internet and nothing will be written. So, a new rule: if absolutely necessary, Google the answer to a highly specific question and then get the hell out. This time around I am exploring memory via possessions, many of which have been hoarded over the years. The idea is to rediscover the forgotten backstories and reconstitute lost aspects and modalities of my younger selves, overlapping with and moving forward from the earlier book, which ended the month before I went to university, where during the first year I discovered writing and sexuality. Back to the poor old washerwomen: Paula recognised the tune, but it didn't trigger any memories or stories on her part. Still, it is a way into this exploration of my record collection – a warm up.

The Mills Brothers: *'Miss Otis regrets'/ 'No headache'*
The label bears the proud boast on both sides: 'No musical instruments or mechanical devices used on this recording other than one guitar.' I loved the close harmony of the Mills Brothers, as I did that of the Ink Spots and the Andrews Sisters. The French translation of 'Miss Otis', on a CD in Paula's studio, has her not coming to dinner rather than not coming to lunch (a question of syllable count, no doubt). [*fig. 49*]

The Ink Spots: *'Java Jive'/ 'Do I worry' (I have two copies, offers please on a postcard; 'A lovely way to spend an evening'/ 'I'll get by'; 'I'm gonna turn off the teardrops'/ 'The sweetest dream'; 'As you desire me'/ 'It only happens once'*
The Ink Spots were well past their heyday when I bought these. 'Java Jive', supposedly, contains references to drugs, 'coffee' and 'tea' being euphemisms for forbidden substances. I remember buying this disc at Dobell's record shop in the Charing Cross Road, on the opposite side from the secondhand bookshops and Better Books – the Compendium bookshop of its day. Sadly, Compendium, in Camden Town, closed in 2000. Dobell's and Better Books were havens I could repair to at lunchtime in the early years of my adult life, while working nearby. Unlike

my friends with their excellent degrees, there was no postgraduate work for me, let alone an academic career.

Still living at home, I obtained the first of my many day jobs, initially as a graduate trainee and then employee at the British Travel Association in St James's Street, followed by a period as a trainee in-house Organisation and Methods person (ironically enough, given my chaos) at the Automobile Association in Leicester Square for a few months. What was I doing at BTA in the first place? At the end of my final university term in 1964, I attended the Cambridge University Appointments Board in Chaucer Road (known to me as the Disappointments Board), where Beetle Raphael would work later. I had not the faintest idea about future jobs or careers, but BTA offered opportunities to travel. Maybe that swung it. In any case, I was appointed to a traineeship at £750 a year (my rent cost £200, approximating to my father's rule of thumb that rent should amount to not more than 25% of income – something that is no longer possible today – which left me with pocket money after travel, food and other expenses). It was the first of several attempts at paid work involving minimal mental commitment and emotional investment, occupations supposedly releasing my energies to do literary things. Not until 1996 did I leave waged or salaried day jobs for the freelance life.

In December 1964, while working for BTA, I was told that an Australian woman had won a competition. Her prize: a week in London on the town. My superiors asked me to take her to the theatre and dinner one evening, on expenses: a new experience for me. Somebody at BTA must have recommended the place – which I would not otherwise have known about: a basement dining club in Great Newport Street, with a band. No pass was made in either direction, perhaps because I was too young or she was too old – or more likely because neither found the other attractive. How old was she? I was twenty-two. She was an 'older woman', probably between thirty and forty. Anyway, my only interesting memory, indeed my only memory, of the evening is that she confided in me that she had been happy in Monterey in California and would I ask the band to play her special song, 'It happened in Monterey'. Now, I knew the lyrics from my much played Frank Sinatra EP, *Songs for Swinging Lovers*. [*fig. 50*] The song's Monterey is 'in old Mexico'... There was a certain sweet absurdity, even pathos in the request: the generous explanation is that she liked the tune and didn't know the words. As a well-behaved

fig. 49

fig. 50

**DUCHESS
THEATRE**

The Reluctant Peer

By WILLIAM DOUGLAS HOME

fig. 51

fig. 52

chaperone, I bit my lip and asked for the song. Before or after dinner, we saw Sybil Thorndike in William Douglas Home's *The Reluctant Peer* – the choice of my superiors – at the Duchess Theatre, a short walk from the restaurant. [*fig. 51*]

My three months at the Automobile Association, in 1967, included a week of utter pointlessness at the Association's Leeds office. However, I took the opportunity to meet a poet I greatly admired, Geoffrey Hill, with whom I had been corresponding. He invited me to his house where I met his then wife Nancy, and took me to the university for lunch. [*Later: Jon Glover, his friend and mine, chatted on the phone about many things, including Hill's recent and extraordinary* Book of Baruch.]

Billie Holiday Album [*fig. 52*]

This collection of twelve 78s was presented to me by Harold George, postal clerk in the Chicago office of the British Travel Association, 39 South Lasalle, where – after fifteen months in the London headquarters – I worked for the first six months of 1966 as assistant manager, or was it assistant to the manager? He was Humphrey Jackson, who lived on the fashionable Near North Side. Humphrey was a smart and cool English guy in his late twenties, with an eye for the ladies. The morning I arrived, bleary eyed on the overnight train from New York, he asked me if I would like to accompany him to the annual Oxbridge-Illinois dinner that same evening. I grimaced. 'Before you say no, this year it's being held in a more interesting venue than usual, the official residence of the Governor of Illinois, Otto Kerner, who was at the same college as you.' So, curious to see the residence, I said yes. A few years later I read that the governor, now a judge, had been jailed for bribery. After a couple of months, my New York girlfriend Linda visited me for a few days at my flat, #311 (or was it #315?), 5465 South Everett, near the University of Chicago in Hyde Park 60615, a residential neighbourhood which was no longer fashionable. I liked living near a great university.

One of my Chicago jobs was to service travel agents in local states, including Michigan, Illinois and Iowa. I put the chains on the office car wheels – early 1966 was a great winter even by Chicago standards, so I was told – and from time to time drove off with free material we, the British government Quango (as it wasn't yet called) responsible for tourism, made available for the travel trade. It was a period when a new kind of American was beginning to travel abroad, a creature who did not automatically go to his or her country of origin, and those few who had already travelled to the land of their fathers wanted to try other places. The UK was in competition with other countries at last. In Davenport, Iowa, I met up with the Irish Tourist Board's Chicago man for a joint presentation. Whom should I brush past in the run-down hotel but Liberace, about to begin rehearsals. In Iowa City I dropped into the office of the Professor of French, Alexander Aspel; he invited me to dinner thanks to an introduction from Yves Bonnefoy.

Back to Harold George: one day, Humphrey was out of the office. As the senior member of the staff of five, I was handed the phone to deal with a request from Marshall Fields, the Harrods of Chicago, the only place where one could buy English tea. Was Mr George creditworthy? I hesitated for a moment and then said, without a shred of evidence either way, but liking him, that he was. Was it after this that he gave me the Billie Holiday album? He is one of the signatories to the goodbye book I was presented with on my last day in Chicago: *Love in the Shadows* by W.J. Weatherby. The other signatories are Humphrey, Marie, Jean and Joan. In Humphrey's writing is the comment: 'How do you spend your spare time, or shouldn't I ask…?' This alluded to a letter to me written by my thirteen-year-old sister Annie, which I had quoted to Humphrey.

I returned home to London at the end of June. A few months later, after I'd moved to pastures new, I learned from a former colleague that Humphrey, while visiting our mutual friend, the manager of the Rome office, Chris Fitzgibbon, went with him on a boating trip and they both drowned. Humphrey's father was J. Hampden Jackson, which triggers a memory of my own father's collection of books in the *Teach Yourself History collection,* with their distinctive black and yellow covers. Jackson *père* wrote several of them. Around the same time, I learned that Harold George [not his real name] was in jail for fraud. The record album was not a Billie Holiday album as such since on the inside front cover there is a printed page where you list your titles; it would appear Harold bought (from Marshall Fields?) or selected from his own collection twelve records and put them in the album as a gift for me. Harold had been a friend of the singer and showed me a pair of shoes he had chosen as a memento after serving as a pallbearer at her funeral in 1959.[40] He took me to a party in an apartment on the far south side of the city. The piano had bullet holes and, so I was told, had once belonged to Al Capone. Some of these records must be quite rare:

'Until the real thing comes along'/ 'I cover the waterfront' (with Teddy Wilson's orchestra. On the Columbia record it says: 'previously unissued'.)
'I've got my love to keep me warm'/ 'One never knows' (Biltmore Record Co, no backing given.)
'I can't face the music'/'Remember' (Clef Records. Billie Holiday and her Orchestra.)
'If the moon turns green'/ 'Autumn in New York' (Clef Records. Side one has Billie Holiday and her orchestra (musicians listed), on side two she is accompanied by Oscar Peterson.)
'Jim'/ 'Practice makes perfect'. (Blue Ace Records. Musicians listed, including Teddy Wilson.)
'This is heaven to me'/ 'God bless the child'. (Decca. Composed by Billie Holiday and Arthur J. Herzog, jnr.)
'You turned the tables on me'/ 'Easy to love'. (Mercury Records. Billie Holiday and her orchestra; musicians listed).
'She's funny that way'/ 'How am I to know'. (Commodore. Side one, Eddie Heywood and his orchestra; side two, Eddie Heywood Trio.)
'I love my man'/ 'On the sunny side of the street'. (Commodore. Both sides, Eddie Heywood Trio.
'Georgia on my mind'/ 'Let's do it'. Blue Ace records. Both sides, Billie Holiday orchestra, featuring Lester Young.)
'I found a new baby'/ 'I'll never be the same'. (Blue Ace Records. Lester Young with Teddy Wilson's orchestra; musicians listed.)
'No regrets'/ 'Did I remember'. (Blue Ace Records. Billie Holiday and Orchestra; musicians listed include Artie Shaw.)
Frank Sinatra: *'Autumn in New York'/ 'Full moon and empty arms'*
I have written my name on both sides of this 78. On the label it states that the record was first published in 1957, but I would have bought it in HMV in Oxford Street in 1958 or 1959. 'Full moon...' is based on 'Rachmaninoff's Concerto' says the label, but doesn't specify which one. This is odd, since if you need telling, you need more information (second piano concerto) and if you don't need telling you don't need the information supplied. I am being a pedant. The phrase clearly stands for 'Rachmaninoff's famous concerto, you know, the one with the great tune'.

Bing Crosby (and others): *'McNamara's band'/ Dear old Donegal'* by Bing Crosby; *'You are my sunshine'/ 'Day dreaming'* by Bing Crosby; *'Let's start the new year right'/ 'White Christmas'* by Bing Crosby (the B side was the big hit, of course. I note here that some but not all of these 78s tell you which is the A side. Either it was obvious or both were equal or they didn't care); *'Moonlight Bay'/ 'Gone fishing'* by Bing and Gary Crosby; *'Mule train'/ 'Dear hearts and gentle people'* by Bing Crosby; *'Apalachicola, Fla'/ 'You don't have to know the language'* by Bing Crosby and the Andrews Sisters; *'I-yi-yi-yi-'/ 'You're a lucky fellow Mr Smith'* by the Andrews Sisters; *'Hit the road'/ 'Oh he loves me'* by the Andrews Sisters; *'South America, take it away'* by Bing Crosby and the Andrews Sisters backed on one record by *'Route 66'* (same artistes) and on another by *'Feuding and Fighting'* by Bing Crosby and the Jesters (3 copies!); *'Swinging on a Star'/ 'Going my way'* by Bing Crosby; *'Rumboogie'/ 'The cockeyed mayor of Kaunakai'* by The Andrews Sisters. The Brunswick label on this last record says 'Fabriqué en Angleterre' *and* 'Made in England'.

'South America, take it away' is an entertaining homage to Latin American dance rhythms from 'the land of the hot-dog stand' and of 'the atom bomb'. 'Route 66' is a better song. Once on Route 66, during my Chicago stay of 1966, I was heading south (as the route does in the song), listening to a programme about English popular music, and looking forward to a quiet evening in a motel, when the announcer interrupted the programme to say there was a tornado in the vicinity and that those heading south on Route 66 should… I forget the exact words but the gist was: get off the road and find shelter. I did not take this in for about five minutes, and then – frightened and exhilarated and feeling like a character in a story or a reader of a story experiencing the emotions vicariously or even the writer of the story – had my delayed reaction and pressed hard on the accelerator. I ended up in a motel in or near Davenport, Iowa, where you could put a quarter in a slot and the bed would vibrate, an experience that had to end up in a poem.[41]

I was not an aficionado of Bing Crosby as a voice, so it is odd I only have one Sinatra 78 and all those Crosby ones. What I enjoyed was the sheer entertainment and jokiness of some of the older crooner's songs. Paula says that I was a few years too young to feel strongly about Bing. [*fig. 53*]

Guy Mitchell: *'Singing the blues'/ 'Crazy with love'; 'Angels cry'/ 'Feet up';* *'The roving kind'/ 'You're not in my arms tonight'; 'Wise man or fool'/ 'Look at that girl'; 'Christopher Columbus'/ 'Sparrow in the treetop'; 'My Truly Truly Fair'*

Guy Mitchell was a clean cut, clean living pin-up singer, and I would guess that unlike Johnny Ray there was no scandal attached to his name. As a performer, he did not have the power and charisma of Ray, Elvis Presley's most important white precursor. Guy's hit 'Feet up (pat him on the po po' is a strange song about a father and his son which is at odds with the persona I remember. It is about a baby 'tiny as a peanut' and contains the line 'I bet he'll be a ladykiller just like his pa'. [*fig. 54*]

Johnny Ray: *'Glad Rag Doll'/ 'Somebody stole my gal'; 'Yes, tonight Josephine'/ 'No wedding today'* (two copies); *'Alexander's ragtime band'/ 'If you believe'; 'Cry'/ 'The little white cloud that cried'*

I remember that Johnny Ray wore a hearing aid and was famous for exciting the bobby-soxers, as Frank Sinatra had done before and Elvis Presley would do later. One read in the papers, years later, that the modern equivalents of bobby-soxers found themselves removing their knickers and throwing them on stage for Tom Jones. Did they engage in this metonymic activity with Johnny Ray? If they did, such downloading did not get into the papers. Even if it had been reported, I, a late developer, would not have understood the symbolic implications.

Mickey Katz: *'Duvid Crockett'/ 'Keneh hora'; 'Tico Tico'/ 'Chloe'* (2 copies)
Duvid (Yiddish for David) Crockett was 'king of Delancey Street', not of the 'wild frontier'. The second of these two 78s is on the HMV label, with the dog facing the ancient gramophone, listening to his master's voice. That dog impacts on the old amygdala, reactivating memories that go back well over fifty years. Mickey Katz (backed by his Kosher Jammers, a klezmer group after the klezmer heyday in Eastern Europe and America and before the klezmer revival familiar to my children's generation) was a phenomenon of the immigrant Yiddish speakers and their children. He was a comedian and recorded songs in Yiddish or in a version of English that presupposed knowledge of Yiddish/Jewish humour. 'Duvid Crockett' is typical of his parodies. For some years he was an entertainer on the now vanished Borsht Belt in the Catskill mountains, and was surely an

influence on Woody Allen, or at least typical of the influences on him; Katz would have to be around the same age as Woody's parents would now be; his son (Joel Grey of *Cabaret* fame) is around the same age as Woody. Mickey spoke from a tradition that lingered into my own childhood (I am seven years younger than Woody Allen) and died with the Yiddish speaking grandparents and the assimilation of the second generation.

While there has been a revival of Yiddish, and diaspora Jewish (as distinct from Israeli) culture and folklore have never been more popular, the social matrix of Mickey Katz has vanished from the face of the earth. In Passaic, New Jersey my late relative Sid Rudolph (the immigration authorities got the spelling wrong, says the English branch of the family) drove me through the run-down downtown neighbourhood where my great aunt Pearl Rudolph Eilen lived. She was born in East Galicia in 1850 and was buried in Passaic in 1935. He took me to her grave just outside the town and I swayed from a branch of my far-flung family's tree. Once as Jewish as the Lower East Side, downtown Passaic became Italian and is now Latino-Hispanic. Hearing Meyer Bogdanski singing in Yiddish; reading Kathi Diamant's biography of Kafka's lover Dora; watching some of the films of Woody Allen, reading Leonard Michaels, I am returned briefly to the lost world of my immigrant maternal grandmother Rebecca Winnick Rosenberg who gave birth to my aunt Fanny in Rodinsky's future room in Princelet Street, Spitalfields (see the post-script to the paperback edition of *Rodinsky's Room* by Iain Sinclair and Rachel Lichtenstein), and later sang Yiddish songs to me.

I email Sid Rudolph to ask if he ever saw Mickey Katz on stage. No, but would I like an LP of Mickey Katz? Yes please. The sleeve calls him a 'dialect comedian'. There is a good parallel between Katz's 'Yiddish' songs and those Irish-style songs – such as 'McNamara's Band' – recorded by Bing Crosby and others for Irish Americans who came to America before, during and after the great East European Jewish immigration which began in 1881, that is after Alexander II – liberator of the serfs, Czar of all the Russias – was assassinated, and ended with the onset of World War I. One difference: the urban poor and rural immigrants knew English although most preferred to speak Irish, according to James Hogan. In Ireland it had been illegal to speak Irish. [*fig. 55*]

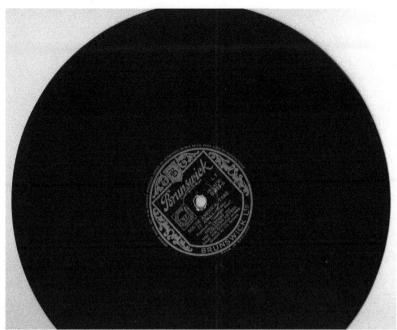

fig. 53

fig. 54

fig. 55

fig. 56

Russ Hamilton: *'We will make love'/'Rainbow'*
Even at the time everybody knew that this first and perhaps only hit by Russ Hamilton was the worst pop song ever recorded, and the competition to win that title was great. I associate the song with an Italian holiday in Viareggio in 1957, at a time when I was corresponding regularly with a friend from Sunday school, known as Hebrew classes, who was in hospital for months, Sue Leveson, now Sue Selwyn. 'Make love' still meant what it meant in the thirties: more Fred Astaire than Mick Jagger, who was still to come. I am uneasy about this memory: yes, I owe Russ Hamilton an apology: I have confused him with Tab Hunter, whose hit 'Young Love', which I do not own, was even worse.

Dickie Valentine: *'The finger of suspicion'/ 'Who's afraid'*
The A side contains the lines: 'Someone broke into my heart and stole a beat or two / the finger of suspicion points at you.' That is mainline popular poetry, and survives as words without the music. Valentine was a heartthrob singer, a big-band crooner. On the other hand, there is his recording of 'Mr Sandman': 'Mr Sandman, send me a dream/ Make her complexion like peaches and cream.' Oy veh, as Mickey Katz would have said. [*fig. 56*]

Lonnie Donegan: *'Putting on the style/ 'Gamblin' man'*
'Recorded during his act at the London Palladium on the 9th May, 1957', says the label. During one phase of my early teens I loved skiffle music more than anything else. Skiffle led some back to Dixieland and traditional jazz, others forward to rock and roll. Donegan, who influenced the Beatles, had something of a revival in his later years, before dying in 2002. To my astonishment, he himself wrote 'My old man's a dustman'. I thought it went back to music-hall days.

Issy Bonn: *'Someday you'll want me to want you'/ 'Sweetheart. We'll never grow old'*
This comes in a sleeve advertising The Wallace Magneto Repairing Company, 202 Walworth Road, phone RODney 3426. I remember Issy Bonn in his cartoon incarnation in the children's comic *Radio Fun*. He was a Jewish comedian and singer, older than Mickey Katz, and with some overlap in terms of audience and output. [*fig. 57*]

The Stargazers: *'A-round the corner'/ 'Dance me loose'*
I have pure (?) nostalgia for this group, which is redolent of my Light Programme heyday. 'The Stargazers are on the air, and to start our programme this time…', their weekly show always began. I am back in my little bedroom above the garage of 41 Middleway. We had a TV by now (rented for the Coronation in 1953 and then purchased, never to leave no more), but my *imaginaire* was radio-bound, and always will be. Unlike on TV, the radio commentator would necessarily describe the action in a cricket match in great detail. Radio plays required 'the inward eye', which was indeed 'the bliss of solitude'. And there were weekly dates with *Sports Report* on Saturday at 5pm and regular programmes (with repeat) such as the *Goons* and *Take It From Here*. My record cannot be played. [*fig. 58*]

Lew Stone & The Monseigneur Band: Vocal refrain by Mary Charles and Al Bowlly (side 2 Al Bowlly only): *'Let's put out the lights'/ 'I can't write the words'*
This record comes in a sleeve from the shop where doubtless the first owner would have bought it: M. Bromley, Music and Gramophone Stores, 36 High Street, Camden Town, NW1. Telephone: 1235 NORTH. There is a sticker on the label: Whatmore 1933, which was the heyday of Al Bowlly who was killed in an air raid during World War Two. [*fig. 59*]

Bill Haley and his Comets: *'See You Later, Alligator'*
This song gave rise to joke rhymes like 'See you later, mashed potato'. Historically important as a pioneer of white man's rock music, Bill Haley did not have an ounce of the talent or charisma of Elvis Presley or even Johnny Ray, but 'Rock around the clock' was on the turntable when Diana Sanders taught me how to jive at the synagogue youth club in 1959 or earlier, although we did not rock till 'the broad daylight'. Dressed up, as all of us were, what were we about to watch or listen to in one of the 1959 photographs of the youth club taken by the *Jewish Chronicle*? [*fig. 60*] Why was the photographer there? Was it perhaps the opening of the first ever synagogue youth club? Apart from myself, I recognise six other people, including Paul Rochman.

fig. 57

fig. 58

fig. 59

fig. 60

Reggie Goff with the Velvetones and Quartet: *'You're breaking my heart'/ 'I'm gonna let you cry for a change'*

The record sleeve carries this message: 'The records recommended on this paper cover are *Long Playing* (33⅓ revolutions per minute) and *Extended Play* (7 inch records with a playing speed of 45 rpm). When playing such records it is very important to ensure not only that the motor is running at the appropriate speed, but also that the *correct* type of stylus or needle tip is used. A stylus or needle suitable for 78 rpm records could cause serious damage to records of other speeds. Do you know that many 78 rpm records are also available on 7-inch, 45 rpm records? With the latter you have all the modern benefits. They are compact, easy to carry, virtually unbreakable, and the quality of reproduction is beautiful.'

The LPs listed are by the Melachrino Strings, Sid Phillips and his Band, Joe Loss 'Dancing Time for Dancers' No 7, Ken Mackintosh his Saxophone and his Orchestra, and Ronnie Hilton. The EP records listed are by Alma Cogan, Max Bygraves (with Peter Brough and Archie Andrews, the latter a famous radio dummy and the former his ventriloquist, but in non-visual media they were one character actor with two voices), Tony Martin, The Deep River Boys, Perry Como and Eddie Fisher. If I carry on injecting in this vein, I'll be drunker than a honeybee on nectar.

Jack Teter Trio: *'Johnson Rag'/ 'Back of the Yards'*

I bought this because of the name 'Johnson'. I had a dear friend called Jenny Johnson, a singer whose range surpassed the five octaves of Yma Sumac. Jenny had been trained by Alfred Wolfsohn, the man Charlotte Salomon calls Daberlohn in her remarkable work, *Art or Life*. I do not recall playing the rag to Jenny, and now it is too late. [*fig. 61*]

'A private recording': 'not to be publicly performed without license'.

What is this 12-inch 78? 'I guess it doesn't matter any more', in the words of the title of a favourite Buddy Holly song. This is what can happen when memories, like the 78 itself, which has not been played for years, are dusted off. Well well, I own a private recording of children singing hymns or songs. In truth, it never did matter, but where did it come from?

Miscellaneous Items

Jimmy Young: *'The Man from Laramie'/ 'No arms can ever hold you'*
Side A was one of Jimmy Young's two number-one hits, the other being 'Unchained Melody'.

Marino Marini: *'Come prima'/ 'Volare'*
These were huge hits. Impossible to know which one was side A since we are not told. The record gives the date of publication as 1958.

'Russian national anthem'/ 'Cossacks' ride through Moscow'
Where this came from is a mystery.

Fats Waller: *'Aint misbehavin'/ 'Don't try your jive on me'*
On this recording he is playing the organ, not the piano. His most famous song and the 'B' side are described on the label as 'slow foxtrot'. [*fig. 62*]

The King Brothers: *'A white sport coat (and a pink carnation)'/ 'Minne-Minnehaha'*
The label on side one is misprinted: 'The King Brothers with The King Brothers and Geoff Love and his orchestra'. This was a cover version of the song written by Marty Robbins.

The Crickets: *'That'll be the day'/ 'I'm looking for someone to love'*
Buddy Holly's name is not mentioned on the label (except as co-composer), presumably for contractual reasons.

Fats Domino: *'Blueberry Hill'/ 'I can't go on'*
The reverse of the record sleeve, from Jupp and Sons, 50 Denmark Hill, says they are agents for Stonia British-made gramophones, prices from 39/6 to £17.17.0, which translated for youngsters means from one pound nineteen shillings and sixpence (£1.97½p) to seventeen guineas, that is seventeen pounds and seventeen shillings (£17.85p). [*fig. 63*]

Percy Ridout: Private recording of two 12-inch 78s
Four liturgical arrangements 'recorded for West London Synagogue in Nov.1954 to celebrate the composer's jubilee as its Organist'.

fig. 61

fig. 62

fig. 63

fig. 64

Tommy Dorsey and his Orchestra: '*Mendelssohn's Spring Song*'/ '*Shine on, harvest moon*'
On the label: 'Swing music 1938 series' – 219/220

I end with a list of the remaining records:

Perry Como: '*Catch a falling star*'/ '*Magic moments*'
Frankie Laine and Jo Stafford: '*Way down yonder in New Orleans*'/ '*Basin Street Blues*'
June Christie: '*I was a fool*'/ '*My heart belongs to only you*'
Tony Martin: '*You and the night and the music*'/ '*Goodnight, sweetheart*'
Lena Horne: '*Stormy weather*'/ '*The man I love*'
Harry James and his orchestra: '*Eli-Eli*'/ '*Music makers*'
Ruby Murray: '*Softly softly*'/ '*What could be more beautiful*'
Little Richard: '*Long tall Sally*'/ '*Tutti frutti*'
Ray Turner: '*Sparky's magic piano*' (sides 2 and 5 of 6-side set)
Rose Murphy: '*Busy line*'/ '*Girls were made to take care of boys*'
Eddie Fisher: '*Cindy, oh Cindy*'/ '*Fanny*'
Paul Anka: '*Diana*'/ '*Don't gamble with love*'
The Crew Cuts: '*Earth angel*'/ '*Ko ko mo*'
Glenn Miller: '*Moonlight serenade*'/ '*American patrol*'; '*Cradle song*'/ '*Elmer's tune*'

My 45s

'*Zorba the Greek*'; '*Never on Sunday*;' '*Jules and Jim*' (and Jeanne Moreau's later '*J'ai la mémoire qui flanche*') [*fig. 64, 65 & 66*]
These EPs take me back to the early 1960s, to my college days, and then to the period of my early day-jobs. 78s were about to vanish from the shops and the Tories from government. 'Thirteen wasted years,' said Harold Wilson. During the run-up to the 1964 general election, while I was travelling around and working in the USA, my close Cambridge friend Terry Eagleton wrote me a letter (post restante?) full of hope and enthusiasm. Harold Wilson, said Terry, had united in a kind of popular front everybody who wanted the Tories out. Wilson has had a bad press in recent years, but his government's social legislation, not least the

creation of the Open University, has stood the test of time and he knew when to say no to the USA, refusing troops to Lyndon Johnson in Vietnam.

Ah, Zorba: the unforgettable dance on the beach, with its *promise*, and Melina Mercouri in *Never on Sunday* with her complexity, humour and allure (six days a week according to the lyrics – hence the title) and Jeanne Moreau, the second older woman par excellence if you were my age: her performance in *Les Amants* to the music of Brahms and, at the time of the EPs, in *Jules and Jim*, imprinted her on my mental template of love. Melina and, especially, Jeanne incarnated possibility: if, following the command of Rilke, whom I would discover later, I were to have the courage to change my life, that is change my mind, things might happen beyond the intellectual and verbal imperatives that seemed to rule my conduct.

Yes, *Zorba the Greek* (1964), *Never on Sunday* (1960) and *Jules and Jim* (1962), all of which I had seen before I left Cambridge, incarnated the possibility that, provided I could forget or put in square brackets Englishness, the constraints of Jewish north-west London, day jobs and our island weather, I would discover feelings deep in the heart of me, which would fuel a life embodying sensuality. Sensuality involved – as I understand my 'thinking' with hindsight – a dialectical relationship between the physical and mental reality of woman and a way of reading the world arrived at through literature and travel. The dance of Zorba was a man's dance, but Quinn *became* Zorba, didn't he? If I could learn the lesson of Zorba, could *become Zorba* (would it work if I was only pretending, wearing a mask?), things might happen. With sensuality, which comes first, theory or practice? Answer: they come together, a simultaneous orgasm of discovery as Paul Feyerabend did not say, but it is a metaphor that this remarkable thinker would not have disapproved of, judging by his autobiography (pressed on me by my late friend Z. Kotowicz), *Killing Time*, a marvellous account of how an intellectual discovered love.

In the mid-sixties, by accident or not, I was reading the Gide-influenced early work of Camus, essays and stories, rhapsodic in their telling of life in the sun, a life that Protestant England knew not (ironic that I write this during the fiercest heatwave ever). South Europe and North Africa were regions of my mind and of my mind's extension, my

fig. 65

fig. 66

fig. 67

fig. 68

fig. 69

fig. 70

body, which I had only rarely accessed before visiting the United States, what with my North European and Ashkenazi Jewish anxiety about the body and its doings. Greece, Italy (where my friends Richard Burns and Kim Landers had gone to live), Spain: those were the lands of undiscovered content.

Another friend from university, Steve Kahn, had a Greek girlfriend, Aliki. She was sensual in a way that English girls were thought not to be (thanks to accent, colouring and other local details), and I yearned for her. Already in 1963 she had given me Kazantzakis's novel *Zorba the Greek* (on which the 1964 film was based) as a twenty-first-birthday present. (For a while she was my father's secretary, slipping through my mother's net.) I had not yet discovered Sephardi Jews or rather Jewesses, who might have delivered salvation: my friend Michael Pinto-Duschinsky lived with his Sephardi great-aunt and pronounced Hebrew in the Sephardi way but really – despite Sephardi synagogue affiliation – he was and is Hungarian Ashkenazi (indeed a descendent of rabbis), more like me in ethno-religious origins than his Sephardic pronounciation of Hebrew and love of olives suggested.

Lorca, Machado, Vallejo, Neruda and other Spanish-language poets began to enter my imaginings, but failed to dislodge Chekhov, Dostoevsky, Forster, Orwell, Hamsun, as, à la Forster, I tried to connect the prose and the passion. But Jeanne Moreau and Melina Mercouri and Juliette Gréco (whom I saw with Steve and Aliki at the Savoy Theatre in 1962) – they spelled danger and freedom, if you were as buttoned up as me. The bisexuality of one Latino male friend – who made a mild pass at me and argued that I was more in love with a mutual friend than with the friend's girlfriend – intrigued me, but nothing more.

'Moscow Nights' sung by Vladimir Troshin, and an English version 'Midnight in Moscow' by Kenny Ball and his Jazzmen, wrongly described on the label as 'traditional', if by 'traditional' is meant 'anon'. [*fig. 67*] 'Moscow Nights' was quite a new song, no more traditional than modern folk songs such as Lonnie Donegan's 'My old man's a dustman' or Pete Seeger's 'Where have all the flowers gone'. I have it in a version by Vanessa Redgrave and one by Marlene Dietrich, who completes a favourite EP with 'Lili Marlene' and two songs from *The Blue Angel*: 'Falling in love again' and 'Naughty little Lola'. I loved the kitschy 'Moscow Nights' (literally

'Suburban Moscow evenings'), which I first heard on my trip to the Soviet Union in 1959, as part of a group of boys from City of London School and from Shrewsbury School. We went on the Soviet liner, the Baltika.

Our party was led by a history master from Shrewsbury, Michael Hart, later to become a well- known headmaster and educationalist. I remember only the name of one boy from the Shrewsbury group, Stuart Martell, the son of an admiral, whom I tracked down via his old school and who, sixty years on, sent me photographs of the trip. Such are the bizzarreries of memory that I cannot remember which of my fellow Citizens were in the group. One night, the liner, which was our residence while in Leningrad, failed to supply us with supper. We may have had to change boats because it was needed for other purposes. On the boat, there was a Finnish girl Picco Elander, who dumped me, perhaps because she realised I was a sexual zero, although at the time awareness of such nuances was not yet on my agenda. She must have left the boat at Helsinki where we disembarked. I spent the day looking round and bought an EP by Anna Mutanen: 'Marja-Lusa'/ 'Karjannan Kunnailla', doubtless as a sample of local talent.

On the boat home some of us hung out with a group of girls who included Ann Taylor, later known as Annie Bright ('Sneakin up on you') and finally as Tracy Taylor ('Bad times have faded away'). Arriving with my new balalaika and 78 records at Tilbury, I arranged with my new Shrewsbury friends to visit the school at an agreed date for a reunion and photo-swap one weekend early in the autumn term, but my father would not let me go. Ann Taylor would eventually marry the jazz musician and critic Dave Gelly, becoming the singer in his group. Forty years later I wandered into the Royal Festival Hall foyer and saw her singing. I said hello and was cheerfully recognised. I bought her cassette of Peggy Lee covers and we mused on the passing of time. [*fig. 68*]

Jacques Brel: '*Les Bourgeois*'/'*Bruxelles*'/ '*La Statue*'/ '*Une Ile*'
This EP has one of those plastic triangles you sometimes had to insert yourself in the centre of a record, if it didn't come with one. I knew I was supposed to find Brel sophisticated and, if I was a woman, sexy, but I didn't and I wasn't, even though his sixties' hairstyle and suit and cigarette on the cover could have served, as a cover indeed, for someone like me. My admiration for him as an artist came later – I went with Terry and

Rosemary Eagleton to a concert he gave in London – ditto for Jean Ferrat, whose *Nuit et brouillard* EP I have and which is on YouTube as I type. Scott Walker's version of 'Mathilde' is better than Brel's own, if a friend of mine, Susan Saffer, is to be believed. [*fig. 69*]

I discovered Georges Brassens at Cambridge thanks to the records of Gisèle, a French schoolteacher, then married to my college friend John Tyler. They lived upstairs at 139 Tenison Road, near the station, and occasionally had dinner parties. Gisèle and I got on very well, initially because I could speak French. Gisèle came from Hinx in the Landes, a small village. I remember phoning her there one summer and, highly amused, asking the operator for 'numéro 3 à Hinx'. At Tenison Road, I recall a 10-inch LP of Billie Holiday and Teddy Wilson. For years I preferred Brassens to Brel, songs like 'J'ai rendez-vous avec vous' and 'Ballade des dames du temps jadis'. This preference cannot have been because his version of a good time involved less angst than Brel's since angst seeks itself out and I had plenty of it, with all that unrealised sensuality afloat like a levitating oasis in my air of lost connections – merely that he was easier to sing along with. This has become less important in recent years. [*fig. 70*]

Trio Avileño: *'Cha cha cha del transito'* [*fig. 71*]
I remember that even with my two left feet I could jive, cha-cha-cha and twist, three great dances which arrived in Britain in the 1950s (jive reached these shores much earlier but it gained a new lease of life with rock n' roll) and early 1960s. Diana Sanders, as I have said, taught me to jive; someone else (whoever you were, thank you) taught me the cha-cha-cha in my homeland, north-west London: the occasion was a party some time in the late 1950s, at the Swiss Cottage flat (my future friend Dan Weissbort was living in the same block, I discovered later) of a girl called Pat Woolf, close to the Odeon cinema. Perhaps the hostess herself taught me. I remember taking a book token as a present, which suggests it was a birthday party, otherwise I would have taken a box of chocolates, After-Eights. (Were such presents unique to me, as recommended by my parents, or was it normal in those circles?) I was taught the twist by Audrey at Cambridge in 1964, during a party in the Real Tennis Court on Grange Road, not long after I first heard a Beatles record at a gathering in Petty Cury, in the Naval Club above Heffers, where I met Anniken for the first

time, with whom I would get together later, even though most of the time there was a thousand miles between us.

Topic records: 'Northumbrian Garland' (Louis Killen, etc), *'Liverpool packet'* (Stan Kelly, etc), *'Blow the man down'* (A.L.Lloyd, Ewan MacColl), *'The collier's rant'* (Louis Killen)

The world of English folk music symbolised by the Topic label (these were the days before the fusion of folk and rock, even now resisted by purists) was part of my sixties education. If the Troubadour in Earls Court was where you went for American blues music, Bunjies off the Charing Cross Road and the Fox at Islington Green (I refuse to tell you what the name has been changed to) were two of the folk clubs that met once or twice a week and you could hear the best performers do their sets, for example my personal favourite Bob Davenport, to whom I am listening on Spotify as I type these words. This world had no points of contact whatsoever with my Mediterranean yearnings, which in truth were beginning to melt in the glare of reality: I was in England. It was a world of beer, not wine, of blue jeans and ponytails and black turtleneck jumpers, not slinky black dresses and eye shadow; of beards and pipes, not moustaches and cigarettes; of youth hostels in the English countryside, not small hotels in Paris. It was the sort of place Harold Wilson, mythologically, might have enjoyed, but not François Mitterand, again mythologically. You get the picture. [*fig. 72*]

There was a kind of purity about the sixties' folk scene, a pre-English Heritage authenticity with roots in left-wing activism and social conscience. I had LPs of Woodie Guthrie, Leadbelly, Pete Seeger and other American folk singers (and here is an EP of Joan Baez: 'Plaisir d'amour'/ 'There but for fortune'). I remember my San Francisco friend and Menard Press author Larry Fixel telling me he had taken over a shed from Woodie Guthrie in Los Angeles in the late thirties when he was participating in the Federal Writers' Project. One day before Michael Heller phoned me to say Larry had died, I faxed Larry to tell me about Guthrie. Too late; the message went unread, another old-timer friend had bitten the dust. I salute a fine and somewhat neglected writer and poet. During the mid-sixties I began to read books on social issues and the political economy and sought to forge a political philosophy of my own, which following Carlo Rosselli I later called 'liberal socialism'; everything

fig. 71

fig. 72

fig. 73

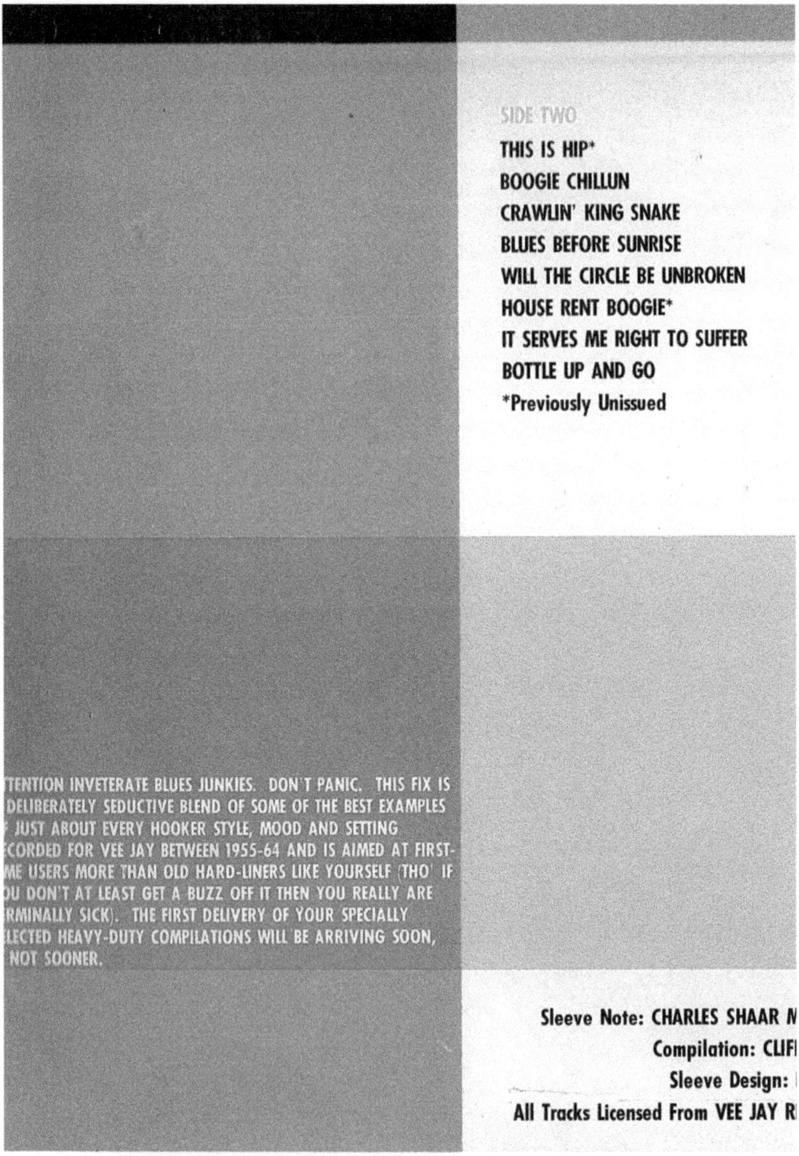
SIDE TWO
THIS IS HIP*
BOOGIE CHILLUN
CRAWLIN' KING SNAKE
BLUES BEFORE SUNRISE
WILL THE CIRCLE BE UNBROKEN
HOUSE RENT BOOGIE*
IT SERVES ME RIGHT TO SUFFER
BOTTLE UP AND GO
*Previously Unissued
TENTION INVETERATE BLUES JUNKIES. DON'T PANIC. THIS FIX IS
DELIBERATELY SEDUCTIVE BLEND OF SOME OF THE BEST EXAMPLES
JUST ABOUT EVERY HOOKER STYLE, MOOD AND SETTING
CORDED FOR VEE JAY BETWEEN 1955-64 AND IS AIMED AT FIRST-
ME USERS MORE THAN OLD HARD-LINERS LIKE YOURSELF (THO' IF
U DON'T AT LEAST GET A BUZZ OFF IT THEN YOU REALLY ARE
RMINALLY SICK). THE FIRST DELIVERY OF YOUR SPECIALLY
LECTED HEAVY-DUTY COMPILATIONS WILL BE ARRIVING SOON,
NOT SOONER.
Sleeve Note: CHARLES SHAAR
Compilation:
Sleeve Design:
All Tracks Licensed From VEE JAY

fig. 74

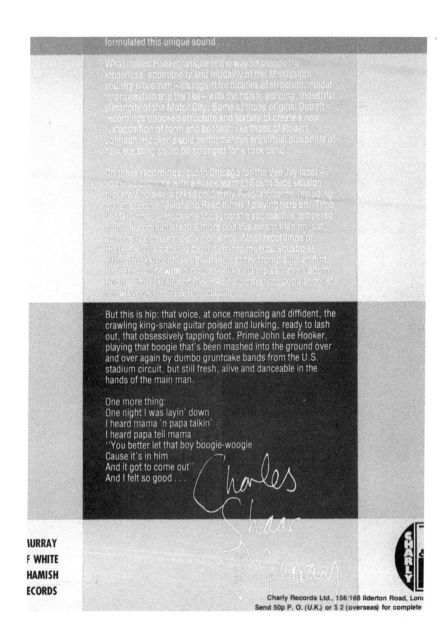

fig. 75

fig. 76

that has happened since confirms me in the belief that such a synthesis (with a non-negotiable green component), now and perhaps always unattainable, would be the best hope for the world. It was in part from the English folk singers that I learned about English and British geo-historical and class differences.

I find in my collection other folk records: 'The Saints'/ 'My Bonnie' by Tony Sheridan and the Beatles, 'Do you ken John Peel' by the Mike Sammes Singers, 'Sinner Man' by The Seekers, and Alexander Bochensky's balalaika ensemble playing 'Black Eyes' and 'Kalinka'. Russia: Russia was one of my passions; Chekhov and Dostoevsky were my favourite Russian writers. Russia's folk music plucked at my heartstrings. I had a vague idea of a personal 'Russian' (i.e. Russian-Jewish) connection, but my geography was wrong: research into family would trace the roots to east Galicia (now west Ukraine) and south Poland. Later too I would scribble on one of those scraps of paper I used rather than keeping notebooks (a disastrous policy which has had a deeply negative impact on my writing life): 'My head is divided between France and America. My heart is divided between Israel and Russia. That is why my body remains in England.' Such a divided self needed or thought it needed a south-European input to be healed and reconciled. To deconstruct the four worlds evoked by 'France', 'America', 'Israel' and 'Russia' is a subject for another time. 'Do you ken John Peel' contains the line 'from a view to a death in the morning': a great line of poetry and the title of an early novel by Anthony Powell, whose entire oeuvre I would read forty years later over a six-month period.

Memphis Slim: *'Cold-blooded woman'/ 'Lonesome'/ 'It's been so long'/ 'I'll just keep singing the blues'*; Ray Charles: *'Hit the road, Jack'/ 'The danger zone'*; Bert Jansch: *'Needle of Death'/ 'Tinker's blues'/ 'Running from home'/ 'Green are your eyes'/ 'The wheel'*; Mahalia Jackson: *'In the upper room'/ 'I have a friend'/ 'Tired'* [*fig. 73*]
I have always loved the blues. In the mid and late 1960s I would go from time to time, alone or with a like-minded friend, to the Troubadour in Earls Court and bigger venues. I heard Blind Gary Davis and, together, Sonny Terry and Brownie McGhee, and my all-time favourite, John Lee Hooker. I have several John Lee LPs and cassettes and CDs, indicative of his survival into my later musical phases. [*fig. 74*]

Blues has affinities with other traditions, such as klezmer and fado, and was one of the sources of rock and roll along with country and western music. Rock music is a synthesis of urban black and poor white country music. The spiral turned and twisted again with the later fusion of folk and rock. I would eventually come to enjoy Van Morrison (who championed Lonnie Donegan during the latter's years of neglect), and post-modern groups such as the Saw Doctors and the Pogues. But the 'pure' blues, as represented by Bessie Smith, John Lee Hooker and others, this music of the oppressed, is the music I like best when I am alone and have had a little too much to drink and am reminding myself that solidarity with the wretched of the earth is my deepest politico-religious commitment (the Internationale shall become the human race, bless Billy Bragg), my gut belief, and that I do not do enough to live up to it. Sadly, I have only a smidgen of hope that the West will wake up to its responsibilities in time. Thanks to climate change and shortage of resources brought about by our own irresponsibility and greed, we may find ourselves in a situation where putting up the shutters will prove to be a waste of effort, for the time will have passed when, out of altruism and self-interest, something could have been done. Still, we have to try, in the name of our grandchildren.

Ella Fitzgerald: *Relaxing with Ella ('Night and Day'/ 'Begin the Beguine'/ 'Just one of those things'/ 'Anything goes'); Relaxing with Ella 2 ('I get a kick out of you'/ 'I've got you under my skin'/ 'What is this thing called love?'/ 'It's all right with me'); With a Song in my Heart ('With a song in my heart'/ 'Every time we say goodbye'/ 'Manhattan'/ 'Blue moon'); Ella Fitzgerald in Concert ('Moonlight in Vermont' and three other songs); Sweet and Hot ('Lover come back to me' and three other songs).* Frank Sinatra: *Songs for Swinging Lovers ('You make me feel so young'/ 'It happened in Monterey'/ 'Anything goes'/ 'How about you?') and Frank Sinatra! ('The lady is a tramp'/ 'Witchcraft' / 'Come fly with me'/ 'Tell her you love her').* [fig. 75]
The first three of these five albums (significantly comprising Cole Porter and Rodgers and Hart songs) were among my most played EPs. Nobody projected sexual fantasies on to Ella (nor for that matter onto Edith Piaf whose 'Milord' / 'Je sais comment' is here), but Ella was a jazz singer of genius, perhaps the most popular one (in both senses) of all time, whereas Frank Sinatra, with his trilby and Windsor knot, was the jazziest popular

singer of all time. What these two shared was a detailed attention – intuitive and consciously judged – to phrasing, a caressing of key words, sometimes legato sometimes rubato reconstruction of small units into a deeply satisfying whole, as individual as any made by the great interpreters of Schubert or Brahms.

The Sandpipers: *'Guantanamera'* [*fig. 76*]
This is a version of Pete Seeger's adaptation of Jose Marti's famous poem. The song – in any good version – is one of my favourites for singing along. I am at this very moment playing Seeger's version on YouTube. I first heard the song at a goodbye party for the Cuban poet and diplomat Pablo Armando Fernandez at Arnold and Dusty Wesker's house in Highgate in 1967, at the end of Pablo's second stint in the Cuban Embassy. It is one of my Proustian madeleines, a trigger mechanism, a memory booster for that period in the mid to late 1960s when hope and promise on private and public levels interacted on the mind of an impressionable young man, with his philosophy of liberal socialism, his yearnings for sensual completion, his goodwill, his dependency, his neediness.

Thanks to Pablo I met Jose and Helen Yglesias in New York in 1964, and through them, Helen's son, the late Lewis Cole, who became a student leader at Columbia University, Robert Scheer and Alan Cheuse; also, Lee and Rosalind Baxandall, who lived near Auden in St Marks Place, and Warren Miller, a novelist who died young and is one of several people I recognise in disguise in Paul Zweig's memoir *Departures*, sent to me by Morris Dickstein, whose Introduction illuminates a new edition of the late poet's story of France. I met the exiled Cuban poet, a member of the Left opposition to Castro, Isel Rivero, who worked at the United Nations, and who alone of all these people became a close friend and remains one, talismanic, forty years on. Now living in Madrid, where she was still working for the UN until retirement in 2003, she visited Oporto in 2004 and, later, Cascais, to attend private views of Paula's shows, and from time to time, sends Paula opera CDs to play in the studio. Andrew Goodman, a friend of my painter friend Linda, was one of three students murdered for civil rights activism in the Deep South in the summer of 1964. That year and later, reading works by Ralph Ellison, Baldwin, Mailer, Lowell, Paul Goodman, Muriel Rukeyser, I was simultaneously enthralled by the USA and appalled: so, what's new?

Yes, at Pablo's goodbye party we sang 'Guantanamera' ('we' included my friend Michael Kustow, Pablo's good friend the recently late Annie Ross, David Mercer and Kika Markham) and drank red wine and danced (the conga), and on that occasion I remember feeling – not for the first or last time in my life – that the experience is real, yet not to the point of taking me over, not to the point of preventing me from processing it. The inability to be taken over is a bad habit, a character flaw: the moment itself in its *finitude* is not enough, it is never enough: rather the *now* is a harbinger of future possibility, of an elsewhere in time and perhaps space when some unrealised potential for life will be realised, that *plenitude* Yves Bonnefoy writes of with such wisdom and power, the plenitude that great literature and music and painting promise or propose as the fulfilment of human destiny in our only world. Yves Bonnefoy's *L'Arrière-pays* meditates upon the road not taken, our unfulfilled aspirations, our need for images, our desire for unity. The melancholy of dance music and the images of intimacy in a painter like Watteau speak of the three-way disjunction between experience, awareness and description, which can never be reconciled despite all attempts to do so, wretched and noble. How often are we released from language? When we dance? When we make love? (Silence, however, is voluntary). And release from language when alone? When I drink? When I look at paintings? When I listen to music? When I sleep? When I die.

'England Swings' by Roger Miller [*fig. 77*]
This dreadful song begins 'England swings like a pendulum *do*, / Bobbies on bicycles two by two, / Westminster Abbey, the Tower of Big Ben, / The rosy red cheeks of the little child*ren*.' My first employers, the British Travel Association, adopted it as a publicity mantra for the so-called Swinging Sixties. BTA's press officer in New York was Andrew Glaze, a published poet. I noted that he had a day job where writing was the central activity. The main responsibility of this Harvard-educated veteran of World War II was to write press releases about the UK. Someone told him that a new member of staff (about to go from London to Chicago via New York) was a poet too. (From time to time I thought of myself as one and must have described myself as such, although usually I had a cover story – poetry translator – when I was feeling insecure, which was most of the time.) So Andrew and I became friends, meeting soon after

my arrival in December 1965 for a six-month stay – the second of several trips to the USA.

Andy did me a good turn, by letting me down gently. I still have the letter in which he critiqued my early poems, telling me between the lines that there was, to put it mildly, room for improvement. He composed a memorable aphorism: 'Always begin a poem as near to the end as you can.' You may have needed to write yourself into the poem with that first stanza, but if you listen carefully it sounds like throat clearing or looks like scaffolding: remove it. He lived at apartment 2N, 803 Ninth Avenue, 10019, an unfashionable neighbourhood, with his tall and truly beautiful half-Hispanic wife Adriana, a marvellous dancer. Now well over ninety and serving as Poet Laureate in his native Alabama, after living for many years in Florida following his retirement from BTA, he is one of the last survivors of the personal pantheon of senior figures I have always needed: to impress, to learn from, to love. Andy Glaze has perfect pitch, although an American-English Vallejo crossed with Neruda comes closer to defining Glaze's aural and psycho-poetic territory than that of the American poets he read closely. [*2016, February 8: Andy has died and my bunch of mentors dwindles once again.*]

'River Kwai March' [*fig. 78*]
This is a *square* 45 bought in 1958 at the Brussels World Fair, which I visited with my best non-school friend, Paul Rochman. There is a picture of the British Pavilion on the playing side of the square; on the other side is a letter from me to my family. Is there a technology to read the faded, well-nigh vanished text written in red biro? Where the address has completely and utterly vanished, I make out the pencil-scrawled name 'Rosalind Altmann' and a SPEedwell number, same exchange as our own phone at Middleway. Out of writerly curiosity, I dialled the number and lo and behold it is still that of Renata Altmann, whose daughter is Baroness Rosalind Altmann, aged two at the time of the postcard; by good fortune Rosalind was visiting her mother when I phoned. We had a brief chat and I congratulated her on a recent unexpected policy statement about social care, which I approved of. Although the name Rudolf rang a bell, nothing emerged. Given her tender age at the time of the card, I must have scribbled down the name years later on whatever was to hand. We agreed that we will never know why. Indeed, it matters only to me, as a writer

interested in what gets lost in the interstices of time – like the use of letters for the names of Exchanges, which went out around 1970 when Altmann was fourteen.

That summer, Paul and I youth-hostelled our way around Belgium and Luxembourg, and received our O level results in Antwerp. He was a boarder at Aldenham School, only a few miles north of Finchley, and yet a world away. One of the things we did together was putting on the green. The green is still there but not the putting. My surviving scorecard records a game I played against myself. I am suspicious about the corrections [*fig. 79*]. I still have Paul's letters with their distinctive left-handwriting, begging for all the latest gossip from the Suburb. We never spoke on the phone in termtime. Today of course he and I would email or text each other. Sadly he no longer has my letters – which would be a rich source, along with the letters (unpreserved) to Sue Leveson in hospital, of material about a vanished world.

Eydie Gormé: *'Yours tonight'/ 'What happened to our love'* [*fig. 80*]
Eydie Gormé, who died in 2013, was a favourite of Paul Rochman's not mine, but for some reason, utterly coincidental, two French friends, brothers, Paul and Alain Sultan, gave me the record: witness their messages on the record sleeve. It was a goodbye present after their trip to London in August 1961. They had come to visit the city and myself, a few weeks after my departure from Paris, where I had spent six months – already mentioned – at the Jewish students' hostel in rue Guy Patin, home to them and other boys, mainly from the Maghreb. They, like so many Maghrebis, later emigrated to Israel ('went up' as the Hebrew has it when you obey the commandment to abandon the condition of exile, that is life in the diaspora) after gaining professional qualifications in France.

Chronologically although not narratologically, my book *The Arithmetic of Memory* ends with the summer of 1961, before I discovered sexuality and writing at Cambridge. I remember that Paul Sultan was very keen to meet girls but the ones I knew were on holiday and I was not competent to be proactive in the search. That summer I had to reboot and upgrade my Russian, essential for my forthcoming Modern Languages studies at Cambridge. I had private lessons with Madame Alhasova-Tomashchina in Notting Hill. These were the final weeks of my sexual and writing latency, although I could not know it at the time.

fig. 78

fig. 77

fig. 79

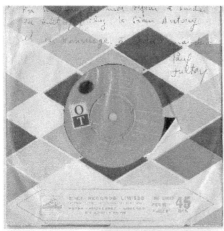

fig. 80

fig. 81

fig. 82

Around two years later, just before my third and final year at Cambridge (when the John Barrell episode involving the rewriting of my poem took place), I would spend my twenty-first birthday at the Biennale de Poésie in Knokke-le-Zoute, having flown to Belgium from Southend with my first patron (if that is the word), Miron Grindea, editor of *Adam*. Among my EPs is 'Biennale 63', with recitals by some of the participitants in the Congress that year (among them Langston Hughes and Kateb Yacine), which a group of young poets, *Jeunesses Poétiques*, gave me as a birthday present. The most significant encounter from my point of view was with the Russian poet Evgeny Vinokurov, the poetry editor of *Novi Mir*, whom I have already mentioned.

I was beginning to reject my father's view of our family's place in the scheme of things: for him, as he once said, there were three kinds of people: those who create, those who are receptive to what has been created, and everybody else. We were in the second group: those who appreciate the arts, read books, go to the theatre, etc. (This traditional attitude was reconciled with progressive politics by the argument that education and arts policy, involving very high taxation, which my father approved of, would bring increasing numbers from group three into group two). Something was beginning to irritate me. There was an itch inside my brain, and this had to be scratched. Just as I had to find out about women and begin my clumsy and ignorant explorations, so I had to find out about writing and begin my clumsy and ignorant explorations.

After the Biennale, on the way to Paris from Brussels, I found myself sitting next to Guillermo Cabrera Infante, the Cuban cultural attaché in Brussels, not yet a famous translated novelist; he told me to contact the poet Pablo Armando Fernandez, his opposite number in London. When I returned to London a few days later, I 'celebrated' my twenty-first birthday by taking a girl called Pat I had met – at a vacation job in Poland Street – to the Café des Artistes in Redcliffe Gardens, where I usually went on my own, hoping someone would talk to me, hoping the music would talk to me, hoping the drink would talk to me. But none of them ever did. On this occasion the girl gave me a present of aftershave, something I have never used, before or since, and did not appreciate or want.

Eventually Michael Schmidt would publish a pamphlet by me and a few years later a book: the book[42] received one wonderful review, in the *Scotsman*, from a real and famous poet, George Mackay Brown. Even now

I hold on to his words whenever I am not sure who or what I am. Later I would turn my attention to literary criticism, poetry translation and, in recent years, fiction, autobiography and writing about art. Imagine if Carcanet's press cuttings had been less efficient and I had not been sent a copy of the review. I pored over the London newspapers which printed nothing, but I would never have known about the *Scotsman*. I sense that not to have read that review would have changed my life for the worse. But I am not about to write a counter-history, although I am beginning to discover that counter-history is one source of fictional inspiration. Don't write about what you don't know, some say. And yet, educated guessing is a strategy for incorporating into your personal knowledge what did not happen but could so easily have done. Another word for it is imagination.

Paul Robeson: *Sanders of the River* [*fig. 81*]
Robeson's singing is too mellifluous, much as I like him. He belongs in spirit to an earlier period: the days of my parents' 78 collection. They had the 'Volga Boatmen' and 'Ol' man river'.

Two Classical EPs: '*Coppélia*' by Delibes (Ernest Ansermet & L'Orchestre de la Suisse romande); '*Eine Kleine Nachtmusik*' by Mozart (Karl Münchinger & the Stuttgart Chamber Orchestra). [*fig. 82*]
These were the first two classical records I ever bought (at HMV of course), in the late 1950s. As such, they are significant, although I have no way of recovering why I chose them. Perhaps I had heard them on what used to be known as the Third Programme or on *Children's Favourites*, if I was still listening to it.

Miscellaneous Items

The first group contains tuneful pop songs, which gave me simple pleasure

Group One

Acker Bilk: '*Stranger on the shore*'
Johnny Duncan and the Blue Grass Boys: '*Last train to San Fernando*'
Jerry Keller: '*Here comes summer*'
Kalin Twins: '*When*'

The Pony-Tails: *'Born too late'*
Conway Twitty: *'It's only make-believe' and 'Mona Lisa'*
The Everly Brothers: *'That'll be the day' and 'All I have to do is dream'*
Emile Ford/the Playmates: *'What do you want to make those eyes at me for?'*
Roy Orbison: *'Oh, pretty woman' and 'Only the lonely'*

Group Two

Mills Bros: *four songs*
Pearl Bailey/Rose Murphy: *two songs each*
Les Troubadours du Roi Baudouin: *Missa Luba 'Kyrie'/'Sanctus' (from If)*
Les Méridiens: *'Verte campagne'*
Jane Birkin and Serge Gainsbourg: *'Je t'aime... moi non plus'*
Billie Holiday: *'Strange fruit'* [See 78s for Billie Holiday]
Pete and Dud: *'Goodbyeee'*
Red Army Choir: *'La Marseillaise'*
Kay Starr: *'Good for Nothing Joe'*
Fritz Spiegel: *'Eine Kleine Beatle Musik' (Ludwig van Beatlehoven etc)*
Bob Dylan: *'Times they are a-changin'*
Sabatino Cantore and I Musici: *Marcello's Oboe Concerto*

My 33⅓s

1

Basil Bunting Reads 'Briggflatts', Bloodaxe, YRIC 0001, 1980
Yves Bonnefoy (in French) Disques BAM, LD 707, 19??
Evgeny Vinokurov reads (in Russian), Melodiya, 1974 (or earlier)
Kathleen Ferrier, recital, Decca BR 3052, 1960
Kathleen Ferrier, boxed set of seven, Decca AKF 1-7, 1968
Ruth Olay: Olay!, EmArcy/Mercury MG36125, 19??
Ruth Olay: Easy Living, Mercury 20390, 19??
Ruth Olay: Olay! OK! Everest 5218, 19??
Ruth Olay: In person at Mister Kelly's, United Artists 315, 1960
Tchaikovsky, 1st Piano Conc., Noel Mewton-Wood, Classics Club (Da Vinci 68), undated

I heard Basil Bunting read his great poem 'Briggflats' at the Poetry Society in Earls Court Square during the 1970s. I was chairman of the society's events committee for three of the six years I was on the General Council. On the occasion of Bunting's reading, my friend Keith Bosley played Scarlatti's Sonata in B minor, a work crucial to the poem. On the LP I am looking at, the harpsichordist George Malcolm is the performer. Until Tommy (as Kenny Smith liked to call him) Pickard rediscovered Bunting in Newcastle – where he was working as a sub on the local evening newspaper – the elderly poet had been as neglected in England as his Objectivist friends still were in America. In the mid-sixties, my Cambridge contemporary Andrew Crozier persuaded one of the Objectivists, Carl Rakosi, to start writing again. I had discovered the work of Reznikoff and the other Objectivists in the Gotham Bookmart and other bookshops in 1964, on my first trip to the States.[43] [*fig. 83*]

Bunting and my late friend and early, perhaps first, Menard Press author, D.G. Bridson are the only two non-Americans included in Ezra Pound's *Active Anthology*. Geoffrey Bridson, a legendary producer for the old BBC Radio Features Department, is now sadly forgotten as a poet but Bunting's reputation is secure. Like the Alps in one of his poems, Basil is here and you will have to go a long way round if you want to avoid him. Augustus Young served as Bunting's minder for the BBC on one memorable occasion and wrote about it entertainingly in his memoir *Light Years*.

The late 1960s saw a flowering of interest in poetry translation. This led to and/or was caused by a sense that England had become too insular as a literary culture. It was good timing for me: initially ignorant, and blissfully so, of the literary world, I had been translating Yves Bonnefoy and the Russian poet Evgeny Vinokurov from around 1963. I have their voices on disc: the Russian record on my desk was signed to me by the poet. [*fig. 84*] The message reads: 'For my translator, Anthony Rudolf, with thanks, this keepsake, Evg. Vinokurov, 24. 11. 74. Moscow.'

Yves Bonnefoy's poetry taught me that creation in a writer is a spiritual vehicle synthesising dialectically the conscious and unconscious mind to convey the nature of human presence in our only world: there was a strange convergence of hubris and humility in the artistic project, that was for sure. I was hooked. What other reasons were there to translate Bonnefoy and Vinokurov, but also, later on, the other French and Russian poets I've mentioned? I discovered Bonnefoy and Vinokurov, as one does, by accident, but I had studied French and Russian and could read them in the original. I loved their work and to translate them was one way of learning how to write better poetry, provided poetry was on the radar in the first place. It also served as a cover story while I practised on the older poets. I know now that some of my early 'exercises' – translations as well as my own poems – should not have been published. Still, the later accident of meeting Alberto de Lacerda, thanks either to Anthony Barnett or Claude Royet-Journoud, and, through Alberto, Nathaniel Tarn, led to my appearance as Bonnefoy's translation reader at the first Poetry International, in 1967, on the South Bank, and to my meeting Ted Hughes, the person at the heart of the war against English insularity – ironically enough given his Englishness (deep as the pike in his poem). Tarn and I are the last living survivors of those who performed at the first Poetry International. My name is not on the programme because I was a last-minute stand-in for Hughes, who had hurt his back.

Ted was fascinated by central and eastern European poets such as Pilinszky, Popa, Holub, Rozewicz and Herbert. Daniel Weissbort had founded *Modern Poetry in Translation* with Hughes in 1965 and, within three or four years, Carcanet Press, Anvil Press and my own Menard Press[44] followed suit, all three starting out as magazines, all three committed to translation. Around 1970, the year we got married, Brenda and I became London editors (i.e. sales reps) of *Stand*, and, with the editor Jon Silkin and others, sold the magazine in pubs and cinema queues around Hampstead and Chelsea. In 1969 or 1970 I wrote to several poets, including Bunting, Hughes, Neruda and Stephen Spender, asking for translations or thoughts on translation for *The Journals of Pierre Menard*, the magazine alluded to above which I began editing in 1968/9 in collaboration with my late friend Peter Hoy. The years I was on the General Council of the Poetry Society (1970–1976) coincided with the interregnum, the Kerensky revolution, presided over by that benign but determined liberal Norman Hidden, who lived into his nineties; we swept away the society's Georgian fustian, and were in turn swept away by proponents of a more radical agenda associated with the late Bob Cobbing and Lawrence Upton. I was on good terms with both of them, although not in complete agreement. Lawrence died in 2020, as isolated as Val Warner, whom I mentioned earlier in the book. [*fig. 85*]

In 1972, the year I became managing editor of *European Judaism*, I was invited along with Daniel Weissbort to be a UK delegate at the Struga/Ohrid Poetry Evenings in Macedonia. There, I participated with Weissbort in various events, and met John Montague, Victor Shklovsky (who disdained me because I was overheard saying 'Neither Washington nor Moscow'), W.S. Merwin, Herbert Kuhner, Zbigniew Herbert and senior Macedonian and Serbian poets. We saw a drunken horse charging across the famous bridge in Ohrid, a political gesture allegedly organised by Albanian irredentists. I published the very first MenCard (a Bonnefoy poem of course – the one and only translation I've never felt the need to revise) as a kind of visiting card.

Brenda was working as a primary-school teacher from 1968 until 1974, when Nathaniel was born, or born out, as he would say later of his baby sister. At one point Brenda took over from me a commission to write a children's book, *The Under-Five Gang*, illustrated by Martin Wiener, which was to be published by Corgi. A few years later she took over another commission, this time to abridge Bernard Kops's *World is a Wedding* for Radio Four, *Book at Bedtime*. During these years, while trying to write my own poems and translate French and Russian poetry and working on various other texts, including my earliest very short stories, my day jobs included supply teaching and teaching English as a foreign language, having gained a qualification in TEFL; later I was editor of a children's magazine for the educational publisher Mary Glasgow and Baker, employee of the antiquarian Covent Garden Bookshop in Long Acre (I was in charge of literary periodicals), translator of a literary historical book by Françoise Basch about Victorian women for Penguin Press, and editor at J.M. Dents in Albemarle Street, helping update the *Everyman Encyclopaedia*, with responsibility for the literature, language and Judaism entries. And there would be other jobs.

One of the poems that Yves Bonnefoy reads in that unique chant of his, scanning the poetry in the English style, is the uncharacteristic 'To the Voice of Kathleen Ferrier', inspired by the singer's sublime rendition of Mahler's *Song of the Earth*, conducted by Bruno Walter. I have a box of seven LPs of Kathleen Ferrier, on which she sings the repertoire from Bach to Mahler. I also have an old 10-inch LP of her singing a selection of folksongs. [*fig. 86*] She is the ultimate contralto. It had not occurred to me till this moment that the great female jazz and jazz-influenced

fig. 83

fig. 84

BASIL BUNTING
Shadingfield
Wylam
Northumberland
10 January 1969

Dear Mr Rudolf

I've written nothing for a long time, and
have no poems, no translations at all on hand or
in hand.
Your magazine sounds like an interesting
venture. There is another magazine, I forget its
name, also busy with translations - I expect
you know all about it - but there's certainly
room for more than one.
I believe Michael Alexander is busy with
Beowulf. That would be worth having.
What's wanted? Current poetry - most of
it, I imagine Spanish. Competent version of
Gongora, swift version of the Cantar del Cid,
an attempt on ~~Metastasio~~ Metastasio, almost
anything Arabic or Persian. You know, I expect,
Omar Pound's bits of Arabic.
I am sorry I've nothing.
Yours faithfully

Delay in answering unavoidable. Forgive it.

fig. 85

BR 3052

ARTISTS' PORTRAITS SERIES

KATHLEEN FERRIER

with PHYLLIS SPURR (piano)

Side 1

1. Ye banks and braes (arr. Quilter)
2. Now sleeps the crimson petal (arr. Quilter)
3. Drink to me only with thine eyes (arr. Quilter)
4. O waly, waly (coll. Sharp, arr. Britten)
5. I know where I'm going (Hughes, adapt. Gray)
6. I will walk with my love (arr. Hughes)

Side 2

1. Blow the wind southerly (arr. Whittaker)
2. Have you seen but a whyte lillie grow? (arr. Grew)
3. The lover's curse (arr. Hughes)
4. Willow, willow (arr. Warlock)
5. Down by the Sally Gardens (arr. Hughes)
6. Ma bonny lad (trad.)

Kathleen Ferrier's remarkable but regrettably short career owed a great deal to the personality that shone through her singing at all times. A radiantly lovely person to see, that radiance and the sincerity that engendered it informed her performance of such things as Mahler's Das Lied von der Erde and Schumann's Frauenliebe und -leben, filling her interpretations with a humanity and sincerity that were almost unbearably touching. The same quality that she brought to these highly polished jewels of the composer's craft she bestowed on those smaller gems, the folk-songs. Most of them are folk-songs or near folk-songs, four Irish (I know where I'm going, I will walk with my love, The lover's curse and Down by the Sally Gardens), one Scottish (Ye banks and braes, a synthetic folk-song with words by Burns) and three English (O waly, waly, Blow the wind southerly and Ma bonny lad). Three more are anonymous, though now accepted as traditional (Willow, willow, Drink to me only—to words by Ben Jonson—and Have you seen but a whyte lillie grow?). The only art-song (to use that convenient but not very happy word) is Roger Quilter's setting of Tennyson's poem Now sleeps the crimson petal, one of the most beautiful English songs ever written.

tender care that goes straight to the heart of the listener from the heart of the singer—an effect enhanced by the unaccompanied singing. The utter simplicity of Miss Ferrier's approach shows a spontaneous love and understanding and an absence of that feeling so common amongst other singers that folk-songs need 'interpreting'.

An English singer with an international reputation, Kathleen Ferrier always showed a special affection for the songs of her own country and there was always a group of them in her recitals. The songs on this record faithfully mirror that love.

© The Decca Record Co. Ltd., London, 1960

FAVOURITE MUSIC IN THE DECCA BR SERIES

BR 3004
Mendelssohn: SYMPHONY No. 4 in A ("Italian")
Israel Philharmonic Orchestra/Georg Solti

BR 3011
Tchaikovsky: SWAN LAKE—Highlights
L'Orchestre de la Suisse Romande/Ernest Ansermet

BR 3016
Adam: GISELLE—Highlights
Paris Conservatoire Orchestra/Jean Martinon

BR 3023
Puccini: MADAMA BUTTERFLY—Highlights
Tebaldi, Bergonzi/Orchestra of the Accademia di Santa Cecilia, Rome/Tullio Serafin

BR 3048
Grieg: SIGURD JORSALFAR—Suite
London Symphony Orchestra/Oivin Fjeldstad
HOLBERG SUITE
Stuttgart Chamber Orchestra/Karl Münchinger

BR 3039
Schumann: PIANO CONCERTO
Backhaus/VPO/Günter Wand

---

fig. 86

fig. 87

fig. 88

popular singers are all – is this coincidence? – contraltos: Ella (see 45s), Billie (see 78s), Sarah Vaughan, Peggy Lee and Anita O'Day and June Christy (see *Miscellaneous* below); Bessie Smith, Mahalia Jackson and Marian Anderson too. Contralto is my favourite female 'voice', and I tend to prefer female to male in song of all kinds, as well as in opera.

Perhaps the cause of the low career profile in jazz of my step-cousin Ruth Olay [*fig. 87*] – who had a magnificent voice in her prime (check YouTube) – is that she is a full-blooded soprano who should have been singing at the Met. Her mother was an operetta singer, her father a rabbi in Hollywood, and she would have heard powerful cantorial tenor voices in the synagogue as a child. Ruth's mother, when widowed, married my father's cousin Zygfryd Rudolf, and to say that he did not get on with Ruth would be an understatement. There is good music in my step-cousin's family and circle: Ruth's nephew Larry Sonderling was a first violin in the Los Angeles Philharmonic, and obtained André Previn's autograph for my son years ago. Larry's mother Mira was a friend of my late friend Annette Kaufman, former grande dame of the Los Angeles music world and widow/accompanist of Louis Kaufman, one of the great violinists in recorded, I mean recording, history, on disc, in the concert hall and on film; Louis, as the solo violin in countless movies, has to be the most listened to violinist ever. His hands can be seen playing in *Intermezzo*, a tiny man crouching unseen behind the star, Leslie Howard.[45]

When I was younger, I preferred music without the human voice, and on balance I still do, the complete opposite of Paula. I would not want to say that music and painting were, and to some extent are, my 'escapes' from the word – words being what I spend my life exploring as a writer, translator and reader – but to experience artistic intensity and vision in non-verbal modes generates new modes of spiritual renewal, even if I sometimes find myself translating what I hear and/or see into words. Music without words, rather than opera, best conveys 'the space of time' – moving me, sometimes to tears, by its aural incarnation of the composer's mind, spirit and let us say soul. These days my musical preference is more austere than it used to be, with solo piano at the heart. I observe that my LP collection, reflecting my classical taste until the mid 1980s when I moved to cassettes and then CDs (78s are mainly from the 1950s, EPs mainly from the 1960s), contains much orchestral music. The most played records, especially in the early days, perhaps inevitably included the grand warhorses of the virtuoso repertoire. Some of my records were bought by mail order from Classics Club and World Record Club.

The soloist on the Classics Club version of Tchaikowsky's first piano concerto was the Australian Noel Mewton-Wood, who committed suicide at thirty-one, younger even than Dinu Lipatti, who died from Hodgkin's disease at thirty-three. After I reported that I had bought this record, my New Zealander piano teacher Douglas Zanders impressed me with the information that he had personally known Mewton-Wood. [*fig. 88*] In later years I reacted against the famous and tuneful symphonies and concertos and found myself despising composers like Tchaikowsky because they were popular. Now that I am beyond such trivial considerations, I have discovered the darker and more tormented Tchaikowsky of *The Queen of Spades* and *Francesca da Rimini* and listen to the popular works. I heard a magnificent rendering of the Fifth Symphony, conducted by Vassili Sinaisky. As a reader and writer of autobiography, as a music lover, as a human being, I am fascinated by this great composer's life.

2

Yehudi and Hephzibah Menuhin: *Beethoven Violin Sonatas 5 and 9*, EMI/HMV, ALP 1739, 1959
I got to know Hephzibah Menuhin in the 1980s, more in her personal capacity as a social activist than as the superb musician she was. Hephzibah was the equal and complementary partner of an infuriating but fascinating man, Richard Hauser, a Viennese Jew who always wore a rumpled suit. Officially a sociologist, he was, in the mould of Nicholas Albery and Michael Young, a conceptual inventor. Richard would describe a hundred problems every day and propose two hundred solutions. A few of these would be brilliant and even workable, given factors that might or might not be under his control. Richard and Hephzibah never stopped worrying about human wrongs and human rights, and the two of them should be honoured. They lived in Ponsonby Place by the Tate Gallery. This is my second copy of the record. I had originally bought it in the early 1960s but I lent it to Nicky Strauss at Cambridge, and he scratched it. Ever the gentleman, he presented me with a replacement copy. [*fig. 89*]

3

Mozart, *6th Symphony in F Major*, Moscow State Philharmonic Orchestra, Cond. Nathan Rachlin, undated

I have here a record of Mozart's 'country symphony in F major' (no K number, no symphony number either) as it is described on the record label, one of a number of records I bought in Moscow in the summer of 1960. Inside the record sleeve are two letters, both undated. I must have made successful attempts to discover which number it was because the first letter, fully three pages, from the Library Research Service of the *Encyclopaedia Britannica* at 67 Great Russell Street, tells me they cannot trace any reference to the description 'country', before listing their bibliographical sources. Someone has then typed out (in those pre-photocopying and scanning days) three quarto pages from a French book of 1912 listed in their sources. Apparently the symphony is important as marking the transition between Mozart's earliest, Italian, manner and his second, Viennese, manner. He was eleven when he wrote it. [*fig. 90*] The second letter, addressed to me at Cambridge, is from Y. Lukin, consultant of the 'Pravda' Literature and Arts Departament (*sic*). He refers to my letter of 1 June (1962) and here too it is clear that I already knew it was the Sixth Symphony. He proceeds to mention a book not listed by the *Britannica* researcher: 'the well-known reference book compiled by L. Köchel, systematizator of the information concerning Mozart's works, givs (*sic*) the following name to the fa-major (6th) Symphony: 'Dorthmusicanten-sesteten' (Sextettes of the country musicians). Here, in the Soviet Union, it is traditionally called "The Country Symphony". Sincerely Yours'. [*fig. 91 & 92*]

4

These days, as I have said, most of my listening is to solo piano: Schubert, Chopin, Schumann, Brahms, Liszt, Debussy. I buy very little modern music, but I listen to Radio Three regularly and try to educate myself in post-Mahlerian, post-Debussyan, post-Stravinskian, post-second Viennese school of music, partly for its and my own sake, partly because I have been writing stories about two female composers, and I need to know what they do, and why. Performances of, say, Beethoven, by modern conductors who are themselves composers, including the main man, Boulez, are particularly instructive.

I go to old music, defined as music with harmonic resolution as a key element, for consolation. I go to later music for the primal demands made upon my inner ear, and that synthesis of thought and feeling which creates and is created by artistic understanding. Modern music cannot be consolatory, redemptive, any more than modern painting. This is an over-simplification but I believe it contains an element of human truth. The earlier work is not easier or less challenging: Beethoven string quartets and late piano sonatas contain enough richness of discordant insight to challenge the ear, but ultimately Beethoven resolves, even if audiences in his own day could not always hear it. When it comes to painting, Manet is on the cusp. He is the first modern painter, far earlier than the first modern composer, let us say Debussy. The composition of Manet's *Déjeuner sur l'herbe* and *Olympia* still has the power to shock, although resolution and therefore consolation are still to be found.

Dinu Lipatti, *Chopin Waltzes,* Columbia 33CX 1032, undated [*fig. 93*]
Dinu Lipatti, *Boxed set of four,* EMI/HMV HLM 7202-5, 1980
Geza Anda, *Chopin Waltzes,* Eurodisk 89754, 1975
(Stephen Bishop Kovacevic, *Chopin and Ravel Waltzes CD*)
One of the records I listened to all the time was by my favourite pianist of those days, perhaps of all my days, Dinu Lipatti: his Chopin waltzes. Later Musa Farhi gave me the box of four Lipatti LPs: Bach, Scarlatti, Mozart, Chopin, Liszt, Ravel, Enesco. One of the pieces is 'Jesu, Joy of Man's Desiring' in the arrangement by Myra Hess, which Lipatti recorded in a studio in July 1950. In December of the same year, in Besançon, the piece was his encore in what he knew was his final recital. As someone who has an unexamined fascination for those who die young (whether suicide or accident or illness), I have no doubt that this was not a 'lollypop' encore, but a considered and heartfelt farewell to live music, to this world, to life. I do not know if there was a strictly Christian element to the choice but, even if there wasn't, the links between the aesthetics of music (and painting) and the stuff of religion until the late eighteenth century were so close that in one sense this element cannot be avoided. But art speaks to our mortality – Chekhov said the village church was the only place the peasant could find beauty – and with that encore Lipatti spoke to his own

fig. 89

fig. 90

Mr. Antony Rudolf
Trinity College
Cambrige
England

          Dear Sir,
     In Your letter on June I You wrote us that in 1960,while
staying in the Soviet Union, You had bought a record of
"The Country Symphony" by Mozart.You ask why this work has
such a name while in England it is simply called "The Sixth
Symphony".
     The well-known reference book compiled by L.Küchel,
systematizator of the information concerning Mozart's works,
givs the following name to the fa-major(sixth) Symphony:
"Dorfmusicanten-sexteten" (Sextettes of the country musicians").Here, in the Soviet Union it is traditionally called
"The Country Symphony".

                    Sincerely Yours,

                         Y.Lukin
                    Consultant of the "Pravda"
               Literature and Arts Departament.

fig. 91

ENCYCLOPAEDI
67 GREAT RUSSELL

A. Rudolf, Esq.,
41, Middleway,
Hampstead Garden Suburb,
London, N.W.11.

With the Compliments of
THE LIBRARY RESEARCH SERVICE
ENCYCLOPÆDIA BRITANNICA LTD.
With apologies for the long delay
caused by heavy pressure of work.

67 GREAT RUSSELL STREET, LONDON, W.C.1

Mozart - Symphon,

We much regret that in spite of considerau....   m
unable to trace any reference to the description of the ....   ne
terms which you cite. We quote the sources which we used in t..
bibliography below.

Bibliography

British National Bibliography 1950-1962

        "Mozart in Music Life Today"
        in Essays and Lectures   Oxford, 1945

Einstein, A.   Mozart, his character and his work   London, 1947

Groves Dictionary of Music, Vol. 5, L - M   London, 1954

King, Hyatt A.   Mozart in Retrospect   Oxford, 1956
        Studies in criticism and Bibliography

Music Index 1957-1961
    This also contains references to articles prior to 1957

Readers Guide to Periodical Literature 1900-1962   New York

Robbins-Landon, H.   The Mozart Companion   London, 1956
Mitchell, D.C.

fig. 92

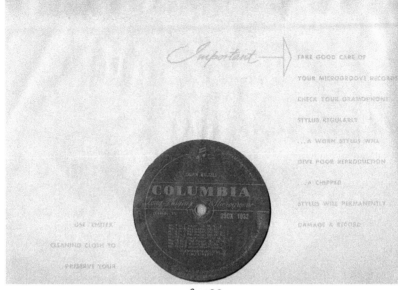

fig. 93

fig. 94

BAND CALL
Duke Ellington and his Orchestra

Side 1
1. 12th Street Rag
2. Isle of Capri
3. Chile Bowl
4. All Day Long
5. Bunny Hop Mambo
6. Satin Doll

Side II
1. If I Give My Heart to You
2. Blue Jean Beguine
3. Echo Tango
4. Band Call
5. Blue Moon
6. Smile

The Ellington band reached one of its great peaks in 1940. This was the period that gave us an extraordinary series of miniature masterpieces, played by what many consider to have been the finest band Duke ever had. The first half of the 1940's was still a fine time for Ellingtonia, despite the recording ban (1942-44) and some major changes in personnel. But by the end of the decade things were not so good. Conditions of work for big bands in the U.S. were getting progressively difficult. In 1950 Ellington was virtually the only man to have a full jazz orchestra in regular activity. There was also disaffection in the ranks, culminating in the bulk departure, in 1951, of Johnny Hodges, Lawrence Brown, and Sonny Greer. Duke made adroit replacements; but there is no doubt that the unsettled conditions affected the band's output during 1951 and 1952, although the acquisition of Willie Smith, Juan Tizol and Louis Bellson from the Harry James band improved matters considerably. Smith in particular, one of jazz's great section leaders, pulled the rather ragged saxophone team together. He did not stay long, but his influence continued to be felt.

By 1954, the foundations of the modern Ellington band were firmly laid. The crisis period had passed, and subsequent changes in personnel were absorbed without undermining the band's character. It was still without Hodges, who did not return until 1955; and around the same time, the Sam Woodyard-Jimmy Woode rhythm

pretty unsuitable) presented in a thoroughly Ellingtonish manner. Duke himself was very happy with the results. He is a man who frequently enjoys making play with the materials of his art; and it is clear that both he and the band took a warm pleasure in making these recordings, with their forthright swinging quality, their frequent sly digs at the popular music scene of the day, and the opportunity they gave to the soloists to show their paces. If there is no new *Ko-Ko* or *Jack the Bear*, there is the strongest impression of a working band (the world's best, as always) enjoying its work in the studio in the most positive manner.

Whenever the Ellington band plays, whether it plays Duke's own music or not, it is quite unmistakable. This is because the Ellington voicings are entirely original, the scores touched with his own creative imagination. Thus a ' pop ' tune often becomes transformed into a miniature Ellington tone poem; and a flamboyant, extravert, hotly swinging effusion has a natural abandon and ebullience no other big band seems quite able to capture. And there is humour in Duke's music, too—a sense of sheer fun that communicates itself through the whole band, and the audience.

Not everyone can take Duke's inconsequential trifles with an easy mind. Such things as *Isle of Capri*, *Bunny hop mambo*, *Twelfth Street rag mambo*, put a wry expression on the faces of the righteous. But Duke is not a righteous man—at least not in that sense. He does

1930. Tongue-in-cheek? Maybe. But it's a good cheek to have a tongue in—especially if it's Duke's!

Another side of the picture is the frequent use of the singer, Jimmy Grissom. At this time Grissom can pass from the pleasantly rhythmic style of, say, *Ballin' the blues*, to the ghoulishly sentimental. Singers have never been a strong point with Duke—largely because the band is so good. But this is a general problem; only a handful of jazz singers are up to the best Ellington standard; and they have appeared no more than intermittently with him. But Grissom is considerably featured here. His abilities are in evidence on the small group version of *Blue Moon*, which has Duke and Billy Strayhorn, Nance (violin), Marshall and Black, backing Grissom.

More authentic Ellingtonia comes with Strayhorn's *All day long; Duke's Band call, Chile bowl*, and a version of the delightful *Satin doll*. (The admirable bass player here is Wendell Marshal.) Also the engaging Ellington/Cat Anderson *Blue jean beguine*. Most of the soloists have a good blow: Willie Cook on *All day*, Terry on *Chile bowl*, Hamilton and Anderson on *Bunny hop*—and so on. Indeed, many of these tracks are settings for the soloists, after the familiar manner. And Duke's piano is prominently (and rewardingly) featured. Close knit orchestral scores are not used to a great extent. And that in itself gives the album its character, as much as anything. One thing is sure : Duke never stands still. Every period in the band's history shows him mortality, and to ours. He left behind a stain, many stains, upon the silence, in Beckett's phrase. Without Bach, no Lipatti, but without Lipatti, no Bach, or more modestly, no Lipatti's Bach. His playing of the Chopin waltzes incarnates the apotheosis of the dance and is, strictly speaking, beyond comparison. Nonetheless Geza Anda, whose Chopin waltzes (his last recording) I have, and Stephen Kovacevic Bishop, survive the comparison. I had a lengthy discussion with Stephen Kovacevic at Marina Warner's house about consolation and resolution in music. He agreed with me but was clearly relieved that I did not consider Bartok and Stravinsky modern. I explained that by listening to modern music I had educated my ear to the point that what I would once have called modern I now considered traditional.

You cannot and are not intended to dance to Chopin's waltzes but the composer takes the familiar idiom of the dance floor, and, on the other side of idealised or essentialised memories or anticipations, even more distilled than those of Schubert, Beethoven, Weber and Berlioz, creates a profound image of the melancholy joy of this activity, melancholy because like love-making and carnival and life itself, it must end, the sheer magic must come to an end. It is a melancholy that Watteau perhaps more than any other painter, Joseph Roth perhaps more than any other writer, Chopin certainly more than any other composer conveyed, and never more so than in the waltzes (and never more so than in Lipatti's interpretation), where we die to ourselves and are reborn each time we listen.

5

Ben-Zion Orgad, *Mizmorim, Cantata for Soloists & Chamber Orchestra*, Gary Bertini and the Israel Chamber Ensemble, CBS, S 72724, 1970 or earlier
Chassidic Dances, Simcha Records, JLP 5, undated
I have here a record of Chassidic dances given to me by my sister Annie at some point no longer determinable. Chassidic dancing and, even more so Israeli dancing, was much more the scene of my two much younger sisters, Mary and Annie, than of my sister Ruth (three years younger than me) and myself. Mary and Annie came of age after the Six-Day War of 1967, and all that the war meant for Jewish identity in the Diaspora. The

occupation of the West Bank and Gaza was initially intended to be temporary but became problematic with the fateful permission granted for territorial religious maximalists to set up homes. In the early 1970s I attended meetings of the socialist Zionist group Mapam, which met in Broadhurst Garden, but later I became disaffected for reasons I have explained in other writings. One member of the group was the singer Naomi Gerecht, whom I discussed earlier.

The cantata by Ben-Zion Orgad was given to me on 5 August 1970 (according to her Hebrew and English message on the sleeve) by Eda Zoritte, the wife of the Israeli cultural attaché of the day, Aharon Megged, a famous novelist. It was to thank me for co-translating one of her plays. Aharon was a pipe-smoking slow-speaking and thoughtful man. Eda, more out-going, was a strikingly attractive woman, with high cheekbones, very oriental, lending credence to a family tradition that an ancestor had fallen in love with a Mongolian neighbour in Russia and converted to Judaism. Aharon Megged was one of a succession of writers – along with Hannoch Bartov, Binyamin Tammuz, Moshe Dor and one or two others – who served as cultural attachés until Menachem Begin became Prime Minister around 1981 and the Israeli Foreign Ministry started appointing junior professional diplomats because no writers supported the right-wing government. The writers were 'soft' in their approach to diplomacy and in those days – pre Intifada and pre Sharon, etc., etc. – the people they mingled with in London intellectual and cultural circles did not need much persuading that Israel was a good thing, or at least a normal thing. Amos Oz, A.B. Yehoshua, Shulamith Hareven, David Grossman and Aharon Appelfeld and, perhaps, Yoram Kaniuk, are Israel's best-known novelists abroad but on the strength of *The Living on the Dead* and *Foigleman*, Aharon Megged, who died in 2016, deserved to be up there with them. Grossman and Yehoshua are still with us.

I met the Meggeds in 1968 at, where else, the flat of Miron and Carola Grindea, 28 Emperor's Gate, South Kensington. On the same occasion I also met Avraham Shlonsky, the leading Hebrew poet of his generation. His English was about as good as my Hebrew, ditto my German and his French. Which left Russian, and I am grateful that in those days I could speak passable Russian, for he was standing in a corner, isolated. His English did stretch to a double pun on my wife's name: Chérie Brenda, Cherry Brandy. On one occasion I found a pun worthy of the master punster himself: he told me he had written a children's book about a 'kengooroo', and its opposite a 'logooroo'. The Hebrew joke depends upon the fact that 'yes' and 'no' in Hebrew are 'ken' and 'lo', thus kangaroo in Hebrew has a punning opposite, a virtual animal. The literal translation – 'Yesgooroo' and 'Nogooroo' – loses the point, but I found the solution: Kangaroo and Kan'tgaroo, and duly attempted to explain this in Russian… Shlonsky translated mainly German and Russian poetry and fiction and drama, but had translated *Hamlet* ('by indirections find directions out') via the German translation of Schlegel and Tieck and the Russian translation of Pasternak. Later the poet Carmi told me that this version was a miracle of intuitive understanding. Carmi, born in New York and the son of a rabbi, was bilingual and himself translated *Hamlet*, as has the scholar and writer Aharon Komem, whose own poems I have co-translated.

All this was background to my Menard Press series of Hebrew poetry in translation.[46] The first of my many visits to Israel until 1995, when I stopped going, was in spring 1969. The day I arrived I attended a Passover *seder* at the apartment of the Shlonskys, 50 Gordon Street, Tel Aviv, where the paintings included a Léger. Shlonsky had compiled the secular *Hagadah* used by the most left wing of the Kibbutz groups, Kibbutzim Artzi, and that naturally was the one we read from. He was a legend, even among the later poets who 'dethroned' him and his aesthetic, who included Natan Zach, until his death in 2020, the senior Israeli poet. Once at Heathrow Shlonsky had to open his bags for a customs official. Not speaking English, he asked a friend to interpret. The customs man picked up a book and asked what language it was written in. Shlonsky told him and added helpfully that it was his own translation of *Hamlet*. 'I thought you didn't understand English,' said the suspicious official. 'Shakespeare I understand, customs officials I don't.' In Israel, I met many writers thanks to Shlonsky, including Carmi and the playwright Yehoshua Bar-Yosef, 'king' of Safed, a town drenched in Jewish history and mystery. I already knew Amichai and Zach from London. Bonnefoy had given me the Jerusalem phone number of Claude Vigée in 1969 and I met the French poet on that first trip. There is an interesting essay to be written on the respective *imaginaires* of my friends Vigée and Jabès, the two major French Jewish poets since the war, who were not each other's favourite writer. Unlike Jabès, Claude does not revel in irony and paradox, he is not a meta-writer. They are both, however, poets of exile and lamentation. Claude remained a French writer, even in Israel. Conversely Jerusalem could be found in Alsace.

Bonnefoy also gave me the phone number of the Romanian-born French poet Lorand Gaspar, whom I saw in East Jerusalem, where he worked as a surgeon. Gaspar later went to Tunis. Vigée suspected he was Jewish. They never met, certainly for political reasons.

6

Duke Elllington Orchestra, *Band Call*, World Record Club, TP 86, undated [*fig. 94*]
I am nineteen years old and two months. I am dancing slowly with a girl called Pat in my room, K8, New Court, Trinity College, Cambridge. We met at the rag fair about an hour ago. She was a student teacher from Bedford. My Duke Ellington LP is playing. The curtains are closed. I put my hand inside her blouse and gently cup her breast. She does not resist. *Au contraire*. The breast is firm and soft, it is cool and smooth. Where had I been all those years? Until that moment I had experienced no sexual feelings and had nothing 'under my belt' (as it were) save French kisses a few months earlier in Paris on the Pont Neuf.[47] Those kisses had not generated morphic resonance elsewhere, at least not in my body. I can't speak for Australia, as in Rupert Sheldrake's theory. (Coincidentally or not, Pat emigrated there). Today in Cambridge, however, is different. It is the beginning of a long journey: my sexual ontogeny. Latency is over: better late than never. We lie down on my bed fully clothed. A few minutes later, still fully clothed, I have changed for ever. We get up, go out and walk to the river. For better and worse (I would discover), I was in a new world, and destiny was manifest.

7

Half Man Half Biscuit: *Back in the D.H.S.S*, Probe Plus, Probe 4, 1985
Some time in the late 1980s, Audrey bought me a record by Half Man Half Biscuit as part of my education in contemporary popular culture. She would have first heard the group on the BBC Radio One programme of John Peel. The bait was the song 'Fuckin' hell it's Fred Titmus': bait

because, to her despair, I was a cricket junky and, rightly or wrongly, she claimed to believe that cricket was to men's minds what sex was to their bodies. The record sleeve lists Jesus Christ as right arm, over the wicket. I occasionally listened to John Peel and his colleague Andy Kershaw [*fig. 95*].

8

Leonard Cohen, *Songs from a Room*, CBS 63587, undated, and others [*fig. 96*]
Bob Dylan, *Blood on the Tracks*, 1975 and others
Leonard Cohen is one of the great songwriter performers, the equal of Bob Dylan. His background is as much 'poetry' as it is music and strictly on the page he is a better poet than Dylan. Dylan's background is folk song, but the comparison is academic. From the troubadours to the chansonniers, from the writers of sea shanties to prison worksongs, from Negro spirituals to the blues, one would be hard put to find a musician wordsmith as great, as various, as prodigious, as Bob Dylan. I remember in the late 1970s Howard Schwartz turning up on the doorstep of our house in upper Holloway after a Dylan concert. Howard was a true believer, owned the bootleg records, knew the words off by heart. I resisted completism and stuck to the old folkways and Folkways, Woody Guthrie being the great hero of Dylan, Moses to his Aaron in the promised land of public awareness. Howard Schwartz and I were putting the finishing touches to our vast anthology of Jewish poets of the twentieth century.[48] Cohen is included. Dylan (or his agent) agreed, but the agent asked too much money for the requested poem. Some might be surprised that in principle he agreed to be included, as did Joseph Brodsky, given that they were Christian at the time, but they did. This raises age-old questions about Jewishness, what with Cohen also being a Buddhist, and so on. We could not ask dead poets to adjudicate but we decided to include Mandelshtam and exclude Pasternak on the grounds that the former would have been pleased, the latter not. We based our decision on the evidence of Pasternak's *Doctor Zhivago* and Mandelshtam's *Noise of Time*. Postscript: I read this paragraph out to Alan Wall, who proceeded to recite the words of 'Desolation Row' and waited for me to reassess my comment that Leonard Cohen is the better poet on the page. I was not persuaded.

But he and I agree that the argument is a waste of time. The two are songwriters and the fact that Dylan's words on the page do not match the ballads of Auden or Villon is irrelevant to his genius as an artist. [*Fifteen years later: Alan now suggests that I might be trying to say that Cohen is more writerly than Dylan.*]

9

Elly Ameling, *Sentimental me*, Phillips, 412433-1, 1984
Yehudi Menuhin & Stephane Grappelli, *Fascinatin' Rhythm*, EMI, EMD 5523, 1975
Elly Ameling's versions of Gershwin, Ellington and Porter form a classic crossover compilation. I usually love crossover and adaptations and arrangements (for example, Igor Stravinsky's orchestrations of Chopin and piano versions by Liszt of orchestral works) but the Ameling record is a mistake although I have heard and admired her in the concert hall and on the radio. It is a mistake because neither nature nor nurture prepared her for this sort of music. I wonder too if Menuhin's collaboration with Grappelli gives as much pleasure to the listener as it evidently did to the players. Psychologically my pleasure in crossover is surely linked to my lifelong involvement in translation (many books and essays). Another version or translation of this is gender bending in theatre and figurative painting. Some of my short stories[49] involve sex-change people.

10

Astrud Gilberto, *The Shadow of your Smile*, EMI/Verve VLP 9107, 1965 [*fig. 97*] Astrud Gilberto's 'The Shadow of your Smile' was a birthday present from my sisters Mary and Annie in 1966: they were still living at home – aged fifteen and thirteen respectively – as was Ruth until she married aged twenty-five in 1970. Their big brother was in his first-floor room in Notting Hill: 2 Powis Square (the building was pulled down later). They must have asked me what I wanted because they would not have known about this singer. Maybe I discovered her in New York or Chicago earlier in the year. I liked that room, which looked on to the square. There was a mouse, but even I learned about Polyfilla and blocked

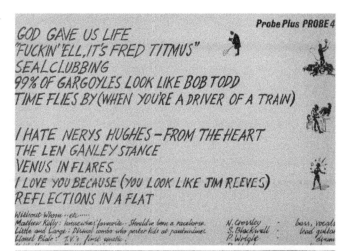

fig. 95

fig. 96

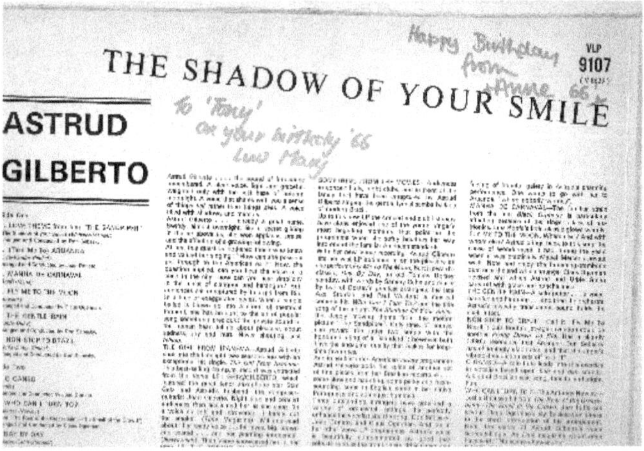

fig. 97

The Lark in the Morning

Dave and Toni Arthur

Accompaniments
Toni *concertina*
Dave *melodeon*
Barry Dransfield *fiddle*

SIDE ONE
1. All Frolicking I'll Give Over
2. The Death of Queen Jane
3. Creeping Jane
4. The Merchant's Daughter of Bristol
5. The Bold Dragoon
6. Cold Blows the Winter's Wind
7. The Lark in The Morning

SIDE TWO
1. Poor Old Horse
2. Hey John Barleycorn
3. Bedlam
4. Admiral Benbow
5. Father Father Build Me a Boat
6. The Press Gang
7. Six Jolly Miners

Recorded by Bill Leader 1968/9
First Published By Topic 1969
Notes by Dave and Toni Arthur and A. L. Lloyd
Photograph Brian Shuel

The Artists

Dave and Toni Arthur make up the most admired duet team on the folk club scene. Dave was born in Cheshire, Toni in Oxford. They met in a London coffee-bar that Dave was managing, married, and now live in South-east London. Toni has formal music training, Dave not. Dave plays guitar though he uses it less and less; Toni plays concertina (and recorder when she has a mind to). Both like to liven their performance by dancing, Dave with Morris jigs, Toni with clog dances. They are accomplished solo singers, but are chiefly in demand as harmony singers (with trial-and-error harmonies that break plenty of rules but contain jubilant surprises). Few young performers in the folk song revival are so zealous in pursuit of valuable out-of-the-way songs, or so conscientious about the pieces they perform. Folk song absorbs them, they say, because they love people; and through folk song one can convey without bigotry so much of what people have gone through—emotionally, economically, politically even.

3. Creeping Jane

How old is this song? Possibly it originated late in the eighteenth century. English racing really began with the formation of the Jockey Club in 1750. There had of course, been racing of sorts before this: Charles the Second raced on Epsom Downs, for instance. The race mentioned in *Creeping Jane* is unknown, what matter? The appeal of the song is in the surprise victory of the underdog (underhorse?), who had been laughed to scorn by the fancy.

It seems to have been a widespread song. Percy Grainger recorded this version from Mr. G. Leaning at Brigg, Lincolnshire, in 1906. It is almost identical to Joseph Taylor's well known version. which Grainger also collected, and which appeared on an HMV record some sixty years ago. Frank Kidson, H. E. D. Hammond, Cecil Sharp and Alfred Williams, all collected versions from districts as far apart as Yorkshire and Somerset. Henry Such, of London, produced a broadside of it. Although also known in U.S.A. (Michigan), *Creeping Jane* never achieved the fame of the other racehorse, 'Skewball', a Yorkshire beast that became a figure of U.S. Negro mythology.

4. The Merchant's Daughter of Bristol

This was collected by Lucy Broadwood from a fine singer, the Sussex cobbler and bell-ringer Henry Burstow. The rhythm gave Miss Broadwood trouble, and she transcribed it in different ways in different publications, but in fact this ballad, like so many others, is in a free rubato time with emphasis rather on the bar-lines of emotion than of academic theory.

Except for the twist at the end, the words are typical of a large number of pieces on the rich-girl-poor-boy relationship, a favourite theme of the period 1750-1850. The motif of the murdered servant lover may derive from a Boccaccio story that circulated widely on English fairgrounds in chapbook form. *The Merchant's Daughter of Bristol* was first published (in 51 verses!) in 1777, and in sundry shapes it was reprinted over and again, making its final appearance on a Such broadside in the 1880s.

5. The Bold Dragoon

When the news of Napoleon's escape from Elba reached Berkshire in March 1815, the Blues, who were stationed in Reading recalled their men, and they marched through the streets, headed by drum and fife bands. One group without a band, marched three abreast led by a fiddler playing *The British Grenadiers*. Such scenes were guaranteed to rouse the people to a frenzy of patriotism and admiration for the lads off to defend the country. If we believe the evidence of folk song, and Hardy's *Far From the Madding Crowd*, the soldiers were not slow to take advantage of the swooning young women. What young country girl could resist the magnificent uniforms of the Hussars and Dragoons?

In the song the girl takes the initiative, and the bold dragoon is only too pleased to oblige. The tune used here is from the singing of Harry List, of Framlingham, Suffolk. The words from the Baring-Gould manuscripts are reprinted in James Reeves *The Everlasting Circle*. F. J. Child prints three versions of the song as No. 299 in his *English and Scottish Popular Ballads*, all three versions from Scotland, but England, Ireland and the upland American South had countless sets of this most popular song.

6. Cold Blows the Winter's Wind

The ballad, usually called *The Unquiet Grave*, concerns a person who feels bound to sit and mourn by his (sometimes,

fig. 99

SIDE TWO

1. Poor Old Horse

Frank Kidson declared in his usual categoric way, that *Poor Old Horse* is a purely humanitarian view of the fate of old worn-out horses. But in fact, in at least three counties, in Yorkshire, Nottinghamshire, and Wiltshire the song was an integral part of the Christmas Ritual performed by parties of mummers, with one of their number disguised roughly as a horse. Celebrated in Kent is the *Hooden Horse*, banned in 1834 for creating havoc among the elderly people, but now resurrected, (it accompanies the East Kent and Ravensbourne Morris Men). The notion of the sacred luck-bringing, even world-creating horse (or bull, ram or billy-goat) is spread throughout the primitive world. In Britain, the ancient Celts had their horse-rituals, and the idea was reinforced by invading Norsemen. There are still plenty of evidences to be seen, from the great Uffington White Horse to the fiery, fecund, May-day Padstow 'oss in Cornwall. Minehead has its town hobbyhorse, and in Wales at Midwinter the baleful Mari Llwyd appears with the dancer carrying a beribboned horse's skull. In Cheshire, the mild-eyed souling horses of Antrobus are famous. Not forgetting the horse-headed man engraved on a bone, found in Pinhole Cave, Derbyshire, the only palaeolithic representation of a human figure discovered in England.

The words sung here are from Alfred Williams's *Folk-Songs of the Upper Thames*. The tune was sung at the Westmorland Festival of 1902 by a Mr. Barber, and noted by Frank Kidson, one of the Folk Song Competition judges. It appears in *Folk Song Journal* No. 5.

2. Hey John Barleycorn

This version of *John Barleycorn* from the singing of the road repairer George Attrill, of Fittleworth, Sussex, was collected by Tony Wales, of the English Folk Dance and Song Society, in July 1958. Mr. Attrill, with a repertory of over seventy songs, was a keen sportsman—cricketer, footballer, player of bowls and quoits, and an excellent shot with rifle or catapult. He also played Father Christmas in the Fittleworth Mumming Play. He died on 10th November 1964, aged 78.

Mr. Attrill's version is more exultant than the usual sets of *John Barleycorn*, and has a good rousing chorus. It dwells less on the life cycle of the corn, to which has been ascribed various ritual meanings including the death and resurrection of the Corn God. Rather, it concentrates on extolling the virtues of English beer and its happy effects on the lucky imbiber. Robert Ford prints a Scottish version in his *Vagabond Songs and Ballads of Scotland*; he presumes it is of English origin though, of course, Burns refurbished a well known version (and did it no good). Certainly, the song seems to have been widespread in England since its first appearance on a blackletter broadside early in the seventeenth century.

3. Bedlam

Henry VIII destroyed most of the monastic hospitals, but left, St. Thomas's, St. Bartholomew's, and the Bethlehem Hospital, called Bedlam.

With the dissolution of the monasteries vast numbers of poor people, cut off from charity, became street beggars, adopting various guises to obtain pity. A favourite 'cheat' was to feign madness. These people were known as Bedlam Beggars, and are mentioned by Shakespeare in *King Lear*. From Elizabeth's time till the end of the 17th century, mad songs remained very popular. One of the most famous was *Tom o' Bedlam* which appeared in 1626 in *Giles Earle's Songbook*. Another favourite

here were collected by Frank Kidson from Mrs. Hollings, a Lincolnshire charwoman. Mrs. Hollings had three verses we do not sing. In these, the young girl writes an anguished letter about the loss of her true love, and is found hanging from a beam by her father. We have added a verse from Gavin Greig's *Folk-Song of the North-East*. The tune is in *Folk Song Journal* No. 3 under the title of *A Sailors Life*. It is reproduced in Ralph Vaughan Williams and A. L. Lloyd *The Penguin Book of English Folk Songs*, p.94.

6. The Press Gang

Considering the dreadful conditions in the Navy during the eighteenth and early nineteenth centuries, it is not surprising that it was necessary to recruit men forcibly, by means of the Press Gang. Whole villages were cleared in the dead of night, and as Frank Kidson said, 'With such happenings in their midst, the folk song makers had no lack of thrilling and appealing material'. The circumstances made it easy for the fathers of marriageable girls to betray the unwanted suitor and have him pressed away to sea. In many of the numerous songs on this theme, the romantic element is not missed, and the girl dressed as a man, sails in search of her love. The words here are from the *Journal of The Folk Song Society* No. 31 and were collected by Cecil Sharp in Somerset. They comprise a shortened version of a broadside text, *The Sailors Misfortune and Marriage* in which the sailor's disguised love, who claims a knowledge of Astrology, tells his fortune and in so doing exposes her own identity.

7. Six Jolly Miners

At Christmas time in the Sheffield area, children used to go round the pubs dressed as miners, with blackened faces, picks and shovels. They sang a begging song beginning : Six jolly miners, we're not worth a pin. But when we get a bit of coal we'll make the kettle sing. And we'll riddle and we'll fiddle, and we'll make the world go round. If you don't mind your troubles, you will have a motty down. (A motty is a miner's tally disc, to fix on the tubs, so that he can be paid according to the number he has filled.) When A. L. Lloyd was collecting material for his *Come All Ye Bold Miners* in 1951, he obtained two Scottish versions of the song, called *Six Jolly Wee Miners*. Apparently the song has been favoured by Scottish miners since the 1830s. The American collector George Korson found versions in Canada and U.S.A., though one of his sets, from Glace Bay, Nova Scotia, had been carried over the Atlantic from Scotland by Lloyd's informant Mrs. Cosgrove, of Midlothian, who had accompanied her miner husband to Nova Scotia some years previously. The only southern English version we know is the one sung here. George Gardiner first noted it from a singer in Cheriton, Devon, in 1905.

Anthony Rudolf 147

B 7738S L   **BBL 7553**

Juliette Gréco
Showcase

Sous le ciel de Paris	Jolie môme
Les feuilles mortes	La rue des blancs manteaux
Coin de rue	La valse
Si tu t'imagines	La fourmi
La fiancée du pirate	C'etait bien
Je hais les dimanches	Paris canaille

Juliette Gréco with the French singer Serge Gainsbourg.
Photo J-P Leloir

"Gréco has millions in her throat; millions of poems which are not yet written. Plays are written for certain actors; why shouldn't poems be written for a voice? Prose writers are faced with regrets and remorse before her. He who works with a pen, who drafts lustreless and black signs on paper, finally forgets that words have a sensual beauty. The voice of Gréco brings this back to them. Soft, warm, light, she brushes past them, lighting their fires. It is

More accurately, the French chanson has no counterpart elsewhere. Songs in general, excluding of course the creations of the great composers, conform largely to a traditional commercial pattern, overwhelmingly obsessed with romance. The chanson, on the other hand, is a vignette set to music, a vignette of all aspects of life.

Some of the songs on this record are immortal: Léo Férré's *Paris Canaille*, for instance and Prévert's *Les Feuilles mortes*. *La fiancée du pirate* is a rarity, an adaptation of a Brecht-Weill song by Maupay. And just to prove Sartre wrong in one respect, Juliette Gréco includes *La rue des blancs manteaux*

fig. 98

fig. 100

the FUGS

ED SANDERS, vocals

TULI KUPFERBERG, tambourine & maracas

KEN WEAVER, percussion

LEE CRABTREE, piano, celeste, bells

PETE KEARNEY, guitar

VINNY LEARY, guitar

JOHN ANDERSON, bass guitar

Groans, yelps, ooos, & harmony by
The FUGS Chorus: consisting of ALL the FUGS
plus Betsy Klein

SIDE 1

1. FRENZY (2:00)
(Sanders)

2. I WANT TO KNOW (2:00)
(Sanders, Olson)

3. SKIN FLOWERS (2:30)
(Sanders, Kearney)

4. GROUP GROPE (2:40)
(Sanders)

5. COMING DOWN (3:40)
(Sanders)

6. DIRTY OLD MAN (1:40)
(Kupferberg, Sanders)

up the mousehole. John Barrell came to stay one night; he was in London from Brightlingsea to work at the British Museum Reading Room. Ian and Gisela Hamilton, on a visit to London from their National Trust pad near Oxford, dropped in for tea. Notting Hill was not a suburb, it was a neighbourhood. This was the first time I had lived away from home in my hometown, after having tasted of the fruits in Chicago. In my own place, at last I could do what I wanted to do, whatever that was, if I got the chance. It was agreed I would go home for supper on Friday evenings, and my mother proposed that I take my washing with me, which I rejected.

Here, at the epicentre of the neighbourhood where the Notting Hill Carnival began shortly before I arrived, I spent a year, enduring day jobs and trying to write poems, trying to improve my translations of Yves Bonnefoy and Evgeny Vinokourov. It was to this room that Alberto de Lacerda came, and whence he took away copies of those early Bonnefoy translations in order to show them to Nathaniel Tarn. Alberto knew many poets, and presented me with his book *77 Poems*, co-translated with Arthur Waley, perhaps Waley's only translation not from the Chinese. De Lacerda was a poet with a capital P, and although he was a difficult man, there was a lightness about his being, a charm and brilliance which I associated with southern Europe, with the Mediterranean. It was some time before I realised that a) being Portuguese in his case meant that he came from Mozambique and b) Portugal was, and is, an Atlantic country not a Mediterranean one. But not to worry, it was all in the mind, or rather in the spirit. For twelve months I entered into the spirit of freedom in Notting Hill, which inevitably included a few joints courtesy of Michael and Frances Horovitz, my neighbours, before entering Avery Hill Teacher Training College (where I met Brenda) to embark on a postgraduate certificate of education in October 1967, reckoning that I would have long holidays to be a writer in – once I had qualified. I failed the exams.

Around this time, thanks to Richard Burns (now Berengarten), I met the late Elizabeth Thomas; she was the secretary of Michael Foot and literary editor of *Tribune*, where she published the early work of many writers – poems, book reviews and so on. I used to go to the ICA in Dover Street and the French Institute, and I was a member of the National Film Theatre and the GB–USSR Association. Yes, I was a busy young man. I was running towards myself and away from myself at the same time, inscribing a circle of late development, still uncentred, still on the margins of my heart, on the threshold of my brain.

11

Juliette Gréco Showcase, Phillips BBL 7553/B77385 L, 1962
I have written about Juliette Gréco and her significance for me as a model of the sexy, by which I really meant sexual, woman in another book.[50] and also in the EPs/45s section above. I played my LP of her most famous songs – including the one Sartre wrote with Kosma: 'La rue des Blancs Manteaux' – more than any other record, apart from the Chopin waltzes. In 2004 I went with Paula to hear Gréco sing at the Barbican. It was a mistake to go, as it was bound to be. [*fig. 98*]

12

(Folk Music)

Woodie Guthrie: *Columbia River Collection; Folkways: a Vision Revisited* (Pete Seeger, Woodie Guthrie, Leadbelly); *Leadbelly Last Sessions: Parts One and Two; Bound for Glory: the Songs and Story of Woodie Guthrie; Woodie Guthrie sings folksongs Vol.2; Pete Seeger: America's Favourite Ballads Vol.5;* Pete Seeger: *We shall overcome (Carnegie Hall concert, 8 June 1963; the Pete Seeger Box (four records); Steeleye Span's Folk Songs of Old England;* Dave and Toni Arthur: *The Lark in the Morning*
Dave and Toni Arthur were fine folk singers and became friends for a while, probably after I heard them sing for the first time, which would have been at the Troubadour. Later I got them to participate in a programme at the Poetry Society. It was no secret that they were white witches. Toni could later be seen on television as a *Blue Peter* presenter. [*fig. 99*]

The Fugs: The Village Fugs; The Fugs
Blake, Ginsberg, Ed Sanders, Tuli Kupferberg: this is late beat, pre-hippy, sixties' stuff, my own vintage. In terms of half-generations, born in 1942, I am a few years older than ageing hippies like my late friend Z. Kotowicz. A new friend, Giacomo Donis, is the singular author of a singular book, *The Empty Shield*, in which the Fugs play an important part. [*fig. 100*]

(Jazz)

The Four Freshmen; Anita O'Day Sings Jazz; Erroll Garner: Moods; Art Tatum Alone; Hamp! (Hampton, Peterson, Brown, Rich)
These are records ordered from World Record Club, which I joined a few years after joining Classics Club. I remember I was trying to educate myself in jazz and I bought what I felt I ought to like as well as what I did like or knew I would like.

Also:

Oscar Peterson Plays Cole Porter; George Shearing: Black Satin; June Christy: This is June; Louis Armstrong selection; Peggy Lee: Black Coffee; A Billie Holiday Memorial; Charlie Parker: 'Bird' Symbols; Lester Young: Pres is Blue

13

(Seven-Inch 33⅓ rpms)

Robert Rozhdestvensky and Françoise Sagan: 'Poets read their verses'; Andrei Voznesenky: 'Poets read their verses'; 'Pasternak speaks' (his voice is heard in Russian, French and German. The record was issued by Discurio, a shop in Mayfair); Apollinaire reading his 'Le Pont Mirabeau'. Here too are Naomi Shemer's 'Jerusalem of gold' and the Classics Club edition of Grieg's 'Peer Gynt', played by the Classics Club Symphony Orchestra conducted by Wladimir Tergorsky.
Given the name of the orchestra, I should have guessed that a Google would not come up with the name of the conductor. Contractual reasons must have required that the orchestra be given a cover identity. A close look at the name of the conductor, Wladimir Tergorsky, reveals Walter Goehr embedded in it. Walter Goehr was associated with Classics Club and my guess is that he is the conductor and that the orchestra is the London Symphony.

SECTION TWO

The Room with Many Names

Here I am, surrounded by time's ruins. An ill-judged tone of voice could get me labelled Firbank with a Baedeker, if I'm not careful. Turning right outside my bedroom, and crossing the narrow hall, I arrive at – what shall we call it, the loo? When I was young, the word word was confined to the upper class: certainly the only person I recall using the word was a girl from a posh public school, Wycombe Abbey, whom I met around in the early 1960s at a New Year's Eve party in Bellmoor, a block of mansion flats in Hampstead on the corner of Whitestone Pond and East Heath Road. Lost and gone for ever is the name of the girl and the host too. In recent years the word loo has become more widespread; it has, figuratively enough, descended the food chain and is beginning to replace toilet and lavatory. In my own childhood, we used the word toilet, but I'm not yet sure if this usage was typical of the professional middle classes into which my father's work as a chartered accountant had brought him. The only other room with more than one name in English is what, as a child, I called the lounge. We shall explore this room in a later chapter. For the time being, we are in the toilet or loo. Research belonging to the discipline of cultural phenomenology, or its virtual clone Perecian endotic anthropology, is called for. Even as I type this, I shall change screens and send an email to regular correspondents, restricting myself to persons who grew up in the British Commonwealth – in one or two cases, the British Empire.

Within five minutes, several people have replied, including three writers, which proves that I am not the only person who peeps at emails while supposedly concentrating on the work of the day. On this occasion at least, I have the excuse that my present task involves email! By noon on the following morning, that is today as I continue with the present chapter, twenty-seven respondents – exactly half my final total – have answered, some with simple replies, others adding a short commentary. It is already clear to me that there is more to the naming of rooms than euphemism and class. What's more, we all use different words with different people, especially when it comes to the bog. This research will be published in a possible future book of Pereciana. But let us move on, for the time being, to the actual site under investigation.

Before me is not the toilet bowl the children and I inherited from the previous owners. Four or five years ago, I realised belatedly that the time had come to modernise the bathroom and toilet. I mentioned to Paula that I would be doing this, and that I could take advantage of a special offer at a local merchant, Plumbase. Immediately she said that on no account was I to allow the plumber to throw away the old toilet (and bathroom sink), since, you never know, they might come in useful at the studio. And indeed the sink already has (see below in the Bathroom section). The old toilet sits against a wall in the studio, to be used in a future picture. It arrived too late for Paula's abortion series, where it could have replaced the bucket, although she would probably have decided against it. While living in Chicago in 1966, I was told that in the famous stockyards (which closed five years later) everything in the pig was used except the squeak. Just so, everything in the studio eventually finds or takes its place in one of Paula's pictures. But, the studio not being a pig (as it happens, this is the animal Paula prefers to all others, rather than a dog or cat or ostrich), even the squeak is part of the equation, for the characters in her pictures have emotions and feelings and they speak their own language, animated by the painter.

On the window ledge above the toilet and below the window, there used to be an antique mirror, which had been a wedding present from Edward and Juliette Pollitzer. Some time in the late eighties, the morning after the night of a great storm, I was distraught to find it in pieces on the floor. Doubtless the window had rattled enough for the mirror to slip down. It was beautiful, an objet d'art, I was distraught. But who knew from great storms?

For many years, two postcards of paintings by Botero have graced the window ledge. I bought these in Paris in 1993, when I accidentally found myself at an outdoor exhibition of the Colombian artist's vast sculptures along the Champs-Elysées, while I was walking to the flat of the poet and critic Didier Cahan, a fellow member of the Edmond Jabès circle. The first card is *Hommage to Bonnard,* which shows the back view of a naked man standing in a bathroom, and the legs of a woman lying in the bath. This is a witty take on the real life situation of the artist, for Bonnard would normally be painting his wife in the bath, not standing beside her with nothing on; the title of the painting refuses the possibility that Botero is representing Bonnard painting a self-portrait. I am reminded of Laura Knight's marvellous self-portrait in the National Portrait Gallery alongside a naked model, and one recalls Lucian Freud's self-image clad in nothing but his boots. Most naked of all is Caravaggio's use of his own head on the platter in his *Salome* in the National Gallery. The other postcard on the window ledge is Botero's Bathroom, the back view of a hugely fat naked lady, with a vague facial resemblance to Frida Kahlo, standing between a toilet and a bath and facing a mirror. It is a different bathroom, and Marthe Bonnard she is not, nor is she Simone de Beauvoir in the famous rear view photo of her standing naked in high heels in Nelson Agren's bathroom.

Also on the ledge are a cracked soup bowl and cracked saucer, from a set of six I bought when on holiday in Portugal with Audrey (see Kitchen section later). This bowl now contains a JC cloth and a sponge. Until I finally succumbed and employed a cleaning lady for the flat, I would mix Flash and Dettol, dilute them, and then, with the leaking soup bowl in one hand, I would kneel on the floor as one might before a throne, and clean the toilet with the other. Such chores demand musical accompaniment: Radio Three or solo piano music on a CD. Alongside the bowl, when it is resting on the ledge, is a Haze container for 'room fragrance'. [*Later: glancing at the listings in the newspaper, I note* Iphigenia at Aulis *at the National Theatre. A name leaps out: Kate Duchêne, highly praised star of a highly praised production. As a resting actress, Kate cleaned my flat two or three times in the late 1980s.*]

Above the window and above the door are two bookshelves, put in for me by Chalky some years ago. The late Chalky White, usually accompanied by his wife Jeannie, was your classic, archetypal odd-job man. After retiring from the council dustbins and buses he was available locally for all who knew him. We met through my former next-door neighbour, Chris. Chalky put up shelves in two rooms and the new curtains in my bedroom. See how memory doesn't work, I forgot to mention this in the bedroom chapter. He fixed lights and the television, straightened ill-fitting doors, replaced windowpanes, and did up my sitting-room balcony, which we will come to later. He used words like 'favourite' and 'previous' in contexts that place him fairly and squarely in a specific class, as befits an old Labour man, indeed Old Labour man. He re-laid the floor of the toilet with fake lino from B & Q, where we went one Wednesday to benefit from his pensioner discount. And he repainted the toilet and bathroom white after the new suite had been fitted. From time to time Chalky went outside his catchment area – I drove him and Jeannie to my mother's place to do the odd job, and they came back on the bus. On one occasion he fixed the windows at Paula's place. Ron is his successor.

The books on the two shelves high in the toilet were taken in an arbitrary fashion from the floor-piled scores of books I had acquired after disposing of my father's library when my mother moved to sheltered accommodation and also when Julia Farrer offered me whatever I wanted from Jonathan Griffin's library following the death of his widow, Kathleen. And now we arrive at the pictures on the wall, including a poster from Paula's Dulwich Picture Gallery exhibition of 1998: *Angel*, one of her noblest and most powerful paintings, with her model Lila holding the traditional symbols of the Passion, namely the sponge and sword. The picture comes from the series inspired by *The Crime of Father Amaro*, in which I posed as the corrupt priest, the central figure in this great novel about provincial nineteenth century Portugal.[51] The author, Eça de Queiros, greatly admired by one of my literary heroes Borges, deserves to be better known here, by which I probably mean, if I am honest, better known by myself, since the books are available in paperback, retranslated for our time by a mistress of the art, Margaret Jull Costa. One of Paula's grandest pictures, one I was particularly proud to be in, *The Ambassador of Jesus*, owned by Charles Saatchi, was destroyed in a fire at a temporary warehouse used by the leading art- storage company Momart, along with hundreds of works by leading artists, including three other paintings by Paula, which she herself owned. Some pundits covered themselves in glory with comments like 'what happened was at worst a mishap, at best perhaps an overdue act of aesthetic cleansing' (Peter Conrad, The *Observer*), the phrase rhetorically updating the Nazi burning of the books in the 1930s with allusion to more recent politics, but attempting to cover its flank with the 'perhaps'. Marina Warner pointed out in the *Financial Times* that not everyone went along with the trashing of Saatchi, the talented Chapman brothers and other younger artists. This was an understatement on her part.

Around the time of the fire, which generated a great deal of publicity, Paula was also profiled by the *Guardian* and, in addition, Robert Hughes's television interview with her was broadcast. So she has been in the public eye. This is inevitable, given how well known she has become, but it is very tiring for her. Still, it's all part of the work. I am lucky to hold a watching brief, to be a participant observer in the life, and sometimes, as a model, in the making of the work. Mind you, the work enters the life even when I am not playing the role of a model: in our many conversations about past and future projects, or when I arrive at the studio of an evening – after she has been working all day with Lila – and give the work in progress my best regards.

We discuss, for example, her *Pillowman* group, a project which involves copying homemade models, sculptural bricolage. These sculptures are an interesting mediating category (a phrase Paula would never use) between painting from your head and painting from the live model. Paint what you know, they said at the Slade. Well, for sure she knows these figures, after all she made them: the exiled king, the dwarf wanker, the cake lady, figures on a beach in Estoril. The face of the girl in the latest picture looks wrong, we agree, and it looks wrong because the image of the doll being copied seems to create a kind of sentimental artificiality that recalls too closely the picture by Doré – one of her favourite artists – that hovers somewhere behind the present one. The solution, we realise simultaneously, is to call in Carmen, Paula's senior granddaughter, to supply the real thing. Paula also changed the angle of the ladder, after I pointed out that it mirrored the angle of the ladder in the first of the triptych paintings, and that this was a mistake unless she had intended it, which she hadn't. It feels good to have an input as a privileged viewer. In the early years my eye was not educated enough to comment. Then the eye improved but I didn't dare speak. Now it's different, and I'm prepared to take the risk of getting it wrong. As for the experience of being a model, that is my story, and I tell it elsewhere.[52]

Another picture on the wall of the room with many names is a poster print of Edward Hopper's compelling painting from 1930, *Early Sunday*

Morning, formerly known as *Seventh Avenue*. This familiar and classic Manhattan view – a row of shops with the apartments above, the pattern broken only by a barber's pole and a fire hydrant – is a meditation on light, that painterly element mediating between time and space. It is, at the same time, a projection of the artist's solitude on to an objective correlative the walker in the city happened upon, sketched and later elaborated into a painting in his studio. As numinous (sorry, Paula, I know you hate the word, but it connotes the mystery) as any Rothko, the painting continues beyond its horizontal margins like a still frame abstracted from a long panning shot in a movie; the changed title re-sites the picture in time, freezes it in time, rather than in the originative space of the avenue. It is not included in a recent book *Hopper's Places*, whose author, Gail Levin, surely drove slowly or walked up the avenue looking for it. Why do I not write and ask her if, sixty years later, she found it? The answer is that although the hoarder of facts, my inner endotic anthropologist, is curious about the trigger image, the human being knows it matters not at all, just as Paula's homemade models are unimportant once they have served their purpose. What matters is that Hopper felt a deep need to paint a humble row of shops, and excluded all indications of human life (he removed a figure originally in the picture), save perhaps the accidental metonymy of the barber's pole. This act of painting, this process of painting, incarnates a profound human awareness of solitude; and his semi-abstract orchestration of horizontals and verticals, his visual musical score, accompanying his poetry of solitude, rekindles that awareness in us. Certainly the picture resists any attempt to colonise it with a counter-projection of Bruno Schulz-like or Hogarth-like characters, sitting in the barber's shop. One recalls that Charles Baudelaire and Charles Meryon – an etcher Hopper greatly admired – never managed to collaborate on a book about Paris, and perhaps Hopperian resistance supplies the reason why. After they died, someone put together a book of Baudelaire poems and Meryon etchings. There is something strange and disquieting about the combination of peopled poems and unpeopled cityscapes. Hopper's *imaginaire* is undoubtedly post-Meryon. The parallel in the case of Hopper would be to pair him up with Charles Reznikoff.[53]

There are six more pictures on the walls of the toilet. One is a poster from an exhibition of American art 1750-1800, which I must have seen at the Victoria and Albert Museum between 15 July and 26 September 1976, certainly before August 16, the date of Naomi's birth. I do not remember the actual visit but I was struck enough by one painting to buy the poster and then write a poem. 'Name' is pronounced 'Nama' but the pun works visually.[54]

Emma Van Name

Emma, what is in a name?
Your creator of no name
Gave us the immortal name
My eyes reflect. They see
That you are good. Oh Emma,
Fecund infanta, baboushka,
Had your local habitation
Been my own, I would have named you
Little mother of the earth.

Oddly enough I remember the book I was reading at University College Hospital maternity wards in Hunter Street during the very night Naomi was born: Octavio Paz's essays *Alternating Current*. I succeed in finding it on a shelf and thumb through it for my marginalia. One sentence I marked at the time serves as a warning to all who would write about works of art: 'Works are mechanisms for creating multiple meanings, which cannot be reduced to the "project" of the person who writes them': thus Paz, in a polemic against Sartre's negative attitude towards Baudelaire. Paz continues: 'Without his poems Baudelaire would not be Baudelaire.' And Paula would not be Paula without her paintings. If a critique of Baudelaire's life does not privilege the fact that the man was a genius, one of the greatest of poets, it is a waste of time. Some approaches to an artist are irrelevant, rather than wrong, as Yves Bonnefoy's essential book on Rimbaud insists. Paz was a generous and thrilling critic, a crucial educator of generations of younger readers, including Richard Burns (now Berengarten), Michael Schmidt and myself. Keith Bosley wrote a birthday poem[55] for Naomi's birth day but conveniently mistook the date as August 15, which enabled him to incorporate a reference to Ascension Day.

During 1970, the year that Octavio Paz spent at Cambridge, in the company of his enchanting Corsican French artist wife, Marie-José, he wrote one of his best and most complex prose books: *The Monkey Grammarian*. Aged fifty-six, eloquent and handsome and possessor of perhaps the most sustainedly brilliant intelligence (above even that of Ted Hughes and more 'public' than Yves Bonnnefoy's) I have ever had the privilege to witness in a long life as an attendant lord and go between, he held court to students and teachers, observing that the best Cambridge poets were at the 'Tech' (now Ruskin Anglia University), not at the university. In my first car, which my then brother-in-law Alan Bell had sold me for twenty pounds, Brenda and I and Michel Couturier drove up to Cambridge for a weekend, staying at Churchill College in three single rooms, since there were no double guest rooms. Michel and I did a joint interview with Paz, Michel for *La Quinzaine Littéraire*, I for *Modern Poetry in Translation*.[56] Later Octavio would say, not disapprovingly, that Michel's interview turned him into a French poet, mine into an English poet, so differently had we edited our joint material. Later that year, commissioned by Michael Kustow, I arranged a series of events on translation at the ICA, including the first public reading of the collective poem 'Renga', written by Octavio, Edouardo Sanguineti, Charles Tomlinson and Jacques Roubaud. I remember too, driving very fast down Sloane Street in that old car, with Octavio seated next to me, and Brenda and Marie-Jo in the back. I succeeded in throwing off the trail a French diplomat with whom we did not want to spend time, for reasons long forgotten.

Twenty-five years later, Octavio and Marie-Jo were in London again. [*fig. 101*] Weissbort, Burns, Jason Wilson and I went to their Knightsbridge hotel for tea. In the photo I am wearing the poetry tie made by Ifigenija Simonovic, and I have included an Ifigenija ashtray. I took along some Menard Press books as a present. Paz observed that their appearance had improved since the old days and that it would be nice to be published by Menard. I stored this up. A few years later, after he died, I wrote to Marie-Jo. Reminding her of this comment, I asked if I could publish his remarkable intellectual autobiography *Itinerario*, which I had read in French and which Professor Wilson, author of a book on Paz, would translate from the original Spanish. She agreed, and it was published in 1999. There was not a single notice of this important book.

I have no doubt at all that had this autobiography by a Nobel Prize winner been published by Faber and Faber or Bloomsbury, it would have been widely reviewed. This surely raises serious questions about the system literary editors find themselves in. While not reflecting on the integrity of individuals, I question the integrity of a system that allows this to happen. One literary editor heard me say this in public and took it personally. He remonstrated and never forgave me. [*Years later, he was congenial at a gathering. I suspect he had forgotten rather than forgiven.*]

Another framed poster on the wall of the toilet is the latest model of the Periodic Table, or latest at the time it appeared in *New Scientist*. In the mid 1980s, I sent that issue to Primo Levi, who replied that despite having written his eponymous book based on the table, he had not kept up with developments in this scientific field, which struck me then as being odd, although it no longer does, perhaps because I have become more aware, thanks to the example of Paula, that you make or do your work and then move on.

Next to the Periodic Table is a reproduction of an old map of Jerusalem, given to me by my sister Mary (formerly of Leeds), of all my family the member most attached to Israel as the place where a Jewish person should live, irrespective of his or her opinion of the policies of its government. She is not militant concerning what other people should do. She and her hydro-geologist husband Mike Krom and married children now live there. Having specialised in teenage obesity and nutrition in Leeds, she is the retired head of public health in a university/hospital faculty in the Galil, the poorest part of Israel. In the words of the liturgy: 'May He who makes peace in His high places, bring peace upon us and upon all Israel and upon all mankind.' One friend of mine who lives in Jerusalem is the poet and painter Miriam Neiger,[57] with whom I co-translated about fifty poems over a quarter of a century. She enters the plot in this chapter because she was commissioned by a German football team to create a poster for them, and I have a copy of it hanging here.

Two more posters before we move on to the bathroom: firstly, one I bought in Leeds City Art Gallery. I was on my way home from a month's residency at Hawthornden Castle in Scotland in 1973. I stopped off in Leeds to break the journey and see Mary. We popped into an exhibition of works associated with the late poet and art critic, Sir Herbert Read. I bought the poster of Barbara Hepworth's drawing of Read reading to three of his children, two boys and a girl. The drawing is typical of sculptors' drawings, being sculptural itself. Lastly, a magnificent screen print published by my dear late friend Felek Scharf, scholar and gentleman, for the International Korczak Society. Korczak, a famous educationalist, was head of the orphanage in the Warsaw Ghetto and deported with his children to Treblinka even though, like Freud, he was important enough to have been offered free passage out of occupied Europe. This screen print contains seven Haiku in homage to Korczak by the Japanese poet Jiri Kondo. Each of the poems is translated into German, English, Polish, Italian, French and Hebrew, the last by my ex-Londoner friend the Israeli poet Natan Zach. Scharf was one of the wise fathers. Eva Hoffman, Peter Gilbert, Colin Shindler, myself: we are only a few of the younger people who would, in his phrase, 'report for duty', to entertain him in return for being instructed. [*fig. 102*]

What are the great scenes in literature and other arts set in the smallest room? (This is a question one would not bother to ask about any other room in a house, since there are hundreds of scenes set in bedrooms, sitting rooms, etc.) One recalls Leopold Bloom in *Ulysses*. In *The French Connection*, Gene Hackman crawls along the floor of a Turkish latrine behind a restaurant, to reach his gun. This was cut in the TV version. *Train Spotting* contains memorable views of a toilet bowl, while Vigo's *Zéro de Conduite* pays a brief visit to the school latrines. Among painters, there is of course Francis Bacon. Lastly, I recall the whimsical photograph of Lartigue's wife during their honeymoon. As Michel Couturier used to say: 'After all, my dear, why not?' I hope it is not unseemly to note that Jorge Semprun and Primo Levi have crucial episodes set in the latrines of Buchenwald and Auschwitz.

The wallpaper on the ceiling is beginning to peel off. There is a cobweb by the bookshelf above the window. Between the window and the bookshelf the wire grill is broken.

Bathroom

Next door to the room with many names is the bathroom, the same word used by British persons of all classes and backgrounds. Unlike the toilet, this room is carpeted, which is probably unhygienic. As already revealed in the previous chapter, the sink and bath are relatively new. Paula's complex and disturbing picture *The Wedding Guest* portrays Lila as a pie-eyed lady, distraught and dishevelled, standing by a sink, copied from the one I presented to the studio. The only male presence in the picture is a metonymic duffle coat, hanging over a wicker chair. The suggestion is rape. Her hand is on the tap, perhaps after swilling water around the basin.

In real life, Lila, as you would expect, is deeply committed to Paula and her work, both as model and also, in recent years, studio assistant. To say that she is a natural model does not do justice to the hard work and sheer intelligence involved in the deadly serious collaborative play with Paula, a collaboration that is rare in the history of art. One thinks of Jo Hopper, but one rather doubts that Jo Hopper or Marthe Bonnard spent much time in playful collaboration concerning their respective postures as models. The story of Lucian Freud's models is manifold and traditional. Perhaps the most interesting of them is Celia Paul,[58] herself a painter of great distinction and one of a number of younger women painters, including the late Sarah Raphael (daughter of my friends Freddie and Beetle), who looked to Paula early in their careers. I have two of Celia's prints. Lila looks like Paula, and this resemblance enables a deepening of Paula's temporary identification with her female characters, some of whom are drawn from life, some of whom are drawn from art or literature or folklore, and all of whom are distilled in the crucible of her imagination.

Yes, the sink in the picture used to stand in my bathroom. My mind wanders back to the time when I had day jobs that involved commuting: if I was not running late, I would take a bath before dashing to the tube. If not, I would ablute at that very sink, brush my hair in front of the mirror on the door of the bathroom cabinet that is still there, and then make my dash.

We have finally arrived at today's bathroom and its contents. The bits and pieces I use regularly are on the window ledge; others are in the cabinet. This is an opportunity to have a clear-out, especially of stuff that has passed its expiry date. Let me check what some of these things are for.

Item: Travelclean detergent
Item: Piroxicam, prescribed 23 January 1993
Item: Boots crepe bandage prescribed for Nathaniel 23 January 1993
Item: Solarcaine (exp. 01/97), Woolworth's suntan cream,

Item: Tiny bottle of Jennie Feldman lavender oil [*Can this be 'my' Jennie Feldman? The address of the aromatherapist is given as Street Lane, Leeds. My Leeds sister Mary has a friend of that name who now lives in Haifa. Perhaps Mary organised the bottle for me, to help me sleep? Yes. I had forgotten that Jennie was once an aromatherapist. Mary introduced me to her about ten years ago because she was a beginning poet and I could perhaps be useful to her. We have kept in touch over the years. By one of those strange synchronicities often referred to as coincidences, Jennie phoned me today, the day I typed the above, and so could confirm she was the same Jennie. She also told me the good and deserved news that her first book of poems and a book of her translations of Jacques Réda had been accepted by Anvil Press.*]

Item: Nystaform ointment
Item: Scholl ingrowing toenail treatment
Item: Betnovate RD cream, expiry date: 1998
Item: Canesten cream, expiry date: 09/98
Item: Boots sting relief
Item: Two small plasters
Item: Small bar of soap from Hotel Roma, Lisbon
Item: Dalacin topical lotion, expiry date: 07/98
Item: Lanes Dual-Lax, expiry date: 11/00

Item: Naturasleep lozenges

Item: 'Hair Brush. Military style. Natural Bristle. Western Germany' [*On the back of the box is a sticker: Owen Owen £5 99p. This was our very own department store in North Finchley. Long gone now, defeated by proximity of Brent Cross, etc.*]

Proceed to the window ledge: hanging above it from the window handle is a splash-proof radio Naomi gave me, which I, good neighbour, use at times when it is not appropriate to play my hi-fi loud. Now I shall move the items on the ledge to the table by the computer; in half an hour, having been itemised below, they will return to their eternal abode, offering me a rare chance to clean the ledge. What have we here?

Item: Kleenex balsam tissues
Item: Lorazepam sedative, expiry date: 25 April 2001
Item: Colgate Plax mouthwash

Item: Eau de Portugal hair tonic [*I don't use the Eau any more. I used to buy it from Johnny the barber, who is ex-Soho and Edgware Road but settled in Golders Green at the side exit of the station years ago. These days 'young Johnny' does my hair once every four or five weeks, while old Johnny the owner spends more and more time on the golf course. Young Johnny has very strong opinions on everything, like a politician or a taxi driver. I have been going to Johnny's for more than fifty years.*]

Item: Ibuprofen anti-inflammatory gel

Item: Valda cough pastilles
Item: Nurofen meltlets
Item: Denman hairbrush [*full of grey hairs; never figured out how to clean it*]
Item: Sponge
Item: Eumovate cream, expiry date: 09/1989
Item: Chanel gel tender
Item: Orsodyl dental gel and Oral-B dental floss
Item: Baldrian Dispert sleeping pills

Item: Caja de Burgos lighter [*Paula and I went to Burgos and Valladolid one year. I was still smoking cheroots.*]

Item: Philishave electric razor
Item: Arnica cream
Item: Interdental brushes
Item: Voltarol retard 100mg, expiry date: 06/2000

Item: Foam rubber earplugs [*These little fuckers don't work. Sure, they shut out the noise, but they are so uncomfortable I can't sleep anyway.*]

Item: Diazepam sedative, expiry date: 05/2002
Item: Piroton allergy pills
Item: Paracetomol tablets
Item: Smint peppermints
Item: Waitrose matches

Item: Wrapped soap from Hotel Saint Rocco, Lake Orta [*Paula and I stayed at this hotel close to the lake, described by Balzac and others as the most beautiful place in the world. Here Nietzsche met one of my favourite women, Lou Andreas-Salomé, and proposed to her and was turned down. Here Primo Levi's relative was arrested and taken to be murdered at Maggiore. Here we were fascinated by the seventeenth and eighteenth century life-size figures in the hillside chapels at Sacro Monte, and in particular the ones at Valaro that so fascinated Samuel Butler, a local hero. These annual trips around my birthday are very heaven. Ah, the concentric rhythms of association, rhythms perhaps more clearly observed on holiday when you don't live together the rest of the year.*][59]

Item: Two shoe-cleaner sponges from some hotel

Item: nitro-glycerine suppositories [*A Portuguese tradition; Paula reminds me that the word is 'glycerine' not 'nitro-glycerine', which might be over the top in this context.*]

A chain or chart could be constructed to demonstrate the changing medications one has taken over the years. These evidently include painkillers for back trouble and sciatica, steroid anti-rheumatic pills for repetitive- strain injury in the forearm, sleeping pills (natural and drug-based, the latter sedative or hypnotic), tranquillisers, painkillers, indigestion tablets, cream for athlete's foot, suppositories, powder and cream against itching. Yet I am healthy in my own way, given the depredations wrought by time in all of us.

The hook on the door holds my bathrobe from John Lewis; my father's silk dressing gown, which I am wearing in Paula's *Rest on the Flight into Egypt*; and a bath towel. The curtain rail above the bath serves to hold drying sheets and towels. Over the bath stretches a crafty space saver, a clothes rack my mother sensibly gave me when I moved to this flat. On it, at any given moment, you will find the results of the latest machine wash: Y-fronts, socks, etc., together with a dishcloth, two pairs of swimming trunks, the old boxers and the trunks I had to buy when we visited Biarritz, because a 'slip' was obligatory in the public swimming pool that happened to be outside the hotel. They have been unused for weeks, while the Finchley Lido pool has been undergoing its latest refurbishment. On the ledge of the bath are my flannels, a bottle of Vosene shampoo, the CIF bath-cleaning cream and the sponge I apply it with. As I have said, except when I was in a great rush, I used to have a bath first thing in the morning. Now that I work from home, I take my bath when I feel like it and almost never on days I'm not going out, as part of my contribution to an ecologically sound way of life.

I lie there, soaping my parts, the sum of which is or is not greater than the whole – depending on which philosophy of mind I currently hold. Thus, my friend Z. Kotowicz dismisses Antonio Damasio on learned grounds, but I find the latter's thoughts on the self quite useful for my sporadic investigations into autobiography. Soaking peacefully, I gaze up at a framed image – signed by Thérèse Le Prat, famous for theatre photography in her day, according to my recently rediscovered friend Henri Béhar – which I have treasured ever since Meyer (Mémé) Cohen gave it to me in Paris in 1961 and which I will keep until I die. It is 'an after-image / of the flesh' (Sharon Nelson), the face and hand of an eloquent mime, Yves Lorelle, a contemporary of Marcel Marceau, and identified for me by Valérie Bochenek, who founded the mime museum in Paris. I love it for itself and in itself, and also because, in the words of Psalm 37, verse 25, '*naar hayiti vegam zakanti /* I have been young and am now old' and this image, surely the earliest one on my walls, has accompanied me everywhere. I Google the name of my fellow resident at Guy Patin: Meyer (Mémé) Cohen. Director of a theatre in Nice: this is promising and, given the nature of the image, it suggests an abiding interest in the stage; I put my brain in gear, but no memory of the old days confirms the suggestion. I shall post him a letter tonight c/o the theatre and return to this paragraph later on. [*A week later: letter received from Meyer Cohen. I translate: 'Yes, it's me, Meyer Cohen. I was at Guy Patin in 1961. I am happy and moved to receive news of you. After spending several years as a pharmacist, I plunged body and soul into theatre, and that is what I have been doing for the last 25 years. I have a beautiful theatre in Nice, my second theatre! I am Director of the theatre, director of plays and actor and full of joy I live out my Passion. Very pleased to renew contact with you after all this time. Amitiés, Meyer Cohen.*] [*fig. 103*]

Sometimes I sit at the other end of the bath – when the shower attachment is not working – so that I can rinse my hair under the taps, and face two posters: one was given to me by Edward Horswell, proprietor of the Sladmore Gallery and world expert on Rembrandt Bugatti. The poster is a collage of work by Rembrandt, *animalier* sculptor of genius, brother Enzo of automobile fame, and son of Carlo, a classical furniture maker. They have an affinity with a Swiss-Italian family of artists, also two brothers and a father, also one genius and two great talents, namely the Giacomettis, although automobile enthusiasts might question that, or agree with it but mean something else. I learned about Rembrandt Bugatti – whom Yves Bonnefoy had not heard of, the only time this has happened when I have mentioned the name of an artist – from Merlin James, a painter and art critic I wrote to after he reviewed (in 1988) *The Unknown Masterpiece*, my little book containing an essay on and translation of Balzac's remarkable story.[60] I was pleased enough by his praise not to mind his reservations. (While one would like only to be praised, I find, strangely enough, that I am more inclined to trust praise when it is mitigated – which in my case it usually is – since one can be more certain it is genuine. Or am I being naïve?). Underneath the Bugatti is a Jonathan Griffin translation of Pessoa published as one of the 'Poems on the Underground', for which I gave permission as his literary executor. [*fig. 104*] Judith Chernaik's magnificent initiative, which took off in 1986, has been copied in cities

fig. 102

fig. 103

fig. 104

fig. 105

fig. 106

– on buses and undergrounds – all over Europe and the USA, and she deserves praise for an idea that has given pleasure to many. The poem is accompanied by a drawing of Pessoa by Paula's Portuguese contemporary Julio Pomar. My own contribution to the series, a Bonnefoy translation, will appear in another room, later in this book.

Following a brief correspondence, Merlin James and I arranged to meet at the Tate, and he entered my life, where he remains, educator and mentor, despite being twenty years younger than me. I bought two of his works on paper and published *Engaging Images*, his remarkable book on how to look at pictures. The back cover states: 'Menard Essays in Art Criticism, No.1'. Note the implication, but the book turned out to be the first and last in the series, which was to have been edited by Merlin James, Audrey Jones and Anthony Rudolf.

Paula and I bumped into Merlin at the Hopper exhibition at Tate Modern (2004), and as always he entertained and instructed with his takes on pictures, especially concerning the use of light by this great and wondrous artist. Paula liked Merlin's own latest exhibition at Andrew Mummery's gallery. Like that of Sickert, Merlin's art is not inhibited by his active intellectual work as a writer on art. I wanted him to take over Menard Press one day, but his reply was good, namely that he was flattered but if he was going to be a publisher he would start his own press. Another candidate, Steven Jaron, had a similar reaction. I realised then that anyone who *wanted* to do it would be the wrong person. One-person-band small presses have a natural life, and when that is over, as Menard's has been for several years, you move on.

The sculptor Rembrandt Bugatti, who committed suicide in 1916 at the age of thirty-one (seven months after another major sculptor, Henri Gaudier-Brzeska, died on the Western Front) was the greatest post-Barye *animalier*, and brought an unprecedented expressiveness to his beasts [*fig. 105*]. Before making his casts, he sketched the animals at the zoo in the Jardin des Plantes, and it is quite possible that he and Rilke eyeballed Rilke's panther, perhaps at the same time. The poem dates from around 1903, Bugatti's 'Panther' from 1904. There is an enchanting photo of Bugatti with a donkey in which it is clear that both are posing. Augustus Young is completing a significant book on Rilke and we both hope that the poet and sculptor met, but sadly there is no mention of Bugatti, admired by Rodin, in the extensive correspondence of Rilke.

Bugatti used to enchant the animals. I gave Paula a print of the photo [*fig. 106*] supplied kindly by Edward Horswell, who told me that a carrot had been doctored out of the donkey's mouth to improve the image. Paula herself sketched a donkey at a sanctuary in the Isle of Wight, when she went there to stay with her friend John Mills, world expert on carpets and ex-National Gallery senior chemist, now sadly deceased. Merlin was working with Edward Horswell on what later became Edward's fine monograph. I was called in and well paid to translate French texts, one of my chief sources of freelance income, although publishers pay far less well than Edward does. Treat Mark Hutchinson in Paris to a double espresso and in turn you will be treated to a splendid rant on the iniquities of publishers when it comes to money.

Certain Louvre papers on Bugatti were difficult to translate – academic art-historical documents – but as compensation there was one easy text, a *feuilleton* by Bugatti's contemporary, the poet and art critic André Salmon. I would bet the money I earned translating him that Salmon, a celebrity in his day, was paid by the word and allowed or encouraged to write as much as he wanted. It was spun out, and obviously composed or dictated in a single draft. Bugatti bronzes are rare. I have caught a few at temporary exhibitions in Strasbourg and Bayonne. Visit the Sladmore Gallery, there is usually at least one on display. His animals, like the grandparents in Robert Lowell's poem, are 'altogether otherworldly now', 'altogether elsewhere', like Auden's reindeer. They always were of course, but no one got closer to their very being than Rembrandt Bugatti. Their stillness, their power, is awesome. The loss to sculpture created by the death of Gaudier-Brzeska cannot be exaggerated. Bugatti's death by his own hand involved an equal loss.

On the wall by the bath are two more posters: one reproducing a Bram van Velde gouache which Samuel Beckett donated to the Centre Pompidou, and one showing the Cyrillic alphabet, which Richard Berengarten (former Burns) gave me after one of his many trips to former Yugoslavia, visiting Arijana, the daughter of his second marriage. Richard phoned me yesterday from Cambridge (that city of 'silent continuities' in the phrase of Elaine Feinstein). Having found letters from me while doing admin, he read one out. Although, like Richard, I keep all my letters, after a few years I stopped filing them properly, and I suffer from this now. I cannot find anything in this flat and I hate myself for making my life so difficult. Yet at the same time I feel comfortable in chaos and disorder. Is this why I like formal, ordered and symmetrical paintings so much? When Richard and I rang off, I recalled that he and his then girlfriend, Diana May (quondam matron of the Avenue Road Clinic and sadly deceased), stayed here to look after me when I returned home from hospital after my first or second hernia operation. They slept in Naomi's bedroom. Richard and I both thought we had piles, so Diana examined us. But I only had one, if that is medically possible. On one occasion I visited Avenue Road for dinner in Diana's private flat. Richard and another matron, Barbara Binding, who later opened the first private clinic for venereal disease since World War I, were fellow guests. I went up in the lift with a short man. 'Do you know who that was?' said Di at the lift door: 'the Sultan of Brunei.'

There are other pictures in the bathroom. One is the poster from Paula's 1997 Tate Gallery Liverpool retrospective, showing a 1986 picture of a girl lifting her skirt to a quizzical and obedient dog. Another is a reproduction of a Balthus painting, *The Moth*, in which a naked woman is holding her nightdress or a towel in one hand, her other arm raised over a disproportionately large moth. She has been read as a spectre, a dream figure, but I read her literally, as someone about to extinguish the light and go to bed, alone. Hopper too painted a woman in her bedroom, alone: the poet John Taggart wrote a whole book about this picture, *Remaining in Light*. Balthus and Hopper: two great painters: they have seen the light.... very differently. What is the light's purpose? The vision is not the whole story, but the story tells a vision.

I lived briefly in Greenwich Village while Hopper was still alive. Maybe I saw him. I probably never even set eyes on Balthus by accident, let alone on purpose. But it would have been possible to meet him: over the years, Yves Bonnefoy's name opens doors, for he is generous with his address book. When I told him I was going to Rome and would love to meet his friend, he authorised me to call the painter at the Villa Medicis, where he was the director: 'Say you are my friend and translator.' But my nerve failed me at the last minute. I cannot claim an altruistic motive, unlike Paul Auster, who told me, some years later, that he stopped visiting Beckett, on the grounds that it was not fair to take up the time of a friendly and courteous old person. I wonder how old old was old at that point?

He draws the light, the sting of memory.
Repose accuses, stillness calls. The silence

of a Balthus virgin screams across
the centuries to Piero and Mantegna.

She whispers, whispers to herself that no
action shall be sister to the dream.

[FROM ONE OF MY BALTHUS POEMS][61]

The fourth in that final group of pictures is a genuine print above the bathroom cabinet, an etching of a figure accompanied by one of my poems, a poem about Claude Vigée that I have re-revised in the years since the artist printed it. Shame on me, I forget his or her name and cannot read the signature. Nor can I send a photograph to Claude in Paris where, aged ninety nine, noble and stoical, he lies on his back, blind, waiting. I phone him regularly. [*Later: he died on 2 October, 2020, four months short of his hundredth birthday. The funeral took place in his native Bischwiller near Strasbourg in the presence of his family, the mayor and a rabbi, all wearing masks.*]

Kitchen

Things happen when you work at home, which you would have missed if you had commuted to an office. A Virgin ambulance helicopter is landing in the garden of the adjacent block of flats, which I am looking at through the bedroom window. My kitchen, however, is at the front of the flat. Will you come into my kitchen, said the spider to the fly. It's a cool web, said the fly, wind me in this angry day. The kitchen is the first room on the right, as you enter the flat, and was last modernised by the previous inhabitants some years before I arrived in 1981. In other words, nothing has changed. At the very least, the cork tiles on the kitchen floor could do with a good cleaning and even replacement. I note a remark about women made by a UKIP Member of the European Parliament: 'They don't clean behind the fridge enough.'

Exercise Machine

Immediately to my right as I enter the kitchen is my cross-trainer exercise machine. I used to run locally, more or less following the contour of Dollis Brook. Those days are lost and gone forever, although I enjoyed the activity, certainly more than I enjoyed swimming. Only yesterday I was in the middle of my daily stint on the machine – my Saturday sessions usually take place during *Jazz Record Requests*, my Sunday ones during *Private Passions* and so on – when I emerged from an endorphin reverie to hear Dina Washington singing 'Blue Gardenia', and caught a line about the eponymous flower being 'pressed in my book of memory'. This kitchen will yield such flowers: the first involves word association with the quondam Gardenia restaurant in Rose Crescent, Cambridge. I could legitimately pursue this line of thought, along the axis of association, but that is not my primary organisational principle, which is to generate memory from objects and documents around me. One of my motives for writing this book is to give myself permission to go through every artefact in the flat, rediscovering lost possibilities, potential achievements or even small victories; enabling the telling of anecdotes and memories; bidding farewell to hoarded paraphernalia; and providing the compost for future stories and poems: my very own uncooked ingredients to trigger the taste-buds of the imagination. It is as if I am returning to the scene of the crime: I am the figure you cannot see – policeman or criminal or both at once – in Atget photographs.

(Around) the Filing Cabinet

Rather than continue my journey to the front of the cross-trainer, I shall begin across the room on the left. Here we find a filing cabinet stuffed with old files – Menard Press, Poetry Society, etc. This filing cabinet is a treasure trove, a well of living and seeing, but I shall describe what is on top of it and then what is stuck to it, since, unlike the contents of the cabinet, these form part of my kitchen life and are therefore germane to my research during this chapter:

Item: Raffle tickets. My three main charitable causes, at the time of writing, are Writers in Prison, Mind and the Medical Foundation for the Care of Victims of Torture. Paula has made a print for this foundation, founded by the late Helen Bamber. I shall spare you a rant on the increasing privatisation of welfare provision and the expectation that, amidst all the sorrow and affliction around us, private charity should replace the state in the retreat from social democracy.

Item: Seven copies of a leaflet describing walks around 'the vanishing Jewish East End'. [*These walks are organised by Clive Bettington, having been pioneered long ago by Bill Fishman, rest in peace.*]

Item: Takeaway Indian menu, still untested, from Hebah, the high-street restaurant that replaced replaced the Greek that replaced the Italian. [*Let us hope that the new arts centre in Tally Ho will have a knock-on effect on this part of London, including the gastronomical provision. Although North Finchley itself has a Waterstones, Barnet, the largest borough in London, is not well supplied with bookshops.*]

Item: two photographs: one of my daughter during her Australia phase, the other of the Cuban poet Pablo Armando Fernandez two years ago, his first London visit for well over thirty years. [*This is signed on the back with his trademark 'always and for ever yours, Pablo',*]

Item: postcards:

   i)   Paintings by Elizabeth Adela Forbes and Harold Harvey I bought at Penlee House in Penzance on holiday with Paula one year;

   ii)   'Autumn Sunlight' by Laura Knight, plus paintings by Murillo and Jan Steen, from Birmingham City Art Gallery and the Barber collection at the University;

   iii)   Laura Knight self-portrait and Isaac Rosenberg self-portrait, National Portrait Gallery;

   iv)   Simeon Solomon's 'Carrying the Scrolls of the Law', Whitworth Gallery, Manchester. [*I bought this at the magnificent Royal Academy exhibition of art from British provincial galleries, a few years ago. The image is a highly erotic, understatedly ecstatic image of an attractive young cantor or rabbi with his hand inside the cover of the scroll, as if under a skirt or other garment.*]

   v)   Family portrait by Sir Thomas Lawrence of the first Marquess of Exeter and his wife and daughter, bought at Burghley House, when we visited Stamford for Ruth Rosengarten's wedding to Ian Garton. [*Ruth Rosengarten is an artist and an art theoretician, and has written several essays on Paula. South African, Israeli, Portuguese and now English, hers is an international mind abreast of theory in all its recent manifestations. Sadly, Ian died after only a few years of marriage.*]

vi) Daumier's 'La Laveuse' and his clay caricatures of
parliamentarians. [*Paula is full of enthusiasms that wax and
wane according to need, but certain artists are of permanent
inspiration to her: Daumier, Doré, Goya, Ensor. Sometimes I will
find a book on the table in her studio or flat, of no apparent
immediate or direct relevance to current work, which is being
metabolised slowly for later regeneration or transformation. Some
say we praise in art what we admire in ourselves, others that we
return to favourite works for inspiration. One writer said recently
that his motive was stimulation rather than inspiration, but this
merely secularises a word with mystical connotations. It's almost
the same thing. There is, however, another motive, neither
narcissistic nor utilitarian: it involves love. Sometimes, quite
simply, we put aside our vanity and self-regard and praise what we
love.*]

Item: Membership card for the Hen and Chickens Theatre and Lowdown
at The Albany. [*This card was acquired when Paula, Lila and I visited the
Albany venue near Great Portland Street tube station to watch Paula's
daughter, Vicky Willing, performing impro, that is, improvisational comedy.
I had seen her before at the Comedy Store. This year her group Sprout are
working the Edinburgh Festival. I performed once with her daughter, Gracie,
in Paula's studio, the big bad wolf to her Red Riding Hood: part of a
commission by Modern Painters. Gracie, aged about seven, did a portrait of
me – which I bought from her for five pounds – during a respite from her
own pose*]

Item: two business cards:

i) Mr Ellinas: he owned a Greek delicatessen in Finchley Central,
up and across from Pedro the Spanish fishmonger, and in my
quondam entertaining days was always good for simple recipes.
[*One day I was leaving the shop when I saw Mrs Ellinas struggling
with several carrier bags. She was going home and I politely offered
her a lift. This was politely refused and I interpreted the refusal to
mean that it was not appropriate for a Greek Orthodox woman to
accept a ride from a man who was not a relative or a close friend*

from within their community. On the back of the card I have written the name of an excellent Greek restaurant Vrisaki, in Wood Green. When we say Greek or Turkish in this context we are talking Cyprus. Pedro too has gone. He had a notice in the window: 'Use me or lose me'. We didn't and we did].

ii) Orexi Restaurant in Hornsey Road. [*I went there a few times. It was around the corner from the famous greengrocer in the Seven Sisters Road, Gibbers, now gone, where you could buy the cheapest olive oil in London. Orexi means appetite, as in 'anorexic'... It served the tastiest taramasalata in London – beige, rather than the artificial bright pink found elsewhere. The young owners had an enchanting young daughter, who was up all hours.*]

The top of the filing cabinet is where I keep my scrap paper. There are at least two thousand sheets of paper with script only on one side. Many of these are manuscript drafts for recycling. I pick out one at random and note an epigraph: 'The true fight is with the Duende': Garcia Lorca.[62] A few more objects crowd together promiscuously alongside the scrap paper:

Item: A Christmas present from Lila, a hamster Hombre who sings and dances 'La Cucaracha' when you press his foot, which I am doing even as I type this.

Item: A swirling glass 'ashtray' from my mother's house. [*I cannot look at this without returning to childhood, when all the grown-ups smoked – the smell as vivid as my grandmother's cinnamon cookies and my mother's chicken soup.*]

Item: Two Father's Day presents: from my son a kitschy golden trophy figure labelled 'Best Dad', and a fluffy Australian animal from my daughter.

On the front and side of the filing cabinet are the remains of round stickers with phrases typical of hippy lapel buttons in the 1970s. Some of them are faded: the one on the left once said: 'Kafka is a *kvetch*' – *kvetch* being the onomatopoeic Yiddish word for grumbler or complainer. This was, indeed, a characteristic of the Prague genius, as I am reminded by Nicholas Murray's fine biography. Murray's account of K's *folie à deux* with Felice

Bauer has never been bettered. The phrase on another sticker was both funny and accurate enough to receive the ultimate accolade of inclusion in Leo Rosten's *The Joys of Yiddish*: 'Marcel Proust is a *yenta*', which is a colourful Yiddish word for female gossip or rumour monger. (This sticker can still be seen on the much later photograph.) 'Demilitarise erogenous zones' is a dated sentiment and as for 'I can't relate to trees' – was it ever funny? ('You are often alone with a person / you are never alone with a tree': Stevie Smith). Among the stickers are a few magnetic objects, including a fried egg, a tiny matryoshka (also in the photo), and a mini-barometer. [*fig. 107*]

The Space Between Filing Cabinet and Oven

There are pictures above and around the filing cabinet, but I shall hoard them till later, when I discuss the kitchen pictures as a group. Now I move on – to the space between the filing cabinet and the oven. Space, as they say, is at a premium, hence the washing line strung above the bath, which I have already described. Here, in this rare kitchen space, I keep:

Item: A 1995 London Residential telephone directory, plus a 2000 London Business and Services directory, liberated from my mother's house, when she moved. [*Telephone directories covering the whole of this great city no longer exist. The assumption is that you only check out local numbers or have a computer with online directories. The free ones are useless. Telephoning Directory Enquiry or other service has become very expensive, as have wake-up calls. In the old days, if you wanted to know the time, you dialled TIM.*]

Item: Other directories, up to date: Barnet local numbers; Thomson local directories: Hendon & Hampstead, Barnet & Edgware; London North Yellow Pages.

Item: Viking Direct office-equipment catalogues.

Item: Large A–Z of London, 2001 and 2002 Automobile Association UK road maps.

Item: Floor-cleaning agent and implements.

Item: Six large cardboard cylinder tubes, containing:

i)   Three large detailed maps of Tel-Aviv, Jerusalem and Haifa. [*Where did the maps come from? What are they doing here? To ask that question might be taken metaphorically or metonymically as a reference to the present work. In which case, these lists enter into the equation. I suggest that my lists (without their material in square brackets) can be read as paratactical catalogue poems, inscribed by me and found by you, or as the verbal equivalent of a miniature installation, such as a Cornell box. Mystery of provenance solved: I find the name of my late friend Felek Scharf on the tube – though heaven knows why someone in Poland sent them to him in the first place. I like lists, poetry is there:* Don Giovanni, The Mikado, *Bible genealogies.*]

ii) Posters sent at my request by an official researcher in the Paris Jewish Communities offices, advertising the now defunct students' hostel where I lived in 1961 for six months, Le Toit familial, 9 rue Guy Patin, Paris X[e].[63] [*The name of the printer at the bottom of the poster is H. Levy et fils, Hagenau. The director of the hostel, Nathan Samuel, and his wife Hélène (sister of the theologian André Neher, of whom, according to Derrida, Emanuel Levinas said: 'He's the Protestant Jew, I'm the Catholic Jew…') had previously directed children's homes in various places, including Hagenau. Like Claude Vigée from Bischwiller, they were scions of these ancient Jewish communities of Alsace. Dollars to doughnuts, or should that be shekels to beigels, the connection went back a long way. Elie Wiesel was one of hundreds of former students of the Samuels: this was in Lyons, pre-rue Guy Patin (see his memoir:* All the Rivers Flow Down to the Sea].

iii) Posters, including a poem by my friend and Menard author A.C. Jacobs, 'London NW2' and a spare copy of my translation of a Bonnefoy poem, both used by Judith Chernaik in her poster series already mentioned.

Item: A very long spaghetti jar. [*This had been given to my sister Mary as an engagement present, and was lying around the garage of my mother's house for quarter of a century before I took it away. Why? Because it was there. One of a number of potential props for Paula's studio?*]

Item: Unplugged telephone. [*It may already be apparent that I have fantasies of becoming a conceptual artist. This phone will be perfect for an installation or ready-made.*]

Item: The tripartite box a Chanukah present of cheese, wine and bottle opener arrived in. [*Perfect for a Cornell box, see previous item.*]

Item: Two dumbbells. [*These were among things James Hogan donated to me when he and his wife Margaret left to live in France. At that time, James was in such good shape physically, his regime of day job, writing books and keeping fit so tightly organised, that retirement to France proved a shock to the system. He has all the time in the world to write, but his body has been playing up, muscles and all. He attends physio and other therapies, and I occasionally forward his treatment plans to my daughter Naomi, herself a physiotherapist, for a second opinion.*]

Oven

In and of itself, the oven need not detain us. When I come into the kitchen in the morning, I heat the first of three cups of Turkish coffee in my small *ezve* with the long handle. Breakfast is usually fruit. Lunch might be a carton of 'Covent Garden' soup with wholemeal bread or a tin of sardines – ever the loyal Portuguese, as I was during the European Football Cup Final, when 'Eo appoio Portugal, obrigadissimo', was my slogan, amidst the natives. In the afternoon, I come down from coffee to tea. When I am at home, I cook dinner, timed for the ten o'clock BBC News. On Thursdays I buy [*Later: used to buy, he's gone*] fish from the Grimsby van at Lodge Lane car park: cod or salmon or kippers; often I grill fish, and serve it up with cooked vegetables, followed by fruit: plums and apricots are favourite. Late-night snack is an apple; Pink Lady has replaced

Braeburn, and one day Pinklady will be replaced, another milestone in the strange and declining history of the English apple. Bread tends to be my carb staple, rather than potatoes, pasta or rice. At Paula's place, a traditional dish is Ervilhas com Ovos: chorizo, onions, peas and eggs, flavoured with coriander, garlic, salt and pepper, etc. Some people add red wine. 'Eat fish, eat fish,' Uncle Juvenal (Paula's son Nick's other name) the dentist would say to the young Paula, pinching her cheek.

Washing Machine (and George)

The space to the right of the oven has the ancient bathroom container for dirty clothes (which I liberated from my mother's house) and my waste bin. Which brings us to the last sector of the left-hand wall: here is the washing machine, which some years ago replaced the vast one I took away alone from George and Sandra Buchanan's flat in Ashley Gardens, Westminster, causing my first hernia. When Brenda and I with our children moved from Upper Holloway to separate flats in 1981, I ended up with the old machine. Now meet another George, who stands close by the washing machine and waste bin. George is a tree Naomi gave me as a birthday present at least ten years ago. He is the only plant that has ever survived in this house. Georgina, a window bush, died from neglect. But George, now almost as tall as me, has survived the rainbow of my will, to misquote Robert Lowell. He twists, turns and recoils, seeking the light around corners, and doubtless water too – when I have forgotten to feed him. He is making a visual statement. He could almost be a sculpture, a living reproach to the sticker about trees on my filing cabinet. He wants to be loved. He reminds me of the Golem or Frankenstein's Monster, but where does that leave his master? George is an intimation of immortality. While George lives, I shall live. Beware of making statements like that, if this was a folk story I would be signing my death warrant. [*Later: He's dead. Fate was tempted.*]

[*Later still: One August evening, driving with my daughter – through the residue of flash-flood water en route to her grandmother – I mentioned George to Naomi. At first she thinks I am referring to yet another George, the mechanical toy given to her by an American friend who long ago lodged at*

Flat One in my block. No, dear, not that George or George Buchanan. As if on cue, she ticks me off roundly for Georgina's demise and says George is permanently drunk on the plant food I give him, about ten times the recommended dose. The two Georges have created a Proustian effect or affect, since she remarks with regret that her childhood is beginning to vanish, what with her mother moving from the first post-marital flat to another place in North Finchley. I say that there is no visible reminder of the years when the end room on the right, now a sort of office, was her bedroom. Makes no difference, she said: you still live in the flat, and that's my room. Curious that my 'sailor' daughter is more sentimental about her room than her 'farmer' brother is about his. And yet, it's not so curious. She, who has moved around a lot, and lived in many places, needs to know that something stays the same. One more reason not to move.] [fig. 108]

On the three shelves which Chalkie built for me above the washing machine are bunches of stationery for re-use: ordinary envelopes of all sizes, stiffened ones, and Jiffy Bags, the last a relatively recent example of a brand name that is used generically, like Hoover or Biro. I have taken this opportunity to chuck out shabby and torn items. I cast a cursory glance at the return addresses on some of the envelopes: here is Andrew Glaze, then in Florida, where I stayed with him in 1998 en route to California, and enjoyed watching one of his puppies dancing around in diapers. These envelopes remind me of the days when Menard had if not a thriving then an active retail trade which I supplied from home – in earlier days I even did the wholesale and trade sales from home too – using the kitchen as an office. Also on these shelves are recipes clipped from newspapers, most if not all never consulted, let alone used, and various supplements, pullouts and newsletters. Here too are books. These I shall describe or list, unlike the ones in the toilet and bedroom, since they are integral to this room, being about food or drink. One recipe is a classic which I still make: Sharon Nelson's Apple Cake, after our lodger in Primrose Gardens. Cinammon never fails to work its magic in the classic Proustian way.

Ingredients
2 large apples; cup of brown sugar; ⅓ cup of oil; 1 egg; 1½ cups of self-raising flour; cinnamon; ½ cup of raisins. Everything can be doubled, if so desired.

Method
  i)   Peel & dice the apples and place in a large bowl.
  ii) Pour the sugar over the apples and leave for about 20 minutes.
  iii) Add oil and egg.
  iv) Add flour and cinnamon and mix all ingredients thoroughly.
       Finally add raisins.
  v)   Bake for 45 minutes on 350 (number 4)

Selection of recipe clippings

Dozens of these, never consulted. In an ideal – dream or nightmare – world, I would list all of them, but in the real world where time and patience, mine and the reader's, are limited, I shall select the ones I tell myself I shall use one day: a tactical (or paratactical) retreat from inclusiveness in the interests of strategic clarity and the imperatives of a catalogue poem. The unselected ones I shall *throw away*. It is clear that the behavioural pattern associated with keeping things to be consulted later 'because they might come in useful' suggests that a psychological need is met by the very act of keeping, irrespective of later use or non-use.

Item: Salt Cod and Parsnip Gratin, *Guardian*, 11/01/97
Item: Baked Sweet Potato, *Independent on Sunday*, 13/09/1992
Item: Cheat's Cassoulet
Item: Pesto, in my handwriting
Item: Pasta with Vodka
Item: Roast Leg of Lamb, *Independent on Sunday*, 02/07/1995
Item: Spice-Roasted Lamb, *Guardian*, 15/04/1995
Item: Basque Eggs, Ruth Brandon fax from Olney dated 09/09/1996
Item: Gigi's Lamb [*This is signed by Gigi, Mrs Eddie Topol of Illinois*]
Item: Salted Almonds
Item: Fish Soup photocopied from Claudia Roden
Item: Hot tips from the Mustard Shop
Item: Baked Potatoes with oil and parsley
Item: Cream of Stilton soup

Selection of other clippings

Item: 'Profile of Helena Cronin', *Guardian* (probably) [*This evolutionary psychologist or socio-biologist or natural philosopher has one thing in common with me: we went to the same primary school, Henrietta Barnett. She tells us she is 'the perfect female shape, 0.7 waist/ hip ratio – the ideal Darwinian curve'.*]

Item: 'How to cope with the morning after', *The Times*, 26/12/2000
Item: 'Seeds of Faith' (on mustard), *Guardian* 20/04/1996

Item: 'Psychobiology and the Mood', Michael Bateman, *Independent on Sunday*, 03/07/1994

Item: 'Jewish Fried Fish' (undated), *Jewish Chronicle* [*This article suggests that Fish and Chips, one of the Great British dishes, is a combination of two imports: Portuguese Marrano fried fish and Lancashire Irish chips. It also says that cold fried fish is a Jewish delicacy, which indeed it is, but fried in matsoh meal, not batter.*]

Postcards

(Not all of these are *integral* to the kitchen, but they have been in a pile above the washing-machine for so many years that they have acquired squatters' rights so here they are.)

Item: from James Hogan, dated 11/12/1983, inviting me over for drinks before Xmas. [*He tells me he is doing a postal survey of dentists' professional reading and might include poetry. It should be pointed out that he was a consultant epidemiologist, and was/is always good for a second opinion on medical issues – even in retirement – and recently has been arguing with passion about Covid.*]

Item: from Ruth Fainlight dated 6/4/1983. [It includes a comment that she is reading *The Brothers Ashkenazi* by Israel Joseph Singer.

Item: from Rabbi Barbara Borts, dated 19/07/1983, reminding me to send two sets of Jewish New Year cards published by Menard Press.[64] [*For a number of years, Menard published Jewish New Year cards, seven in all, donating the profits to charity. At that time, only hyper-schmaltzy commercial cards could be bought. Cards eventually went out of fashion, mainly because the relative cost of long-distance phonecalls and postage has changed in favour of the former, and that was even before emails and texts and other messaging entered the scene. Barbara was one of a remarkable group of rabbinical pioneers whom I met in the days when I was involved in the Jewish community. Others included Aviva Kipen, Julia Neuberger and Jacquie Tabbick.*]

Item: card signed off 'love from Auntie Judith'. [*Judith Thurman, now a biographer, has addressed the card (postmarked Brooklyn, April 4, 1974) to me, Brenda and Nathaniel, then six weeks old. She agreed to review a book for European Judaism.*]

Item: BIFF card (one of several around the flat) headed 'Any Questions with Krazy Frank Kafka, the Bore from the Bronx'. [*This, judging by the jokey message on the reverse from Jill Grey, was sent to wish me well before my first hernia operation. It shows a heavily bandaged man on a hospital bed, saying, 'Why me? Why now rather than then? Why here rather than there?'. On the floor is the creature from* Metamorphosis, *saying, 'You think you've got problems.' Having posed nude as Kafka's creature for Paula, I can relate to this situation.*]

Item: image of a Turner painting from Joyce Bridson, widow of Geoffrey Bridson.

Item: mint postcards: the cricketer Bob Willis, 'Prayer for Peace', Chagall's *Rabbi with Torah*, poem of (and probably from) Paul Auster, portrait of John Clare, Picasso's *Le Dessert*, portrait of Wordsworth.

Item: 'Free Vanunu' postcard. [*Of the causes I have embraced none has been less popular than that of the Israeli whistle-blower, Mordechai Vanunu, who was championed by Susannah York. He belongs at the interface of two of my main and continuing concerns – Israel and the wider nuclear issue, the latter concern centred on Star Wars, terrestrial weapons, new nuclear technology and intelligence sharing with America agreed by Britain without even a discussion by the parliamentary Select Committee let alone a full debate in the house.*[65]]

Item: postcards from Amber Jacobs. [*This beautiful, enchanting and scatty child, then in the sixth form, was chief baby-sitter here until the day the children informed me they didn't need a child minder, let alone a babysitter. She is now a mother herself, and lectures at Birkbeck in psychosocial studies.*]

Item: postcard from Maggie Gee postmarked April 1984, containing the phrase 'You were sweet to me at BAND.' [*What on earth does this mean? Aha, memory kicks in: Maggie Gee and Ian McEwan had been giving a pub reading under the auspices of Book Action for Nuclear Diasarmament. When it ended, I had gone up to them and, as I recall, had talked to Maggie, an old friend, but corrupted my discourse by trying to impress Ian McEwan. And then apologised in writing to Maggie. Maybe it didn't show, or maybe Maggie is sparing my feelings. Either way, it does not matter any more – if it ever did – but in that case why do I tell the story now? Whatever, trying to impress people is an old trait which I have attempted to self-treat, with luck obviating recourse to aversion therapy or cognitive psychology.*]

Item: postcard from Michael Sheringham with Raymond Mason's wonderful polychrome sculpture from Saint-Eustache in Paris on the other side. [*Raymond Mason, in a photo on the washing machine signing books with Yves Bonnefoy, has lived in Paris since 1946. The same age as Anthony Caro and William Turnbull, he too is a major sculptor. I introduced him to Paula: they understand each other well, as knowledge of their work would lead you to expect. He is much admired by Ron Mueck. There is a witty photo by Cartier-Bresson of Raymond sitting atop the photographer's house on rue de Rivoli, cap on his head rhyming with the chimney cap, while working on a topographical drawing of the view. Later: Raymond has died: peace, respect and affection unto him.Michael too. See Pereciana 1 in the appendix to this book.*]

Domestic appliance leaflets

Item: Here are the Bosch warranty details for my dishwasher. *[My father used to say that it was a waste of money to insure appliances like ovens and fridges, dishwashers and washing machines. The odds are good that the machines will last long enough before they break down, justifying purchase of a new one or repair of the old one without insurance. He was right. On 8 May, 2014, I reached his age at his death – seventy-one years and eight months and two days – which was from a heart attack outside his office at the southwest corner of the roundabout where City Road meets Old Street. But these games are pointless, too many variables in terms of genetics, diet, exercise, and, what's more, one has two parents, four grandparents: my father's father lived till he was nearly hundred, my mother's father till he was about sixity-three. Nuh? As we say, in Yiddish.*

The matron of Waverley Manor, a home for old Jews, told me the story about grandfather Rudolf: she came into his room to find that he had not got up for breakfast: 'I am going to die today, please bring me a cup of tea and my prayer book, when you have a moment. There is no hurry'.

As a member of the Hendon United Synagogue (where he was the zakan, the elder), he would have opened his Singer's Prayer Book *at the page headed 'Confession on a Death Bed'. He would have recited the prayers in Hebrew, beginning with Modeh ani lefanekha (I have modernised the antiquated translation):*

I acknowledge to you, Lord my God and God of my fathers, that both my cure and my death are in your hands. May it be your will to send me a perfect healing. Yet if my death be fully determined by you, I will in life accept it at your hand. May my death be an atonement for all the sins, iniquities and transgressions of which I have been guilty against you. Bestow upon me the abounding happiness that is in store for the righteous.

Make known to me the path of life: in your presence is fullness of joy; at your right hand, bliss for evermore. You who are the father of the fatherless and judge of the widow, protect my beloved kindred with whose souls my own is knit. Into your hand I commend my spirit; you have redeemed me, Lord God of truth. Amen and amen.

Then the following, said three times:
The Lord reigns; the Lord has reigned; the Lord shall reign for ever and ever.

Then this, also said three times:
Blessed be His name, whose glorious kingdom is for ever and ever.

And then, seven times:
The Lord He is God.

Finally, the single most important sentence in the Jewish liturgy, the first sentence of the prayer known as the Shema, *chanted by Jews at peace and at war, in sickness and in health, in normal situations and in extremity – entering the gas chambers for example – and here, on the deathbed, as spoken by my dear grandfather who, unlike many members of his family, was spared not only to live in freedom, but to live until he was ninety-nine.*

Listen (usually translated as 'Hear'), Israel:
the Lord is our God, the Lord is one.

Sophie Urman, the mother of my late cousin Jerzy Urman, whose war diary[66] I edited and published, told me she said Modeh ani lefanekha *every evening and the* Shema *every evening. One non-Orthodox liturgy has a version of* Modeh, *plus the identical prayers that follow it but said only once. It is under the rubric of 'Prayer during a Dangerous Illness'. I pointed out this shift from 'Confession on a Deathbed' – it has a Victorian aura, and* Singer's Prayer Book *was first published in 1890 – to Alan Wall, who reminded me that it parallels the Catholic shift from 'Sacrament of Extreme Unction' to 'Sacrament for the Sick'. I phone my friend Howard Cooper, rabbi and psychotherapist, and announce that I have appointed him chief adviser on Judaic tradition following the death of top maven Hyam Maccoby. He protests that he has one-tenth the knowledge of Maccoby. I tell him he is being modest: let us say he has one-third the knowledge of Hyam – that is already vast. Given that I have one-thirtieth, I remain in good hands. I ask Howard if 'Confession on a Deathbed'* (Vidui shahiv morah) *has been known as that for centuries or if it is indeed a Victorian naming, almost the title for a Pre-Raphaelite painting. His reply is fascinating: the Hebrew means*

'Confession while lying sick' (so the latter part is correctly rendered by the non-Orthodox translation) and goes back to Talmudic times; Singer's translation is therefore inaccurate in respect of the Hebrew (but true to my grandfather's situation) and Howard fully agrees with me that it sounds like a Victorian invention, although one would have to check pre-Singer United Synagogue liturgy translations to be sure.]

Books

Item: *Tous les Cocktails*, signed and dated 'Paris, 1961'. [*I cannot come up with a reason why I bought this when I was nineteen, given that I did not drink cocktails, unless it was to impress myself with my own sophistication.*]

Items: *Soups* by Marguerite Patten; *The Soup Book* by Brigid Allen. [*I love soup. The Portuguese cooking Paula grew up with and the Jewish cooking of my childhood both emphasise soup*]

Item: *The Jews of Poland: Recollections and Recipes* by Edouard de Pomiane, a Gallicised Polish aristocrat. [*This is an eccentric and fascinating book originally published in 1929 in Paris and intelligently edited by the amusingly surnamed translator, Josephine Bacon. She does not allow later developments to back-shadow her reading of a number of comments that might not pass muster today. The author himself recalls at one point: 'On one occasion, at the table of wealthy Parisian Jews, a well-trained servant asked me softly: "Does Monsieur eat pig?", while presenting me with a dish on which slices of ham were wrapped around eggs in aspic.' What is the point of this anecdote? To hint that the presumably Catholic servant thought Pomiane was a Jew? Pomiane tends to exaggerate the wealth of French Jews and the poverty of Polish Jews. The Polish dishes include 'Tyrolean Strudel' and 'Algerian Chepchouka'.*]

Item: *Suzy Cookstrip* by Suzy Benghiat and Peter Maddocks. [*This is my favourite cookbook, a gift from Michel Couturier; it is written by a friend of his; Benghiat has a similar Sephardi background to Claudia Roden's, whose own fine book I have given to people as a present and who in some photos is a dead ringer for Paula. Who knows, in addition to being a quarter Italian, maybe Paula is part Marrano, which might explain why the pig is her favourite animal. Suzy's instructions are cheerfully and lightly given. No idiot cook ever felt more efficient than when he deploys her recipes, which are impossible to ruin.*]

Item: The Book of Garlic *by Lloyd Harris. [fig. 109] [This fascinating and beautiful book was published by a San Francisco small press, Panjandrum, in 1975. I also have a copy of the first issue of the newsletter of the Lovers of the Stinking Rose, Garlic Times, edited by Lloyd Harris, Head Garlichead, in 1977. We learn that in Gary, Indiana, 'It is illegal to take a streetcar or go to the theatre within four hours of consuming garlic.' For a town known as the armpit of America this has to be the mother of all chutzpahs. One survey has shown that the most hated odours in the USA were garlic, lard and olive oil in that order. The favourite odours were hot coffee, strawberries and apples. I visited California in 1975, mainly to spend time with and interview second cousin Zygfryd Rudolf in Los Angeles, but also to meet Menard's North America Berkeley-based distributor, SPD Inc. – which remained Menard's distributor till 2019 when the annual fee finally exceeded income from sales.*

On arrival in San Francisco, still jetlagged, I was taken by my host, Larry Fixel, to the lunchtime launch of Harris's book. Everything, including the ice-cream, was garlic-flavoured. Later on, Menard and Panjandrum co-published Fixel's Book of Glimmers *and Leah Goldberg's* Selected Poems. *A New York publisher eventually issued a facsimile edition of* The Book of Garlic, *and a huge success it was too. The recipes are simple and good. The first one is for 'Roasted Garlic': '... garlic as it should be treated – as a vegetable and not merely a spice, herb, seasoning or flavouring... Serve as appetizer with toast or as a vegetable side dish.' Various cures are listed: for haemorrhoids, apparently, a garlic clove oiled with lard works a treat when inserted.*]

Item: Evelyn Rose's Jewish Cookbook. *[This is a much-thumbed book. It is for my generation what Florence Greenberg's book was for my mother, whose own mother remembered the tradional East European Jewish dishes from her childhood near Bialystock in Poland]*

Items: A Taste of Heaven *by Rabbi Lionel Blue and June Rose and* Bedside Manna *by Rabbi Lionel Blue. [The first of these two books contains Lionel*

fig. 107

fig. 108

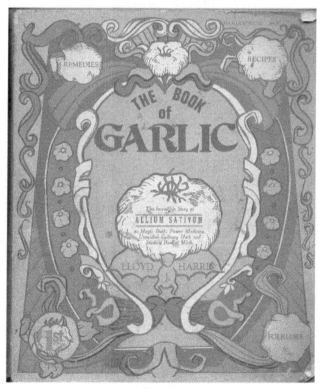

fig. 109

fig. 110

fig. 112

fig. 111

Blue almost at his best. Some of his later books are mannered and repetitive but here he makes schmaltzy Jewish humour and traditional Jewish recipes come to life again. He does not have the hard edge of Leo Rosten when it comes to humour, perhaps for pastoral reasons. He is always concerned to spare people's feelings. We were good friends at one time and made up after the mother of all rows. Living not far from me in Finchley, Lionel is ill, but hanging on and hanging in. The obituary of him already written by Albert Friedlander has been overtaken by the one Lionel wrote very quickly on Albert when the latter died sooner than expected. Lionel is working on a novel and I expect it will deal with being gay, although Bedside Manna has an anecdote about the young Lionel which makes clear that this was not always or not only the case. Long ago, when he was living with a famous yacht designer, Kim Holman, they lent Brenda and me their house in West Mersea. Just as I recall what I was reading while Naomi was being born, so I remember a book I was reading during that holiday: Before the Flowers of Friendship Faded Friendship Faded, the Penguin selection of Gertrude Stein. I remember too that we ate oysters and drank Chablis on the beach, as you don't if you are obedient to the laws of Kashrut. Lionel's mama, Hettie, was in charge of checking parcels for bombs (and tasting food?) at Isaac Woolfson's office. She never minded about Lionel's partners, regretting only that they tended not to be Jewish. [Later: on my most recent visit, I learn that an Orthodox rabbi is trying to convert him. Later still: Lionel has died.]

Item: Dictionary of Symptoms by Joan Gomez. [Pharmakon: remedy or poison? Autobiography, certainly. Medical as well as culinary texts float around the shelves above the washing machine. This is my second copy. Audrey liberated and probably threw away my first copy, on the grounds that the book encouraged my alleged hypochondria. It is not a good book, old-fashioned, coy and confusingly indexed, but it has its moments. I have just brought home today's Daily Telegraph, having been alerted by my sister Mary, who phoned to tell me about an article on her paediatric work. What with my other sisters Ruth and Annie working as special-needs teachers, Brenda a former primary school deputy head, and even myself with my five years of remedial university teaching, not to mention uncles and cousins and in-laws who were or are teachers, education has been a family trade.]

Item: Aromatherapy for the family [*The recommended oils for various mental/emotional symptoms and the historical and diagnostic accounts of the oils make interesting reading*]

Item: The Allergy Connection by Barbara Patterson.
Item: The Mitchell Beazley Pocket Guide to Cheese; Pocket Wine Book.
Item: Chambers Scotch Whisky by Michael Moss.
Item: Irish Potato Cookbook by Eveleen Coyle.
Item: The Food Pharmacy Cookbook and *The Food Pharmacy* by Jean Carper.
Item: Complete Calorie Counter.

I have never consulted any of the following items, not once. The conscious reason for writing this book is to sift through the piles of stuff hoarded in every room and either throw away what I define as rubbish, donate it – but to whom? – or sell it – but who would want to buy it? How does one choose a restaurant in a great metropolis like London? Habit and chance play their part. The choice can depend on the dining partner. My friend the late Z. Kotowicz and I went regularly to Caprini in Waterloo. Musa Farhi always insists on a Turkish restaurant. With Susannah York, it used to be a post-performance restaurant conveniently near to whatever theatre. Paula and I were regulars at the Delancey Brasserie – I called it our default restaurant because it was OK and near the studio and you didn't have to reserve and the basic dishes were fine – but it went off and we stopped going when a waiter started to sweep up before we had finished. It was deservedly savaged in a local newspaper. And now it has closed.

Item: Time Out Breakfast and Brunch Guide and special food issues.
Item: Which, *including: emergencies; stain removers; home security.*
Item: Guardian *food and drink supplements.*
Item: Observer *Tippler; 30-Minute Suppers; Bar Guide.*
Item: Independent *Eating Out in London on a Budget.*
Item: Takeaway leaflets for local restaurants.
Item: Sainsburys *leaflet on sensible drinking.*
Item: World Cancer Research Fund *leaflets and newsletters.*
Item: Schwartz *herbs and spices free gift leaflets.*
Item: Majestic Wine *bulletins.*

Item: Food Safety Advisory Centre: *Questions Answered.*
Item: Les Routiers *Guide to Britain* 1993.
Item: IKEA catalogue 2002.
Item: Hatchards Pocket Wine Book 1989.
Item: Green Catalogue, 1992,
Item: *BBC Health Check* by Barry Lynch.
Item: Sainsbury's *Easy Meals for One and Two; Vegetarian suppers; Meat Cooking.*

It's time to say goodbye to the washing machine. Having removed and gone through everything piled up on it and on the shelves above it, we are left with a few forlorn objects but each one plays its part in the scheme of things –if that were not the case, none of them would be here in the first place, as Lichtenberg might have said.

Item: a toolbox with the beginnings of a tool collection that never really got going.

Item: a broken Lazy Susan.
Item: a rolling pin.

Item: bottles of rarely used liqueur: Cointreau, Benedictine, Menard (but of course) Cognac, Martell Cognac, cheapo Slivovitz from Montenegro, Martini Bianco.

Item: a wood and fibreglass object made by Nathaniel in carpentry class at school.

Item: various bowls, including a good square ceramic baking dish.

Window Ledge

Having made our way along the left-hand wall, we are now facing the window wall [*fig. 110*]. On the left is the boiler. Next to it, stretching along most of the rest of the wall, are the windows, which look over the entrance driveto the flats and – above the hedge – Nansen Village next door, residential halls for postgraduate students with children. To the sound of young children wafting up from the village nursery school, I stand, doing the washing up, chopping onions for dinner, making a cup of tea.

The window ledge contains a number of items that have been there for years, as well as temporary residents parked there when other surfaces are full to overflowing. The first to catch my eye is a corkscrew in the form of the Belgian Manneken Pis with an erection. It is a visual joke, since it doesn't work well for practical purposes – and has never caused any reaction, whether amusement or otherwise, doubtless because nobody has noticed it – with the exception of one cleaning lady. One day, a few hours after she had left the flat, I received an abusive and threatening phone call from a Latino-sounding gentleman saying that I had insulted his wife. I had no idea what he was talking about since he refused to sully his lips by explaining my offence. Eventually he yelled that she had been in my flat that morning. I still had no idea what he was talking about but he unnerved me to the extent that I thought he might come round and pull a dagger on me, or something. Finally, in a roundabout way, he referred to an obscene object in the kitchen, and I finally twigged. I said that if she was offended by it, I was very sorry, but she did not have to look at it. He put down the phone without a word. That was the last I heard of the matter or saw of her until a few months later when, much to my surprise, she was taking photographs at a large family gathering at my sister Ruth's house. The cleaner punished me not including me in any photo.

Next to the manneken is an elegant ceramic vase, the smaller of a pair of wedding presents from Michael Pinto-Duschinsky, one of those rare gifts which could be divided up without being broken in half when my wife and I divorced. Sometimes I buy flowers and Michael's vase is where they go.(The top of it can be seen to the left of the plant in the photo). On the other side of the manneken is an empty pot, once home to the late Georgina. Straight ahead of me is a hand-painted pebble, quite large. When we lived in Primrose Gardens, I used to browse in a shop on Englands Lane owned and run by an American woman called Charlene Gary. She sold prints, fine edition books, little magazines, art postcards, objets d'art and so on. Some Menard Press titles were on sale. I asked her if she would like to see samples of pebbles a local artist had painted. She said, why not, or words to that effect. I walked home (about thirty yards) and told Brenda, who had done one or two for fun. She did more, they were sold, she was paid. Farther along the window ledge, I spy a bottle of Fairy washing-up liquid (visible in the photo) and Ajax powder in its old-fashioned container, and next to them my Zippo lighter, a fiftieth-birthday present from Audrey. In those days I smoked, albeit lightly Café Crème cigarillos and the occasional cigarette in the company of real smokers. I was still smoking when I met Paula – in 1996 – but my mild habit, a style accessory rather than an addiction, soon ended, given the company of a full-on ex-smoker. Close to the Zippo are a beautiful flower-patterned [*fig. 111*] ashtray/lighter pair, of the size that used to adorn many a lounge, such as my parents', whence these. I pick up a small glass salt container, pentagon-shaped with a lid. Again, this beautiful object, a powerful memory booster or nostalgia gizmo, came from my mother's house when she moved to sheltered accommodation: at least fifty years old, it once had a pepper pair. They were part of the special Passover dishes, used for eight days every year.

Food

As I face the window and window ledge, the dishwasher is to my left, with the draining board above it, and assorted pieces of crockery that have not been put away – like my unfiled papers. To the right, and right again, is a right-angled Formica surface, with a bread-bin, a pair of scales and other kitchen items, as well as framed photographs. I shall return to the non-food items later. But I now describe my food arrangements. Above my head to the right are orange-coloured cupboards that, along with an almost unused microwave, serve as the larder I do not have. There are cupboards too, running from the right of the dishwasher and then along the wall at right angles. The row of cupboards incorporates my fridge.

For years now, I have kept regular supplies of the same food: replenishing as and when required, and almost never requiring a shopping list. In the fridge are apples, pears and oranges; also my favoured plums and apricots. Bananas perch on the formica surface above and to the left of the fridge as you face it, next to the bread bin, where a wholemeal loaf tends to be on the go. Occasionally I buy plaited *challah* bread or bagels. Certain vegetables are always in stock: onions, carrots, cucumber, mushrooms, tomatoes – the last strictly speaking a fruit.

[*My grandfather loved onions. I would smuggle into his room at Waverley Manor in Hendon onions, herring, black bread and schnapps, like a midnight feast in a school story. At home, I like to cook onions in olive oil with carrots and tomatoes and eat them with grilled fish or lamb chops and bread for dinner. Half a bottle of red wine, and I'm all set up. Later: one glass of red wine is now the rule.*]

In the fridge I also keep extra-strong cheddar cheese, and eggs; lemons and garlic; prunes; St. Alfour black-cherry jam and Mexican honey; reduced calorie mayonnaise. I keep in the freezer compartment the extra portion of fish I buy [bought] from the Grimsby fish man and some pitta bread. The cupboards that serve as my larder and the right-angle formica surface host various staples:

Item: brown sugar.
Item: Uncle Ben's long-grain rice.
Item: split red lentils.
Item: *matsohs* and *matsoh* meal.
Item: sea salt and pepper.
Item: spaghetti.
Item: vegetable stock cubes.
Item: Lea & Perrins sauce.
Item: Telma chicken-soup powder.
Item: Hermesetas sweetener.

Item: Assam, English Breakfast, peppermint teas; Turkish and various varieties of strong ground coffee: Moccha and Arabica for use with filter paper and a plastic filter. [*Tea rather than coffee was the childhood drink. My mother's mother drank black tea, with a sugar lump between her teeth; my mother poured the milk after the tea on the grounds that English aristocrats did this. The memory of instant white coffee at my school canteen and in college rooms and for years later makes me shudder, and, in particular, the thought of hot milk in it makes me want to throw up. In the days when I was a coffee addict, it caused me to hyper-ventilate one morning in Regent's Park*]

Road opposite Mustoe's Bistro, and having to be prevented from falling down by a visiting American friend, Ron Aronson. I remember too driving home from a visit to the Griffins long ago at their annual rental in Aldeburgh, Regent Cottage, Crag Path, and failing to drink enough coffee to counteract the copious wine. When we were within a couple of miles of home the windscreen of the little Austin, our first car, shattered, but we made it home safely enough.]

Item: soya sauce. [I buy large bottles from Atariya, the Japanese shop near here, which services the large local community. I used to take sashimi to Paula's studio every few weeks, and we would enjoy it for dinner, but our taste for it fish-tailed off.]

Item: Rose's Lime Juice Cordial. [I have permanent craving for lime. Before dinner, I used to enjoy a variant of Philip Marlowe's drink of choice: a Gimlet (lime with gin), except I used vodka]

Item: olive oil.

Item: mustards of different kinds. [When Stephen Cang had a flat in Paris he would go to the mustard shop near the Madeleine and bring me back different flavours. I use it in cooking – as a leitmotif in cheese dishes, to gloss fish or meat, and to give an edge to salad dressings.]

Item: Schwartz's (now Bart's) spices and herbs: garlic salt, ground coriander, chilli seasoning, tarragon, chilli powder, ground cumin, paprika, marjoram, cloves, cayenne pepper, chives, basil.

I have already described the drinks above the washing machine that are hardly ever opened. Apart from the wine and beer in the fridge, I keep other alcohol on the surface by the bread bin:

Item: port in a decanter.
Item: sherry in a decanter.

Item: whisky in a beautiful cut glass slightly chipped decanter. [The decanter was a present to my parents on their twenty-fifth wedding anniversary *from the late Jean and Peter Davis, aka. Lord and Lady Lovell-Davis.*]

Item: bottle of vodka.
Item: bottle of gin.

[*Later: I no longer stock any of these except whisky.*]

Crockery, Cutlery and Other Utensils

My crockery, my cutlery, my pots, my pans, all doubtless have their place in the scheme of things but they are higgledy-piggledy in the kitchen. I am not a tidy person: both cause and effect of my hoarding. The only time utensils saw service in quantity was the annual party I gave for close friends Michael Heller and Jane Augustine, visiting from New York. On these occasions I would prepare salmon and chicken or lamb; egg and onion (a favourite dish of my grandfather and my son); multi-vegetable salad; vinaigrette; potato salad; wine; fruit; cheese.

[*Mike and Jane, her provenance WASP, his Polish Jewish, are members of my extended family of friends too young to be parental figures but old enough to join Elaine Feinstein, Musa and others already named as older sibling figures. I wonder if I am dramatising or over-dramatising a simple fact, namely that some of my friends are simply and accidentally a few years older than me? Be that as it may, Mike and I have much in common beyond the fact that my mother's mother's family and his father's father's family come from the same Polish White Russian Jewish town, Bialystock, and a village nearby.*

Mike's paternal grandfather was a rabbi in Brooklyn at the same time as my maternal grandfather's cousin, Rabbi Israel Rosenberg, but we cannot yet prove that they met. Rosenberg was well known in his day as a senior Orthodox rabbi and, as such, a member of the delegation that visited Roosevelt in 1942 and demanded action to help the Jews of Europe and promise justice against the Nazis after the war. This may have been the only occasion in Israel Rosenberg's life that he knowingly or willingly met a non-Orthodox rabbi, the once legendary Abba Hillel Silver. My mother and aunt remembered a visit from Israel Rosenberg in London in the 1920s, and how he walked with a silver cane. During one of my 'genealogical' phases I elicited from my aunt that Rabbi Rosenberg had been the rabbinical authority for Manischewitz, the bakers of Passover matsohst. I wrote to them in New Jersey. They forwarded my letter to Rabbi Rosenberg's lawyer son, Mitchell, whose nieces – Judy Rappaport, psychoanalyst, and Ruth Perlmutter, professor of film – later became friends of mine.

On the lowest and most practical level, Mike Heller and I have had a mutual arrangement, acting as bankers for each other's incoming and outgoing cheques, to avoid iniquitous bank charges. We also exchange poems amd prose texts. As explained in another chapter, I have a huge collection of faxes from Heller, now fading and overtaken by email. Heller is an unusual poet in that he has a background of science and engineering and this is sometimes reflected in his imagery and architectonics as a poet. Jane has a sporadic dialogue with Paula, whose work has spawned poems and texts within the matrix of Jane's radical and explicit but not dogmatic feminism. They have a tiny rent-controlled flat in Stuyvesant town and intend in principle to retire to the neighbourhood around Grand Central Station, nearer the Opera and the Metropolitan Museum, one day, but they won't.]

My pots and pans and stuff are on the oven, on a shelf above the washing machine and on the draining board: a whistling kettle, a sieve, three stainless steel saucepans, a heavy casserole, three small cast-iron Le Creuset saucepans donated by my sister Ruth, a chopping board, two identical Pyrex measuring beakers. I have a Teflon frying pan. I mentioned earlier the pair of scales on the flat surface by the bread-bin. This serves two purposes: weighing food and weighing parcels. Menard Press's office is in or rather *is* the kitchen. Until there is a dedicated Menard room, probably Nathaniel's bedroom, Menard has no choice but to be domesticated. I am my own kitchen man whom, like Bessie Smith and hers, I can't do without. The parcel weigher is a witness to pre-inflation times – and indeed I recall buying it in the early seventies, pre-Yom Kippur War and the hike in oil prices – for screwed into it is a price sheet, listing first-class stamp: 9p, second-class: 7p, etc, as if they would never change.

The majority of my utensils are in the drawers and cupboards under the right-angled surface to the right of the window. Here are:

Items: 21 spoons, 18 forks, 18 knives; carving knife and fork. [*The spoons, forks and knives are not sets; they are conventional shapes and sizes, except for* a long silver spoon that was a gift on my birth from my godparents, Aunt Fan and Uncle Jack. I have never used the carving fork but sight of it transports me to my childhood house, to Sunday lunch. Friday night was our traditional Ashkenazi diaspora Jewish dinner: chopped liver, chicken soup, etc. Sunday lunch, however, was roast beef, properly kosher it goes without saying, but roast beef. To me belonged the 'corner': when my father started carving – after the thrilling ritual of stropping (if that is the right word for a knife rather than a barber's razor) the knife – he would cut off, circumcise if you like, the tip of the beef, a succulent fatty bit, and that was my perk as senior child. The weekly combination of those two meals incarnates a certain kind of Anglo-Jewish household, now virtually defunct. The centre no longer holds.]

Item: 19 glasses of different shapes and sizes.

Item: 18 large plates and 9 small plates. [In addition there are two plates made and designed by Naomi, one by Nathaniel, at Moss Hall Junior School, and an enamel one portraying 'The Owl and the Pussycat', a fiftieth birthday present. Many years later I bought Paula a runcible spoon because she loves the poem and we sometimes read it.]

Item: 18 coffee mugs. [There are seven special mugs: one sold by the friends of John McCarthy, a local boy, to raise funds for the hostages in Beirut; one with images from her own work given to me by Paula – but it isn't there! Ah, I moved it for safe keeping to the 'treasure' shelf in my lounge. This is a sneak preview of my cornucopia, the only objects in the lounge that are not books or pictures or piano or hifi-related; and, lastly, five hand-made mugs by Ifigenija Simonovic (plus three of her dishes or ashtrays). Ifi, as she is known, is a great favourite of her close friends who miss her now that she has returned to her native Ljubljana following the death of her husband, Veselko, the head of the Slovene Section at Bush House. Pottery and poetry, so similar as words, are her two arts. Most of these she gave me as gifts, but over the years I bought many: perfect presents. One dish was commissioned: 'Menard 25'. Each piece has her characteristic Dubuffet-type cartoon figures and/or writing, with words occasionally misspelt to the delight of connoisseurs. As I said earlier, we worked together on translations of her poems, published as a Menard book. Ifigenija devotes her life to art and craft – financed by hard work as a journalist and prose translator – and friendship.]

Striking Root[67]

you must listen
    to the song of your eyelids
    crushing air
    cutting light
again and again

to hear grass grow is nothing
    hair crack is nothing
allow
    your eyelids to close
    as loud as they can

never open them again
never open them again

Item: beige-coloured large soup bowls, small soup bowls and small plates; small yellow soup bowls; plain old soup bowls. [*The beige set was bought in Portugal – at the instigation of Audrey – while we were driving south from Vila do Conde to Figueiró dos Vinhos, north of Lisbon, where we would be spending a night as the guest of my friend, Z. Kotowicz before flying home. There were six of each, but kack-handedness has taken its toll. When my mother moved from her house she could not take all her possessions, so I acquired the yellow soup bowls, which had been for Passover use.*]

Item: three blue Stilton jars. [*It seems a shame to throw the Stilton jars away. I used to enjoy serving myself a Bloody Mary in one of them, for the colour contrast, but now I've given up this drink, they sit there, unused and unloved, like a boring dream.*]

Item: three teacups and saucers. [*These are never used. Like fountain pens and typewriters, they are* terra incognita *to my children's generation, except perhaps in a hotel or restaurant. When did mugs definitively replace teacups? In the late 1970s, I'd say*]

Item: The drawer next to the drawer for knives, forks and spoons. [*What have we here? Unsexy bottle openers; wooden spoons and spatulas; hard-boiled*

---egg masher; two whisks; soup server; sharp knives including a non-stainless medium-sized Sabatier; garlic press; chopsticks; six Pukeberg designer knife-rests/card holders – perhaps a wedding present; carrot peeler; cheese-slicer.]

Cleaning Materials/Medical

Before proceeding to the cupboard and drawer below the formica surface to the left of the fridge along the wall at right-angles to the window, I should mention that certain cleaning materials are kept on the floor below the boiler. To begin with, Persil non-biological washing powder sachets: I used to suffer serious back itch until the sussed Audrey suggested that biological washing-powder was a possible culprit. The change did the trick. Also in that floor area are salt, rinsing agent and powder for the dishwasher and extra compost soil for George, who has finally grown out of his pot and needs to be rehoused. The Hoover, usually based next to George, is being repaired at the moment by Mr Warren in the High Street, as well as two Anglepoise lamps. He telephoned to say that he will be bringing these round on Tuesday, together with a reconditioned television I reserved and a 'freeview' modem so that I can watch BBC 4. I rarely use the Hoover, preferring the heavy-duty industrial brush and dustpan, also perched next to George.

Back, or forward, to the 'medicine drawer' and the cupboard. What do I find in the drawer?

Item: Elastoplast in various shapes and sizes; stocking support. [*And a stretch roll bought in Italy while Paula and I were visiting Lake Orta. While there, I turned my foot over, stepping off a kerb. Also, a gel for the swelling, and the stocking support.*]

Item: bulbs of different wattage; batteries of different voltage

Item: small silver candlesticks and old Parker pen. [*These and various items in other rooms will one day belong to my children. The Sabbath candlesticks were a wedding present from my mother; the old Parker Pen, probably dating from the forties, needs to be repaired. It belonged to my grandmother Rudolf, and counts as a family heirloom. But will it be used? I'll put it, as is, on the treasure shelf in the lounge.*]

Item: two torches. [*A torch used to be required for trips to the attic when heading for the (now defunct) water tank beyond the electrically lit and floorboarded front section that the two Dennises sorted for me when I came to this flat in 1981. Prior to Chalkie, little Dennis and big Dennis, as they were known, did various jobs around the flat. I met them at Musa's house where big Dennis did the carpentry, and little Dennis everything else, including rewiring. I have made an executive decision that the attic does not count as part of the flat for the purposes of this book.*]

Item: ball of string.
Item: spare buttons that came with a new suit.
Item: tube of Bonjela.
Item: aluminium foil for the oven.
Item: shoelaces.
Item: Barnet Council leaflets.

Item: boxes of matches, including one from Lemonia restaurant in Primrose Hill.

Item: box of Smints.
Item: a finger-wipe I picked up in the casino at Estoril.[68]

The cupboard contains medical things and cleaning materials.

Item: cleaning wipes: surface cleaning wipes, oxy-wipes, clean and dust wipes, all-purpose wipes, floor wipes, window wipes, glass wipes. [*No longer do I clean the kitchen floor with a mop dipped in liquid Flash, although the Flash and Dettol are kept in the kitchen, in this cupboard, for service in the toilet, as already detailed in that chapter. No longer is the kitchen floor as clean as it used to be, which is not saying much. Note: this was written before I employed a regular cleaning lady*].

Item: Spare hoover bag and anti-allergy freshener.
Item: Polycell mould cleaner.

Item: scrubbing brush.
Item: household candles.
Item: Ambre Solaire (Men 12), Solarcaine, Coppertone, Soltan.
Item: greaseproof paper foil, cling foil, aluminium foil.
Item: mop.
Item: insect powder.
Item: duster resembling candyfloss.
Item: white spirit.
Item: bath stain remover, all-purpose cleaner.

Item: Vicks. [*Vicks is a eucalyptus-based decongestant whose smell when I open the bottle, indeed whose mere name on the bottle, is redolent of my childhood bedroom overlooking the garden, and my mother's dab hand. You don't have to have read Proust to appreciate the generative power – via whatever psycho-neurological prism of the mind – of smell, and how the re-remembering of childhood moments leapfrogs – in this instance – the role reversal of doing the same parental work for one's children. All you need is to be a father (and a son) in late middle age. Ay, there's the rub.*]

Item: Tiger Oil.
Item: sore-throat rinse.
Item: Boots multivitamin and iron tablets.
Item: Boots sodium bicarbonate.
Item: Arnica [expiry date November 1999].
Item: Stanley knife.

Item: Celebrex and Diclofenac anti-inflammatory tablets. [*The former was prescribed for what I feared was Repetitive Strain Injury in my upper arm, caused by too much use of the computer. Perhaps this condition is displaced from the mind. Plenty of writers repeat themselves. The latter was for a bad back.*]

Item: Tineafax. [*For athlete's foot – non-athlete's right foot to be precise: the sexiest condition this side of the body.*]

Item: Kiwi leather brushes and twist-and-shine polish; box of shoe-cleaning materials: brushes, rags, polish, etc.

Item: Elnahar wax earplugs and Boots foam earplugs. [*The latter are a great improvement on the former. Even for me, the lightest of light sleepers, no amount of noise reduction could compensate for the discomfort of wax. I don't think insomnia is caused by excess of food or drink or stress. I have had trouble sleeping since I was a young child. Yves Bonnefoy's line 'To take a long time dying, as in sleep' comes to my lips.*]

Item: Paracetamol; Disprin; Nurofen.
Item: Rennies
Item: Nirolex lozenges
Item: Interdens

Item: Immodium diarrhoea relief (expiry date June 1992, more than ten years ago). [*Logorrhoea: if someone comes up with a cure for this condition he or she will deserve a medal. It is amazing what you can get a medal for. At the Imperial War Museum yesterday I visited an exhibition of World War II paintings – including work by Anthony Gross, who taught Paula at the Slade – and the D-Day Exhibition. Here I learned about Gustav, the carrier pigeon who earned the Dickin Medal, the animal equivalent of the Victoria Cross. After regularly dodging gunfire and foul weather during the war, Gustav died in retirement when his breeder stepped on him. Not even the PDSA, whose founder gave her name to the award, could have saved him.*]

Item: rubber gloves (yellow). [*My late friend the radio playwright John Casson could be highly theatrical in an understated way. We overlapped in the same day job for some years, and understood each other only too well when it came to the conflicting calls upon our energy, but you never complained since you had chosen your life. As befits a playwright, especially a radio playwright, John had a perfect ear for speech rhythms but there was one mute gesture he used to make that always had people in fits: if a colleague, male or female, made the slightest remark that could be interpreted or more likely misinterpreted as relating to a gynaecological matter or indeed any internal examination, he would mime the rolling of a rubber glove with his right hand on to his left hand. Someone only had to mention the name of an elderly retired colleague – whose gusset obsessed him – for John to pretend to be pulling her tights or knickers over his head. In his private life, John tended towards smaller women. Mind you, it was not difficult to be smaller than the six foot five inch*] *former fountain-pen salesman. John's diminutive girlfriend, Lesley Howling, who also died prematurely, was a professional photographer; wearing the large hat I bought at Mister (or Master?) Bates the Hatter (in Jermyn Street since 1892), I posed a few times for her non-jobbing experimental work, in exchange for which she would take photos at Menard Press gatherings gratis. On one occasion, we were about to start work on Waterloo (?) Bridge when a man threw himself into the Thames, and the police moved us on. As a playwright, John Casson did the police, and south London villains, and boxers, in different voices.]*

Item: Mr Muscle Oven cleaner, Mr Sheen cleaner.
Item: stainless-steel reviver, car-body filler.
Item: liquid carpet cleaner; stergene; Vanish stain remover; Bio-tex, sugar soap.

The Remaining Cupboards (Known as Menard Cupboards)

I have already explained that I use the kitchen as my Menard Press office and some of my papers are stored in these cupboards and drawers to the right of the fridge, along the wall which is at right angles to the window. Little by little we are approaching the fourth wall, and finally the door with its pinboard. The table in the middle of the room need not detain us, since it is piled high with a temporary installation of Menard documents and personal papers that get shuffled around daily, along with cellotape, envelopes, stamps, pens, chequebook, and the contents of my jacket and trousers, emptied there every evening. Money and keys emerge from the trouser pockets. The jacket contents too are always the same:

Top pocket: Glasses case containing either reading or driving glasses.

Left-side pocket: Diary (month to a page) and Sylvine notebook. [*I have used Sylvine products for years. The notebook is an unofficial filofax, a way of organising my life; at the time of writing, it includes the following pages:*

exhibitions I want to see, and the date the exhibition closes (how many times have I attended on the final day); a list of people I owe letters, real letters not emails; the state of my personal and Menard bank balances; books to buy; current or new projects before these become detailed enough to warrant a proper file, paper or computer. The inside covers of each successive notebook are covered with phone numbers and often no name,] [fig. 112]

Right-side pocket: mobile phone.
Inside left pocket: comb and pen.
Inside right pocket: wallet.

A quick glance behind the fridge, before I move on: I see nothing that would confirm the ideas of the UKIP MEP mentioned earlier: no dead spider or mouse, no aborted foetus, no broken egg or mouldy cheese. Before opening up for inspection the remaining cupboards and drawers along the third wall, let us take a look at the top of the fridge and the surface to the right, as we face it: we find miscellaneous things that have been based there for years:

Item: washers and clips for envelopes and Jiffy Bags.
Item: paper clips.
Item: coffee grinder.
Item: eye prescription.

Item: wax seal with my name on it plus equipment. [*This was a present from my son and daughter-in-law, Helen Gordon. When – accompanying Paula – I found myself in a small group presented to the then Prime Minister Tony Blair at the 250th-anniversary party of the British Museum in 2003, I wondered what to say. Avoiding controversy, I told him my daughter-in-law had met him three or four times and received a letter from him. He appeared interested and asked me who she was and I explained that she had been a Labour candidate in 2000 for the first London Assembly and unexpectedly lost, and that he had added a personal note of commiseration at the end of a letter sent to all defeated candidates. Helen and my son, both former Labour Councillors, are new Labourites. I, on the other hand, am old Labour and, as such, seen as irrelevant rather than wrong. My daughter Naomi is issue-oriented rather than party political and when younger would ring up* for a discussion on the Bomb or Israel or whatever. I was fearful of nuclear war in the early sixties, fearful in the early eighties, and now, more than twenty years on, equally fearful given the demonisation and vilification of Vladimir Putin by the Democrats and the virulent hostility towards China on the part of Trump's United States. The military-industrial complex Eisenhower warned against needs a demon. Some things will not change under Biden].

Item: passport, metro tickets, Euro coin of the realm, Eurostar timetable. [Also on the fridge is my ticket for an imminent holiday in Switzerland with Paula. If you send a eurocheque from France to Germany, there is a bank charge. I found this out when trying to avoid charges on a transaction. While economic issues are important – the advantage to us of the single market etc – the political arguments for a deeper British commitment to 'Europe' are compelling and indeed unanswerable: namely to reinforce the community as a counterweight to the sole hyperpower – and to counter East European nationalism. Sovereignty issues are a red herring at best, a euphemism for English nationalism in many cases.] [Later: this was written well before the referendum on Brexit, that co-morbidity of corona policy, that gleam in the eye of Ubu-Johnson.]

The surface to the right of the fridge is largely taken up with Menard Press flyers for all the books published since the 1999 thirtieth birthday catalogue, the latest MenCards (for the eightieth birthdays of Hyam Maccoby and, by one reckoning Menard's first author, Michael Hamburger), compliments slips and copies of the editorial statement that was inserted with each copy of Dan Plesch's 2002 Menard pamphlet, the final one in the series.[69]

Item: details of the congestion charge.
Item: details of my Orange Nokia phone.
Item: a packet of Able-Labels.
Item: an iron (unused).

Item: small-reel films. [One of these films has a label on it: Josef Rudolf, ninetieth birthday, dating from December 1970. It is time to transcribe this film to video. My grandfather always seemed old. My mother, when she was

*well over ninety, seemed nothing like so old, partly because I had almost
doubled my age since then*]

Item: Premium Bonds [*£5 dated 17 September 1958, £5 dated 18 March
1964, £1 dated 25 September 1964, £5 dated 7 January 1966, £2 dated 27
May 1970. Premium Bonds were introduced in 1956. Before that I had small
sums in National Savings.*]

Item: sketchpad and Faber Castell colour pencils. [*This was a present from
Paula, calling my bluff when I said I'd like to have a go at drawing. When
Paula paints or fashions what she sees in front of her, e.g. Lila or me or a
younger model or mannequin, this is rarely portraiture or illustration. Despite
her insistence that all she is doing is copying and that anyone can do this with
hard work and years of practice, we know that the end product is a fascinating
story and a beautiful artefact: patterned meaning to the highest degree: not
anyone can do this. Over the years I am slowly improving my skills in gaining
a purchase on the visual. It is good to be at the receiving end as she works with
and on the likes of me. Please put me in the picture. With my sketchpad and
pencils, all I could do was attempt to look and then see, and draw my
conclusions. Over a period of seven weeks I made twenty-two sketches. The
first few are boxes of the kind I used to doodle when I was at school. 'Do you
ever doodle?' an interviewer asked Paula. 'No', was the reply. After the first
few early non-colour pencil-drawn boxes, I added a bottle, pen and mug.
Then we find coloured images: three pencils, a diary, a comb, Paula herself
from a photograph, rosette, Sabatier knife, a saucepan with a glass in front of
it, a box of matches, another comb.*

Whenever I enter Paula's studio[70] *and look at the latest picture or pictures
on the go, I cannot 'tell' how it is done, how it got there and where it is going,
even if I am in the picture. In this sense, composing music is more like writing
than painting is, and yet, although I can do a hopelessly bad drawing, I cannot
write even hopelessly bad music. I can, however, imagine moving the pen
around and adding to what I have already composed. In painting, the
beginning is spatial rather than temporal but you have to start somewhere: I
have seen Paula start at the edge but more often somewhere in the middle.
With writing (literary or music) too, you can start in the middle if you want
to, although it took advice to that effect from the writer Ka-tsetnik 135633
to make me understand this after I had said of some project or other that I*

didn't know where to begin. When completed, the music will move across time, as will a story. Paintings work differently: yes, you read the story in Paula's or Doré's work or in Poussin's Dance to the Music of Time, *but you cannot help experiencing these synchronically.*]

Above the cupboard to the right of the fridge there is a quarter of an inch of space where I store the menu – signed by the proprietor, Guy Gateau (Mais, oui!) – of a restaurant I was taken to in Vichy around 1988 by my late friend Robert Ford.[71] The cupboard contains for the most part old Menard papers: accounts, flyers, order books. This stuff is not integral or intrinsic to the kitchen, it's just stuffed into available space. Like the material in the filing cabinet you encountered near the beginning of the chapter, it belongs, if at all, in another chapter or another book. But I cannot help re-reading some of the many letters from the 1980s, with their orders (and cheques) for pamphlets in my nuclear series. It was a time when the traditional radical pamphlet still played a part in public education and sold in large numbers. Judging by the evidence of Dan Plesch's pamphlet, which sold unexpectedly few copies, many of the customers from the 1980s. now get their information from the Internet. The issue has, dangerously, gone dead or under the radar. One of the letters, dated March 1987, is from someone in New Zealand less impressed by its then Prime Minister, David Lange, than I was. Lange stood up to the United States, not allowing military vessels to dock in his country unless it was confirmed that they did not carry nuclear missiles. America's policy was neither to confirm nor deny. I had written to Lange, told him I would buy exclusively New Zealand dairy products in future, and would he please send his autograph for my son – which he did.

In the left-hand cupboard is a box of entries for the translation prize of the British Comparative Literature Association/British Centre for Literary Translation. For three years I was one of the judges. The late Dan Weissbort and I, with similar views on translation, regularly reinforced each other's arguments in favour of a particular candidate, for example, Timothy Adès, whose remarkable translations of Jean Cassou's Resistance sonnets won first prize one year.

The drawers above this cupboard are so chock-a-block with bits and pieces that they might have furnished the wet dream of a depressed bricoleur.

Item: two spectacle cases, each containing a pair of old glasses. [*That pair was bought from Mr Freedman, an ophthalmologist at the far end of Roman Road. Mr Freedman had invented a technique for testing eyes which had been widely adopted, but my main reason for going there was his recommendation by Moris Farhi, and my father always recommended recommendations. It is only in recent years that I am happy to go up the road to the high street where I live, and make local, Colin Gaunt for teeth and Michael Sharpstone for eyes. For how many years did I schlepp across London to the Uxbridge Road in order to visit the family dentist, 'Uncle' Doddy Sigaloff? As for the actual glasses, even without my astigmatism, a condition that complicates contact lenses, I would only ever wear spectacles. I like wearing glasses.*]

Item: three *yarmulkes*, also known as *kappels*. [*These are worn in synagogue, or at weddings when grace after meals is recited, or at the cemetery. By me, that is. A pious Jew like my maternal grandfather wore a hat everywhere, all the time.*]

Item: three old wallets. [*Semi-agog with expectation, I find two notes, but they are Portuguese escudos (3000), the pre-Euro currency. Maybe a bank in Lisbon will exchange it for Euros: about 30.*]

Item: gold fob watch that belonged to my father, a gift to him from his old friend Ralph Leigh. No manufacturer's name on it. Possibly an Omega, according to the repair shop in Hampstead. [*Ralph taught me French at Cambridge. For years and years I believed that I only got a university place thanks to his intervention. More than twenty years after I graduated and a few months after my father died (and shortly before Ralph himself died), I confronted him with my belief. He said I was wrong and that my Russian had been good enough to get me a place, irrespective of my French. During the war he was at Bletchley. Later he became a world authority on Rousseau. His family were the poorest of the poor in the East End. After the suicide of his mother and in the care of an alcoholic and disorderly father, Ralph was often at my grandmother Rudolf's flat and exerted an enormous influence on my father and other members of the circle, including my father's maternal cousin Reggie Flashtig, later Forrester, one of whose three sons was the psychoanalyst John Forrester, who died too soon.*]

Intellectually, although not emotionally, Ralph was the towering figure in the wider circle of clever sons and daughters of immigrants. He was also gay. I did wonder sometimes if his relationship with my father went closer than I shall ever know, but it is unlikely, and my mother was decisive in keeping Ralph at a distance for some years, before she relented. Uxorious to a fault and fundamentally heterosexual, my father, I am certain, did not have a gay tendency. Still, it's a wise son who knows his own father, and what do I know about Henry Rudolf in other and more important respects? Far less than I would like to. People would not talk about him after he died. My feelings and thoughts belong rather in fiction, where attempts to understand are deepened in – indeed made possible by – the process of verbal invention.

Paula has made images of her mother that she could never have verbalised in directly autobiographical writing had she been a writer. This suggests that paintings which have emerged directly from the artist's life are fictions, and all the more truthful for that. I would like to write an essay comparing Stendhal's Life of Henry Brulard *and Wordsworth's* Prelude, *foundational texts of Western literature and masterpieces of self-understanding; they are perhaps the first autobiographies in the sense that we understand the word today, along with De Quincey's* Confessions of an Opium-Eater*). Rousseau's* Confessions *is in the background to all three. Even though Wordsworth may never have read* The Confessions, *the anxiety of its influence is palpable, as W.J.T Mitchell shows in an important essay. I would want to compare the way each of these great books relates to fiction. Having written those sentences, I serve notice on myself to deliver and now I kick the ball into touch, until the time comes to retrieve it, if ever.*]

Item: a ring-bound recipe book with blank pages and sundry: bulldog clips, address stamps, cotton thread, high-lighters, dry markers, matches, staples, rubber bands, envelopes, London streetmap

Item: notebook. [*This notebook, redolent of Laura Ashley and second-generation hippies as opposed to my generation which could be described as second-generation beatnik, is something I would never buy. It was certainly a birthday present from my junior sister Annie, who might even have made it. The ring-bound cover has tree leaves stuck on and what look like Hebrew letters on the back. The paper is handmade, deckle-edged. All three of my sisters have had homes that reflect their personalities and styles. Mary's house in Alwoodley, Leeds [until they left for Israel in 2015], was a big comfortable busy place, full of visitors from Israel or the USA, with Mary and husband Mike rushing in and out, off to the university to give lectures or whatever. Their style is old Israel, their world very Jewish. Annie's Bauhaus style house in Hampstead Garden Suburb has an improvised air to it. Her creativity is classic Arts and Crafts, quite appropriate for a part of London inspired in part by that very movement. As I said, she knows how to make things that I would never even buy. Where Ruth and Mary are direct and forceful in stating their opinions (like father,) Annie and I are more periscopic (like mother). Ruth's house, also in the Suburb, is understated and elegant, with classic prints and symmetrical arrangements of furniture. The taste of her second husband – a retired American compliance lawyer, Michael Blane – has reinforced the mood of this beautifully designed Suburb house. I have mentioned Mary's and Ruth's husbands. Annie's husband Jack had a busy professional life as a clinical psychologist, culminating in a book on the subject, but he has never stopped researching his life-long project – the quantity of data is enormous – namely imaginary countries, e.g. Charlotte Perkins Gilman's* Herland.]

Item: gold table lighter. [*This was a present from my mother. She freely admitted that the reason she started smoking in 1938, when she got married, was because smoking was stylish and glamorous; we would now say cool. It will astonish younger readers to learn that cinemas and theatres had ashtrays, and you could smoke during performances; and in buses, aeroplanes, everywhere. It was normal: conjure up Mastroianni, Belmondo, Brando, Bogart. Here too is a tin of my old cigars, the smell redolent of ancient days.*]

Item: Zodiac watch. [*fig. 113*] [*This was the bar-mitzvah present from my grandfather Josef Rudolf in 1955. It cost three guineas – the online multiplier says that three pounds would be seventy four pounds today: expensive. The sum recalls* The Three-Guinea Watch *(published in 1883. Three pounds would be three hundred and twenty seven pounds today), a once famous tale by Talbot Baines Reed, ex my alma mater City of London School, typical of the school stories I read as a child.*]

Item: printer's block, with the word 'Shema' in Hebrew. [*This survives from the first of the Jewish New Year cards Menard published back in the 1970s.*[72] *The card contains Primo Levi's modern version of the* Shema *prayer, his own midrash. This also became the title poem of his first Collected Poems, which I was proud to publish in English. The poem caused trouble in the context of the card because it ends with a terrible curse, and some people felt this was not appropriate at New Year.*]

Item: six traditional dinner place-mats. [*These have an attractive design involving trees and nympsh: a wedding present from the art historian Judith Bronkhurst and her family.*]

Photographs, Posters, Pictures

Almost every inch of available wall space has a framed painting, print, poster or photograph on it, and propped up on various surfaces are photographs. I would like to take you on a tour of the artworks that give pleasure in the kitchen. I need their company and, without being metaphysical about the matter, I believe they need my company, to complete them, *à la* Duchamp. I confess that the positioning of the pictures was random to begin with – although they have learned to interact, have grown together – and therefore I need not be too specific about where each one hangs or rests. A bunch of photographs face me in the days when I used my cross-trainer machine four or five times a week, until it died the death. This ritual required choosing a radio programme as background to work out, making sure my notepad was to hand on the table, all the while trying to lose myself in the body rhythms for thirty to forty-five minutes.

The photographs are, in the main, a non-systematic family album, my children and grandchildren at various ages and stages. There are three early ones that I enjoy always, sometimes questioning them, sometimes questioned by them: in the first, the two children are together, holding each other, very young, very serious; in the second, Naomi is about three, wearing a fringe and with a searching smile; in the third, Nathaniel is about five, looking quizzical. The old question raises its head, a question with a fringe on top: were these photographs taken because the parents loved those particular expressions, or has the photo consecrated more or less accidentally one of a large number of slightly varying images, of changing faces? I guess the answer is 'both', and for sure the percentages cannot be calculated. This is not Cartier-Bresson, it is not even rocket science. There are photos of the two in their Dame Alice Owen's School uniform and later on in their graduation garb, Nathaniel at Warwick, Naomi at Birmingham. Another question raises its head: is it my imagination or am I right in suggesting there is a dearth of autobiographical writing about people's children, a dearth amounting to a taboo? Parents, especially when dead, are considered fair game, but children?

This selection from a large number of photographs kept in carrier bags is completed by one of my son and his wife, Helen, on holiday in India. There are photographs of Paula too: one is of her in cap and gown, after receiving an honorary degree from the London Institute, another taken by me in the Azores against a landscape, a landscape! (Paula doesn't do landscapes or nature, seeing their role as places that contain fast roads to the nearest nice hotel.) Two more photos are on another wall, taken while she was waiting to be interviewed for Portuguese TV. There is a particular edge to one of them because she didn't know I was taking it: wearing a favourite Missoni top, anxious, determined, ready to go (and get it over with), she is grooming herself, an ultra-focused cat. Shortly she will tell the interviewer part of her truth.

There are other photographs dotted around the room, including, perched against the wall amidst a chaotic surface, one I took of Jon Silkin's tombstone at Bushey cemetery [*fig. 114*], where he lies not far from my father and from Miron Grindea, and from his own mother – but not his father, who was cremated. (Perhaps Jon Glover, Silkin's biographer, will solve this one.) The authorities bent the rules in allowing the wording to include Silkin's profession or vocation ('poet') and an additional quote that is not from a traditional Jewish source but chosen by me: beneath the peaceable kingdom verses from Isaiah are the words from Silkin's poem 'Into Praising', which the authorities authorised: 'The word surrounded / so by light'. Not for the first or the last time, I recited the *Kaddish* for someone who was not the usual close relative, or indeed a relative at all. Ken Smith, Manny Litvinoff, Jon Glover, other friends, assorted lovers, wives and children of the poet, were present as we said goodbye to a difficult and remarkable 'old trouper.'

Mention of Ken Smith [*fig. 115*], yet another old friend who has died – prematurely, from Legionnaires' disease and a hospital bug that delivered the *coup de grâce* when we thought he was getting better – allows me to segue to the wall cupboard left of the fridge that serves as my larder. Stuck on the door is a thoughtful image of Ken, whom I met through Silkin in 1965 in Exeter, and with whom I had an irregular poetical and political dialogue for the rest of his life. This is a Bloodaxe publicity poster of Ken with an extract from his magnificent London poem, 'Fox Running'. Ken wrote a book about being a writer in residence at Wormwood Scrubs, *Inside Time*. The reviews were favourable, even enthusiastic, and rightly so. But you could tell that only one of the reviewers had read his poetry (modesty forbids…), since had the others read it they too could have quoted from poems such as 'Fox' to show that the themes of the prose book echoed closely the poet's own preoccupations and troubles. You can guess what animal interrupted the proceedings during Ken's funeral. https://vimeo.com/412232987 (better quality than YouTube) takes you to Neil Astley's fine film about Ken, which includes footage from a reading he gave in Colombia. The subtitles are taken from Isel Rivero's translations done specially for this occasion.

There are three other unframed posters stuck on cupboard doors. One is a joint Royal Academy and London Poetry Secretariat poster advertising a reading on 10 November 1983 by an old friend, David Gascoyne, together with Menard author Jeremy Reed. Next to it is a wonderful photograph of Edward Thompson [*fig. 116*], used for the poster advertising his memorial meeting at Logan Hall, London University, on the afternoon of 7 November, 1993, ten years almost to the day after the Gascoyne reading. I remember dashing home to prepare a dinner: the guests included my sister Ruth and her husband Michael and Rabbi Aviva Kipen. The starters – homemade soup and homemade humus – were copious and tasty, which was just as well since nobody had room for the disastrous main course, whiting in cheese sauce. Whiting! The last poster is an image of two noblemen, boyars, fighting, and was given to me in Cambridge in 1962 by Agnes Barto, a once famous Russian children's writer whom I met when she gave a reading.

We are coming to the end of this cook's tour of kitchen ingredients, with short stops at the framed pictures on the four walls. To the left of the window, around the boiler, is a beautiful photo of Yves Bonnefoy taken circa 1993. I begged the Bonnefoy off a young professional photographer at the great Giacometti exhibition at the Musée d'art

fig. 113

fig. 114

fig. 115

fig. 116

fig. 117

fig. 118

moderne de la ville de Paris. To the right of the window there is a photograph of Yves taken about forty years earlier, at the time of *Du mouvement et de l'immobilité de Douve*. The intensity was still the same, the magnificent intelligence – surely inscribed in the face and not projected by me – was still the same, but the later photograph is softer, with a smile bespeaking a wise father, fatherhood being celebrated in *Dans le leurre du seuil*, a book of the 1970s that set the seal on a poetic vision which began so potently with *Douve*, the book of his that Paula loves best, sharing as she does its surrealist world. Bonnefoy's poetry changed after *Dans le leurre*, for reasons to do with the changed nature of his prose. The interaction between the two is the material matrix of his *imaginaire*, not a subject for the present book.

Next to the 1993 Bonnefoy photograph is a little drawing of a flower by Jane Joseph, a superb graphic artist and etcher, as you can see from her two Primo Levi editions published by the Folio Society. The flower, stubborn, strong, retiring and gentle, reminds me of the artist herself. Adjacent to this drawing are one by Maurice Blond and an etching by Wilfred Fairclough, which come from my mother's house. Maurice Blond was a distinguished minor figure in the Ecole de Paris who arrived in the city from Poland around the same time as Chagall from Belarus. I recognise the noble face in Blond's drawing: it belongs to René Cassin, the Nobel Peace Prize- winning jurist. Sometimes Google turns up trumps: we learn that Blond's dealer after the war was Jacques Spreiregen, who was my father's client and friend, and Polish/French founder of Kangol berets, made in Cumberland. According to the same website, the art critic Claude Roger-Marx called Blond 'Le Bonnard slave'. My mother was surprised to learn that Jacques had been a dealer – she thought he was a collector, his Fitzroy Square office was bursting with paintings. This is a minor error on her part and, in any case, the categories of collector and dealer sometimes overlap. David Sylvester was both and an art writer too, although he always denied that dealing in Bacon paintings affected his critical judgement on the page. My mother told me that Jacques set up his mistress, Janine Hardy, in a boutique opposite Claridges, where he stayed when in London. Kangol (silK ANGora wooL) eventually added a kangaroo to their trademark because when berets became fashionable, women asked for Kangaroo berets by mistake. Is Madonna's beret a Kangol? Even to ask the question is at best whimsical, at worst corrupt, for I do not care, and by asking it I collude in a (celebrity) myth I do not cherish. The website page of Blond asks owners to email the painter's son with details of their pictures for a catalogue raisonné. [*Months later: no reply from the website. Years later: no website. So it goes, with reputations. More years later: I met Madonna at the Marlborough Gallery when she expressed interest in Paula's work. No beret.*]

I move now to the next wall: propped up against it, by the bread-bin, is a small painting of a poppy against a semi-abstract background, done on a copper plate by a Menard poet, Brian Coffey. When Augustus Young and Margaret Hogan moved to France they gave me various things, including this picture. Augustus tells me he used it as a clipboard while writing *Light Years*. It was a peace offering after he and Brian had quarrelled around the time Menard published Young's *Lampion and his Bandits*. Next to it, on the wall, is a classic Mexican image done on tree bark that was a wedding present from the late Helene Koon of Los Angeles, whom we met through Jonathan Griffin. She was the biographer of Colley Cibber and was writing a book on Shakespeare and the Gold Rush.

For some years I have kept tucked into the frame of the Mexican figure two postcards published by the International Institute of Human Studies (*sic*). The cards are from a series, essentially tabloid astrological in style, about people's names: Nathaniel: 'He talks logically, his actions are only brought on by necessity, he strides out with the intention of arriving in some place of interest. He is a perfectionist!' And Naomi: 'No one else is able to live your life for you, you have done fine so far. With your willpower and strength you will achieve far more than you can imagine. You are wonderful – stay wonderful.'

Farther along this wall, above the fridge, we find a Maurice Blond gouache of a house, perhaps in Meudon or Ville d'Avray. Underneath it is a linocut of a boat by the Israeli artist Dorel Pascal – Miron Grindea's nephew. To the right, behind the row of mainly family photographs that faced me on my trainer, and below the posters of Gascoyne/Reed and Thompson, are two gifts: a lithograph by Tamara Rikman-Charny and a painting by Yitzhak Greenfield. These date back to Menard's heyday. Tamara is the first wife of the late Israeli poet Carmi. He was born Carmi Tcharney. When he arrived in Israel he turned the names round and became Tcharney Carmi – or T. Carmi as it says on his books. I used

Tamara's delicately energetic drawings on the covers of two Menard books. Yitzhak Greenfield's image could be a fragment of parchment or part of a wall. As with many of his works, the image contains Hebrew words, for words or the logos are deeply characteristic of Jewish religious understanding and if, in addition, you buy into Kabbala then there are hidden meanings in every letter and combination of letters, based on numerology or *gematria*. For Greenfield, the Jerusalem landscape as imaged in his work requires words. If you cannot read Hebrew or if, as in my case, you can read it but have difficulty understanding it outside the liturgy or poetry (when the vowels – dots under the letters – are printed), it appears to house mini-worlds, as if each letter is a Chinese ideogram.[*fig. 117*]

The wall facing the window and where we will soon reach the door has the only screen print in the kitchen, made by Carol Wheeldon: Richard Burns's 365-line poem *Tree*, which I was the first to publish as a book, back in 1983. To its left is a linocut of a squat earth mother by the Oxford artist, Heinke Jenkins: this was included in an issue of *Journals of Pierre Menard*, the predecessor of Menard Press; to the right of *Tree* is a poster given to me by the artist whose work it advertises and portrays – the late Ivar Ivask – when I was in Oklahoma City in 1986 as a juror for the Neustadt Prize. Ivar Ivask was the editor of *World Literature Today*, which sponsors the prize. Ivar was a poet, artist, critic, consummate networker and major-league *makher*. This was the only time in my life I have been a VIP in my own right: we the jurors were accommodated in fabulous apartments, with whiskey in the cabinet, etc., etc. I had worked immensely hard on my presentation. It is a good prize to win; many winners have gone on to get the Nobel Prize. My candidate was Yves Bonnefoy. Maya Angelou was defending Wole Soyinka. In the end, I came third, she came second, and Adolf Mushg's candidate Max Frisch won, entirely because – as cunningly pointed out by Mushg in his final speech – no previous winner had been a playwright.

The remaining pictures on the wall before we reach the door are two black and white etchings by Paul Coldwell and a collage painting by his wife, Charlotte Hodes. Paul and Charlotte are good friends of mine, independently of their friendship with Paula. I have written about Paul's work on more than one occasion, and I reviewed a show of Charlotte's. In particular I have a strong affinity with Paul's thematic concerns and we are plotting a second joint venture. We met thanks to a vegetable. I had read somewhere that Margaret Atwood claimed poets could eulogise round vegetables but not crooked ones. This was a challenge and I wrote a poem about broccoli, and mentioned the subject to my friend, the painter Julia Farrer. She laughed and said how amazing, she had a friend who was obsessed by broccoli, and she took me round to the Coldwell/Hodes house off Balls Pond Road, where, not yet on my radar nor I on hers, Paula had already begun her etching collaboration with Paul, who in addition to being a printmaker is a sculptor – just as Julia is a painter and printmaker, and Charlotte a painter and ceramicist. The dinner at Paul and Charlotte's – another guest was Stanley Kubrick's daughter – led to other meetings, and eventually our first joint venture emerged: a book[73] containing Paul's broccoli etchings (a proof is on the kitchen wall) and my broccoli poem…

Above the door is a small lithograph by H.A. Freeth called *Firegod*, dated 1966.

He is the father of the Royal Academician Peter Freeth whom Paula and I have met at the RA and at the house of our friends, Michael and Mary Rowan-Robinson. Next to the Freeth is a haunting photographic collage by Carol Rosen that shares a page with a David Vogel poem, translated by the late Arthur Jacobs. One of the pleasures of being a poetry publisher has been that artists sometimes write asking for permission to use a poem. Mostly it is not a question of money, and in this case, after consulting the translator's copyright holder, his sister Sheila, it was agreed that the artist could use this poem, in return for an artist's proof for me, and one for Sheila.

We have reached the last wall. Above the filing cabinet, which you will remember from the beginning of the chapter, are three drawings by Merlin James in one frame, which can just be made out in the photo. Two of them accompany my sequence of poems *Mandorla*, published in 1999.[74] This poem started life a few years earlier when Julia Farrer invited or challenged me to write a poem for her to illustrate. I was unable to deliver, the residue of a snobbish and ignorant idea that such a proposal was somehow contaminated by contingency – an occasional poem (what's with the broccoli then?), whatever next! Or maybe, I was too lazy, uptight, hidebound. Nothing happened. Then one evening I received a phone call at Bush House where I happened to be working: 'I'm meeting you for a drink after work, I want to show you something.' The something was a set of drawings. The ball is in your court, she said. One week later I had written my sequence of poems. *Homo ludens* at last. Julia then reworked her sketches and eventually was ready to create the artist's book, a lengthy and complex process given the way her psycho-geometrical imagination works. In such collaborations, the visual artist's temporal and therefore financial commitment is incomparably greater than the writer's. This has to be built into the ultimate agreement over copies and payment, if any. However, things went wrong. Julia and I had a series of misunderstandings and the book didn't happen. I write so few poems that when I do I want to see them published. Since these had been written with the visual in mind, I was especially pissed off with Julia (and vice versa, *nicht wahr*, Julia?) and I went round to Merlin's studio. He was happy to oblige and we found some drawings to fit the story. But there is a second happy ending: some years later, Julia came round and showed me the mock-up of the new *Mandorla*.[75] The eventual book was beautiful. There is something quite magical for a primarily verbal person about collaborating with visual artists: Paul Coldwell, Merlin James, Julia Farrer, Jane Joseph, Jane Bustin, Cathie Pilkington and Arturo di Stefano. Paula too: she has done three drawings for my book[76] of fables, *The Mermaid from the Azores*.

Below Merlin's drawings are four drawings by Julia, which were given to me by Kathleen Griffin. They are the works Julia made to illustrate Jonathan Griffin's Menard book, *Commonsense of the Senses*. And below hers are four lithographs by George Nama, which accompanied *The Grapes of Zeuxis*, a sequence of Bonnefoy poems translated by Richard Stamelman. To the right of these multi-image frames and also to the right of the oven is a linocut I bought from Manou Shama-Levy – who is a daughter of the same Cairo Jewish world as Gabriel Josipovici and my late friends Edmond Jabès and Carlo Suarès. Under Manou's moody image is a lithograph of a woman's head by André Minaux and a poster that I remember vividly from my childhood: a still life advertising his exhibition at Galérie Sagot-Legarrec, 24 rue du Four.

To the immediate right of these works, above and around the waste bin, are three more pictures: in one frame there are two drawings I bought from Irene Gunston, of a woman on her back with her feet in the air, certainly sketches towards a future sculpture. Beneath these robust images is a 1cm/2km map of the Stanislawow region which I have pored over many times, deriving energy and inspiration from the names that are so familiar to me from the conversations I had with my grandfather, with second cousins Zygfryd Rudolf and Friedl Trevor and with other relatives born in that part of the world. Kalush, where my grandfather was born. Dolpatow: the tiny village where the priest would visit my great-grandmother's house on a Sunday to eat her famous gefilte fish; the village where my great grandfather with his wooden teeth (like George Washinghton) had his inn until 1911; the village in west Ukraine, east Galicia, south-east of Bruno Schulz's town Drohobycz, south-west of Joseph Roth's town Brody, a few miles from Sigmund Freud's and Henry Roth's ancestral town, Tishmenitsa. My grandfather left Dolpatow in 1903, never to return. I have visited the region twice, it is remote in every sense. Even though east Galicia is the birthplace of only one grandparent, he lived till I was thirty-eight and so he is the closest to me, and on an important level of feeling it is mine. Yes, the region is mine, and it is also a mine, full of good gold, the gold of ancestral feeling, which purchases a return ticket to one's origins. I raise a glass of shnapps, what else, and toast him in his father's inn. Over dinner at Musa Farhi's flat in Brighton, I discussed Jewish Central and Eastern Europe with the Budapest-born Geneva-based writer Judit Kiss and told her that my grandfather lived there for a year around 1903. Now, whenever she is in Budapest to visit her mother, she emails me with an account of meeting Josef Rudolf down by the river.

The other picture in this group is a poster of Paula's 1997 Tate Gallery Liverpool exhibition: 'Turning Back' shows three girls and a small dog, the girls colluding in an auto-erotic fantasy. This picture was one of the last Paula did before I entered the scene. That might be the reason that it seems almost as remote to me – temporally that is – as works like her earlier opera collages. Perhaps there is a hint of retro-jealousy, as if being a component of her present and future is not enough. This is imperialism, albeit a colonisation of time rather than space, and I am ashamed of myself. A less grandiose explanation is that as I only met the artist three or four times before we started going out (in June 1996), pictures done before then feel as though they were painted by a stranger, which indeed they were. Last picture of all, high above the washing machine and next to the clock, is a signed linocut by the Australian artist Horace Brodzky, biographer of Gaudier-Brzezka.

Pin Board

We are back where we started, at the door of the kitchen. On the door is a cork-tile pin board where I place messages and leaflets and other necessities for the competent administration of things required by good self-government (reference Marx and Lorenzetti).

Item: opening hours at the British Library Reading Room. [*These days I go far less often to the Reading Room. The internet solves many problems I would once have taken there. I can truly say that some of the happiest hours of my life have been spent in the Reading Room (in particular at its earlier location at the British Museum), often on fool's errands, looking for fool's gold, while pursuing scholarly or poetic will o' the wisps. The copy of Beckford's* Vathek *I was consulting (I no longer recall why) had belonged to one of his most important admirers, Mallarmé, unless some reader forged the great man's signature. The last time I went to Panizzi's magnificent circular room I was checking out illustrated editions of the Comtesse de Ségur's once best-selling* Les Malheurs de Sophie, *a book Marina Warner and Paula both grew up with. I had conceived the idea of a triple collaboration: Paula would illustrate, Marina would introduce and I would translate the first new edition of this book in English in perhaps a hundred years. Nothing has come of my idea. I have cooled on it, Paula was never warm, and Marina had no inkling of the project.*

Miron Grindea organised my first Reader's Ticket around 1960 as a researcher for ADAM magazine. I particularly liked the North Reading Room, where the undisputed king was Vincent Brome in his cashmere pullover, whom I had first met either at George Buchanan's salon in Westminster or at Nigel Foxell's European Society of Culture gatherings in Chelsea. Vincent, as countless young ladies could tell you, had droit de seigneur. With some of them, no doubt, he opened the book for the first time, entering into the spirit, a troubadour of the body. Unusually in modern times, Vincent wrote whole books for a living, of which three were biographies: Frank Harris, H.G. Wells and Havelock Ellis – a suitable case for treatment. He was in a sense the last of the 'Edwardian' writers, although he is rivalled in mentality – and vastly exceeded in quantity of words – by my new friend, Michael Moorcock, whose surname would have suited Vincent. I last met Vincent, aged around ninety-three, when Nigel Foxell took me to their club the Savile for lunch. He smiled sweetly and gesturing down informed me: 'You-know-what has finally given up the ghost, I can't get it up any more.' I told him he had had a good run, to which he graciously assented. There was something of the knight about him. Kinky Friedman tells us, 'They don't make Jews like Jesus any more.' Well, they don't make rogue male writers like Vincent any more. When he dies, the template will be broken, and many a retired female head of department will toast his memory and dream of the soft look her eyes had once. Or maybe not.

[Later: October 2004: the very day my obituary of Fermin Rocker was published in the Independent, *I noticed adjacent to it a death announcement for Vincent Brome.] Another sixties salon was at the Kensington flat of the economist Ruth Troeller, where people took their poems and drank red wine. Once every three months, she gave notice as she fidgeted with her worry beads, that she would lock the door against the world and enjoy privacy and intimacy for a few days with her philanderer husband Gordian. She would smile mysteriously and the young me sensed a mystery deep in the female spirit, and probably body too. The rest of the year Gordian was a globetrotting photographer. A quick check reveals that she later taught economics and liberal arts in Mexico and has since died.]*

Item: the phone number of the fado singer Mariza in Lisbon.
Item: opening hours of local libraries (in my handwriting).
Item: the cheapest car park at Luton Airport.
Item: Three Valleys Water card.
Item: Naomi's mobile number, now memorised.

Item: Ronald Brown Opticians leaflet and my latest prescription from Michael Sharpstone.

Item: piece of paper with a triangle, a square, a circle and the figure 3 drawn on it by Paula, as instructed by her friend Colette. [*What you have to do is make your own drawing, joining up three squares, two triangles, one circle and one figure 3 any way you want. The resulting shape tells you something about how you connect sex and love and money.*]

Item: instructions for radio-controlled wall clock, no longer working.

Item: invoice for the chair I am kneeling on even as I type this. [*Bought at the Back Shop in New Cavendish Street on 29/09/94: the mechanism that lengthens/shortens it broke a few years ago, but Chalkie saved the chair by immobilising it.*]

Item: Envelope of letter posted from Jerusalem by Claude Vigée. [*I kept it because one of the stamps celebrates gefilta fish, complete with carrot.*]

Item: New and old TV licences.

Item: Antiquarian, Rare and Second-Hand Bookshops in North London. [*Later: most of these have closed now that their owners trade from home over the Internet.*]

Item: Anti jet lag regime – downloaded from the Internet.
Item: Diagram of physiotherapy exercises.

Item: faded fax from Augustus Young. [*Advice about the causes of itching: 1) avoid polyester, go over to cotton sheets; 2) if there is a rash, it might be caused by an allergy; 3) check out flat for bugs; 4) dust!*]

Item: information about the Médiathèque. [*The Mediathèque is the multimedia library of the French Institute, one of my key nodes in the last forty years. Here I sometimes borrow a CD or DVD to take round to Paula's. Last time we watched Jean Vigo's entire output of four films because Paula had somehow always missed* L'Atalante. *She enjoyed this masterpiece less than I expected, but revelled again, after many years, in* Zéro de Conduite. *Had Vigo not died at twenty-nine, he might have rivalled Bunuel.*]

This kitchen man could do with a glass of wine, if not a bottle of beer and a pig's foot. God bless Bessie Smith. Next stop, the hall.

SECTION THREE

Hall

I wouldn't be surprised if the hall has more square metres than any other room in the flat. It is very long and quite narrow and can't be used as a living or working space. Over the years I have lined its walls with shelves and pictures. It would once have been possible to sashay the length of the hall, if that was the way you walked. One of the teachers at my children's secondary school was known as 'glider'. He didn't walk, he glided, that was his default mode. Yes, that teacher would have liked my hall *in the old days*. But now, if you were to come through the front door and walk straight ahead, you would risk taking a trip, that is to say a tumble, although it is indeed a kind of journey. Yes, once upon a time you or I could have walked the length of the hall unimpeded until the hall cupboard at the other end had been reached.

To the left and right as you enter the flat are shelves from floor to ceiling until you reach two doorways – the lounge door left, the kitchen door right. They are always open. In front of the shelves on both sides of the hall are various objects, leaving only a narrow path, which a stout person would have to negotiate sideways. Proceeding along the left side before we reach the lounge door, we find on the floor in front of the shelves:

Item: suitcase. [*This is larger than needed for outward journeys but useful for catalogues and other acquisitions after travels abroad, including our annual week in early September to celebrate my birthday. It was bought in Bloomingdales. Retail therapy for me is bookshops, for Paula it is department stores. A few blocks from Bloomingdales and the Mark Hotel where we were staying is or was a wonderful traditional secondhand bookshop. Here I bought Musa Meyer's book about her father Philip Guston, which Paula had (rightly) praised in the most glowing terms – I read it on the plane home. I like to accompany Paula to department stores, where she not only makes purchases but also susses out local attitudes to fashion, a deep interest of hers since childhood and one that feeds into her paintings.*

Trips abroad sometimes involve the private view of one of Paula's shows (thus Manhattan) but the September tradition around my birthday is to visit a European city where there are great paintings: Paris, Florence, Venice, Munich, Amsterdam, Antwerp, Zurich, etc. Our Swiss trip was partly inspired by Paula's admiration for the work of Félix Vallotton, whom she believes influenced Edward Hopper. At the Kunsthaus we were fortunate to see Vallotton's undisplayed pictures. This was one museum where the curator knew my name in addition to Paula's, because I had translated – for an exhibition centred on the friendship and professional relationship between Cartier-Bresson and Giacometti – a long catalogue essay by Yves Bonnefoy. Not only did we see these marvellous Vallottons in the vaults, Paula also spotted a fine Ensor and an equally fine Degas pastel. The curator informed us that, after refurbishment and enlargement of the museum, there will be less room for paintings, not more…]

Item: stationery supplies. [*Menard Press still services a vanishingly small number of direct retail orders in my kitchen, but trade orders go through the distributor Central Books [Later: now through NBN] and the small press consortium Inpress. The backlist is almost all that is left of Menard. Only in exceptional circumstances is a new title countenanced, such as the poems of Caroline West, a strip-cartoon book by Matt Barrell and a revised edition of Nigel Foxell's* A Sermon in Stone. *Fifty years old, Menard has had its day. I have done my share of weeping for Jerusalem, as Auden wrote. But it would be a shame and waste not to shift more backlist books,*[77] *if only to raise money to pay for a Menard anthology. And expenses and charges have to be covered.*

What a lovely flat this could be if it were ever tidied up, and the rooms returned to their proper use. Then the kitchen would be a real kitchen, the hall a real hall, the lounge a real lounge, the bedroom a real bedroom. But for each room to become a real room, I would have to sort out my brain, which would involve getting unreal, given the mindset. I'm sure that one day a gene will be discovered that would enable a Wallace Stevensian connoisseur of chaos to live in order. Fatuously, I comfort myself with Rilke's comment that if he were to rid himself of his demons, he would also be rid of his angels. Rilke has been one of my talismanic writers, whose lives compel my attention in addition to their work: Beckett, Rimbaud, Kafka, Laura Riding, among them. Rimbaud in particular fascinates me. By 1875, when he was twenty-one, he had announced the great themes of twentieth century literature, just as 'Tiepolo painted nineteenth century pictures in the eighteenth century,' or so our friend the sculptor Raymond Mason told Paula and me when we met him, quite by chance, in Ca Rezzonico in Venice, at the Tiepolo frescoes: 'modern art begins here'. And yet with other writers whose work I revere – Browning (who died at Ca Rezzonico), Joyce, Baudelaire, Joseph Roth, Emily Dickinson – I am content not to explore the life in detail.

One of the large envelopes piled high in the hall was for the dispatch of Will Stone's Menard translation of Nerval to a woman who had phoned me, complaining about the long time Hampstead Waterstones said it would take to order. The book was for her undergraduate daughter, who was studying Nerval at Cambridge. When the cheque arrived, it was from the account of her husband, a prince no less, though not from Aquitaine. I hope the word spreads that this is a great crib for Les Chimères. There were no such cribs when I was a student nearly fifty years ago – the renaissance in poetry translation had not yet started. Paula has just phoned me from Heathrow on her way to Oporto for her new show. I reminded her of the Tiepolo incident: 'Ah', she said, 'the father (Gianbattista) was a genius, the son more like us.' Modest and flattering at the same time.]

To the right, before we reach the kitchen door, standing on the floor in front of the shelves, are various things, including:

Item: my Hoover. [This is an old-fashioned upright Hoover, a Hoover with a capital H, which survived the move from married life in Upper Holloway. I read much of the night, and handfuls of dust are at the ready, as pervasive as allusions.]

Item: small bookcase. [This particular bookcase has been in the hall for ages, and is likely to stay there, since there is no space for it elsewhere, at least not until the repository rooms are cleared. Apart from books, I use it as a kind of out-tray: thus I have placed on it papers to take to Hatfield on Monday for the start of my weekly stint as Royal Literary Fund fellow at the University of Hertfordshire, helping students improve their essay writing. I am finding the work difficult, at a structural level beyond the sentence, because, as you are *discovering in this book, linear writing is not my preferred mode, favouringas I do association and collage – certainly not the way to write an academic essay.*]

The shelves on the right do not quite reach the kitchen entrance, unlike the shelves on the left that reach right up to the lounge entrance. In that gap stands the cardboard filing cabinet Octavio Paz gave me when he and Marie-José left Cambridge for the USA in 1970. It can hardly be seen for all the books on top of and around it. This filing cabinet is now completely chock-a-block with unsorted letters. The same goes for the cupboard at the other end of the hall, thirty feet from the front door – in parts the hall is only four feet wide, and even less where the space has been encroached on – and filled with Menard folders and personal stuff.

Perched between the bookcase and the filing cabinet is a bound volume of the *New Statesman* for July–December 1934. I started reading the journal regularly when I was sixteen or seventeen. I became aware of this old volume at some point. Until then, it had lived undisturbed for years in our converted loft under a window seat next to my father's theatre programmes, which were later thrown out by my mother, anti-hoarder par excellence. My guess is that 1934 was when my father started reading the magazine; enthusiastic, he bought the binder and thus preserved the issues for posterity. Although he continued reading the paper till around 1980, when he began rethinking his politics, he clearly gave up having the issues bound after the first six months – unless my mother threw those out, but why bother to keep the first set?

I loved dipping into those old issues, not least the advertisements. I open it now at the issue dated 6 October, the week of my father's twentieth birthday. One cannot fail to note the name of the co-author of the *Encyclopaedia of Sexual Knowledge*: A. Willy (although the word did not have the slang connotation then). The large advertisement for the encyclopaedia's third edition states: 'Where Havelock Ellis gives information, this book also gives advice.' One wonders what the 'consequences of self-abuse' were said to be. The book cost 36/- with a pre-publication offer of 29/6, that is twenty-nine shillings and sixpence in the old money. Above it is a book review with the intriguing sub-heading of *Le Chef d'oeuvre inconnu*, and yet the review contains no explicit or even implicit allusion to the Balzac story,[78] discussed earlier, that you would expect it to be referring to. The review, by K. John, is of two critical books, Pelham Edgar's *The Art of the Novel*, Macmillan, 10/-, and *Women Novelists from Fanny Burney to George Eliot* by Muriel Masefield. The reviewer has a go at Professor Edgar, clearly an old-fashioned and somewhat puritanical Canadian who is 'distressed by the predominance of sex in modern novels.' Apparently Edgar quotes Miss Lavinia Spenlow (good thing I checked on Google, it's a long time since I read *David Copperfield* – probably a year or two after I first looked at these bound copies of the *New Statesman* – and I was going to make a joke about the writer's name being perfect for an old-fashioned romance) as saying 'love is modest and retiring, it lies in ambush, waits and waits.' The reviewer likes Muriel Masefield's book but would have welcomed 'a short chapter on Mrs Inchbald', whom I shall, in my invincible ignorance, leave the reader to check out.

The advertisements too are interesting: Norman Haire, general editor of *The Encyclopaedia of Sexual Knowledge*, turns up as one of the lecturers in a series at Essex Hall sponsored by the World League for Sexual Reform on a Scientific Basis. One advertisement is for a book called *Bachelor Woman's Cookery* – so, the word spinster was already considered inappropriate as long ago as 1934 – invoking 'all the odds and ends a girl can do when she is on her own', presumably not a reference to the activity whose consequences were discussed in the encylopaedia mentioned earlier. Gertrude Lawrence and Douglas Fairbanks Junior were starring in Clemence Dane's *Moonlight is Silver* at the Queen's Theatre (telephone number Ger [i.e. Gerrard] 4517), while at the Empire Leicester Square Sophie Tucker and Florence Desmond were in *Gay Love* (it had an 'A' certificate). Who was the author who wanted to let a few rooms in his country home near Edenbridge? Then, a young Viennese lady 'gives German lessons; also wants to meet an Englishman graduate with good German, for literary co-operation'. Doubtless she's tired of bachelor girl cooking, ditto the 'intelligent cultured gentlewoman [who] wishes to meet another of her own unconventional inclinations, attractive, independent, not over 35'. This tour has been on the lighter side, and why not? After all, we sometimes need a break from Matthew Arnold's

> ... burden of the mystery,
> ... the heavy and the weary weight
> Of all this unintelligible world

which we live with much of the time, but I should not move on without one reference to the politics of the day as seen in that issue, for politics would have been the reason why Henry Rudolf, a serious-minded trainee chartered accountant, read the magazine every week. The issue of 6 October ends with a full-page advertisement drawing attention to German student refugees. My father, for financial reasons, did not become an LSE student on leaving school in 1931; nor, for the same reason, could he enter the law. Instead, he joined a firm of chartered accountants as an articled clerk, which is what he was at the time he would have read this issue. For accountancy, a premium payment was not required. Henry would certainly have known and been concerned about the situation in Germany, and not only because most of the cases given as examples had to leave as a result of 'the Aryan paragraph', that is they were Jewish. Hitler had come to power the previous year. The editor of the *New Statesman*, Kingsley Martin, wrote of Oswald Mosley after a recent Manchester rally: 'He blackguarded the Jews, big and little, international and local. He taunted Mr Citrine and the TUC with openly supporting the conspiracy of Jewish finance..... The truth is that Sir Oswald Mosley, with his wild talk and swashbuckling methods, is doing more than anyone else to make Fascism stink in English nostrils.' My parents came of age in the mid-thirties and were radicalised, like all their friends, by what was happening around them, literally so in the East End of London. Although, unlike a good few of their friends, they never became Communists (not even before the show trials drove many out), they would soon support the Popular Front.

Here I am (in 2005), reading one of the issues of the 1934 *New Statesman* that I first read in (let us say) 1958. I remember distinctly sprawling on the floor of the loft, dipping into these bound copies. Later, from 1964 till about 1990, I would read the current issue regularly (and in recent years I have rejoined the readership); I even contributed an article or two, one lead book review – of Jonathan Schell's *The Fate of the Earth* – and a poetry translation in the 1980s. I remember too in 1958 thinking how strange it was that cinemas and theatres in the advertisements still had the same phone number (I looked them up), that the same features were still in the magazine and, indeed, that the magazine still had the same editor. *But in 1958, 1934 was only twenty-four years ago.* Well over half a century has passed since 1958, and yet I leapfrog the years without effort. Seventy something (at the time of the current revisions of this book) is not *old old* these days, but it is old enough when it comes to memory, for my memory is not getting any better, and there are signs that it is getting worse.

> And now, with gleams of half-extinguished thought,
> With many recognitions dim and faint,
> And somewhat of a sad perplexity,
> The picture of the mind revives again:

Wordsworth's picture becomes a home movie in my head. I see my father at twenty. An alumnus of Raine's Foundation School (headmaster Mr A. Wilkinson Dagger, still there fifteen years later when Elaine Feinstein's late husband Arnold attended the school; Feinstein a scientist with a good eye – he spotted the influence of Tiepolo on Paula), Henry is in training to become a professional man, he is courting his future wife, Miss Esther Rosenberg, whom he met at Shabbos School (held at the Jews Free School in Bell Lane) when he was sixteen; he is in the beginnings of a mild revolt against his Orthodox background that will last at least until his first two children are born and decisions have to be made. On Friday mornings, before taking the bus or walking to the city office, he buys the *New Statesman* near his home in Alie Street, a few yards from Leman Street, and doubtless devours the journal during his lunch break.

Fast-forward to 1938: Henry marries Esther – after her 1937 solo cycling trip to Denmark and Germany, a bold assertion of independence and also a way of encouraging him to declare his intentions – in the Great Synagogue, Dukes Place, which was later bombed in the war. He gains his qualification as a chartered accountant. The scene is set for a life his ancestors, Rudolfs and Flashtigs and Foxes and Stadlens and Vogels from Poland, Russian Poland and East Galicia, could not have imagined. Courtesy of his immigrant parents, Josef Rudolf and Fanny Flashtig, he is here. They would have hoped that he would – in words they would not have used – become integrated into England, but not assimilated. Fast-forward four more years to the Salvation Army Mothers' Hospital in Lower Clapton Road, Hackney: the boy is born who will direct this home movie.

It is time to emerge from reverie and move along the hall, past the doorways to the lounge and the kitchen, and address two facing cupboards. These are the only survivors of my childhood furniture and date from the year of my bar mitzvah, 1955. Badly designed, they supported a desk top, long gone, which was in my first-floor bedroom in Middleway, prior to my moving upstairs to the newly reconstructed loft, quite likely the second in the Suburb after the Penguin Classics translator J.M. Cohen's in the same street. On top of the cupboard at the left, by the lounge door, is my Sharps telephone/fax machine. A succession of such machines – the first one illegally wired in at a time when you could only buy imported ones – saw much traffic until I belatedly discovered email. Apart from professional activities, such as sending off articles or urgent proofs, my main purpose in using fax was to correspond with two mates Mike Heller in New York and Port-Vendres denizen James Hogan then living in Hendon, four miles away.

Heller and I rarely phone each other, and Hogan while still in London was not a man for the phone. His faxes were handwritten. One of the repository rooms contains my collected faxes, hundreds, from both friends: there is material to keep me busy for years to come but they are fading fast, a suggestive thought.

Here are my old diaries, with phone numbers typically uncopied into a proper (presumably electronic) telephone book. In 1981, when I moved here, I attempted to keep a loose-leaf book that I was supposed to update, but it foundered on my pathetic inability to organise my life. I find a page headed 'miscellaneous', which contains the names of persons not from the UK or America, France or Israel, including

Pablo Armando Fernandez, Cuban poet: still at the same address.

Evgeny Vinokurov. Russian poet: deceased in 1995.

Johan Polak. Dutch publisher: deceased in 1992.

Vasko Popa. Yugoslav poet: deceased in 1991.

Guido Lopez. Italian critic: presumed still at the same address in Milan. [*Guido, a friend of Primo Levi's, was one of the people I met through the*

magazine European Judaism. In 1971, Rabbi Michael Goulston and I drove to Rome – where we met Richard Burns (now Berengarten), a fellow editor – for an EJ conference with Italian writers and editors, including the poet Edith Bruck. There, in a hotel lounge, Michael conducted the first ever non-Orthodox service held in Italy. We drove on to Milan to see Guido and returned via Paris. It may have been on this trip that Michael caught the bug that would kill him aged forty the following year. Guido died in 2010.]

Lada Klaboch and Dora Sebestova. [*Lada and Dora were two of my London TEFL students in the tumultuous days of the Prague Spring. I lost touch with them long ago, as you do. I still hope to visit Prague. I am tempted to look them out, in between a detailed inspection of every inch of the Kafka trail. I have written in articles about how I was indelibly marked by the twelve months period which saw the Six-Day War, the May events in Paris, and the Prague Spring.*]

Harry Kuhner: still at the same address in Vienna. [*Harry conducts a one-man war against anti-Semitism and other dangerous stupidities that survive in Vienna. Poet, drummer and polemicist, he sends me accounts of local goings on that leave an innocent like myself astonished at the human race: fecal orgies, for example, and cruelty to small animals. On hearing of Elfrieda Jelinek's Nobel Prize, I emailed him to ask if she was a sister or condemned to outer darkness. In reply he sent his account of Elfrieda's exploits with Valie Export. Harry reports that during the Third Reich children were taught to kill birds in a camp called* Kinderland, *'Children's Land', the play J.M. Barrie never wrote. I first met Harry at the Struga/Ohrid poetry festival in Macedonia in 1972. When Paula took me to Vienna for my sixtieth birthday, we had dinner with him and his wife Irmgaard at a restaurant facing the building where, according to a plaque, Auden died in 1973. A few years ago, I bought Paula a cassette of Auden; now he is one of the poets we read to each other every night on the phone. Paula's taste – poetry, fiction, folklore and other primary work – is a great lesson to anyone (no names, no packdrill) who reads biography and especially criticism when they should be reading the works these are based on. Exception made for Elizabeth Hardwick's essays on the Brontës, which Paula has read several times.*]

Gitta Holroyd-Reece. [*Gitta, who lived in Vienna, sent Menard her translation of the Austrian poet Gerhard Fritsch, which I accepted and published in 1978. This was one of the very rare Menard books that came, out of the blue, from someone not actively involved in the poetry translation sub-culture, although the translator evidently knew enough about the scene to contact Menard. Gitta was the daughter of a world-famous musicologist Otto-Erich Deutsch (think Schubert D-numbers). When my son aged about twenty needed to have papers signed for his membership of the Middle Temple so that he could enter a pupillage, he went to the chambers of a top judge, Simon Brown, who asked him how he knew the man who had recommended him, Konrad Schiemann, also a top judge. Doubtless to Brown's amusement, Nathaniel replied, perhaps stretching a point: 'I'm a friend of Konrad's mother-in-law.' Gitta's partner, Engelbert Broda, was a leading physicist and leader in the anti-nuclear struggle in Austria. Gitta remained a radical – perhaps milder than her friend Erich Fried – to the end of her days. She died in 1998.*]

Various unsorted things lie on top of the cupboard alongside the diaries and address book, including Orange mobile-phone literature, clothes brush, small hammer, coin of foreign realms, plug adaptor and British Telecom codebooks from 1990. Underneath the cupboard, which does not reach to the ground, are Menard books brought down from the attic for immediate access. On top of the cupboard facing this one are reference books. In front of the reference books are cassettes, often in the wrong plastic case, or with the wrong notes attached, or gathering dust outside their plastic case. And everywhere, books in no particular order.

Given the nature of the present work, there is no escape from the situation I find myself in, namely dealing with the mother of all administrative priorities: unsorted possessions. Yes, there is escape (I hope not escapism) in writing poems or stories or anything that draws on mainly right- brain thinking. Yes, there is escape in translation and criticism and certainly in publishing activities, etc. that draw mainly on left-brain thinking: this book, however, needs both in equal measure. Writing the present paragraph, better late than never, I understand in the context of creativity and chaos Wallace Stevens's line (in 'Connoisseur of Chaos'): 'The squirming facts exceed the squamous mind.'

I cannot even tidy up as I go along because the draft has to be finished before I am too old to do anything else. I must press on, trying to find stories of the past that seem to generate interest and/or amusement, and sometimes significance, although that will only emerge when the work is done. From time to time I dream the same dream, a nightmare: I lose a briefcase full of important papers and travel long distances on impossible vehicles through bizarre and alarming citiscapes, a cross between Piranesi and Chirico. It is a warning to get my act together before it is too late.

The cassettes on the cupboard by the kitchen door in the hall: either they had never been 'filed' in the first place, or they were taken from the big box in the repository room that was Naomi's bedroom, where my collection is stored, and not been returned. Let me sample them:

Item: recital of Spanish songs by Victoria de los Angeles and Alicia de Larrocha; Jobim; Tom Waits; Art Blakey and Thelonius Monk; Blossom Dearie (including 'Doing the Ooh La La' and 'Rhode Island'); American Theatre Songs: all copied for me by James Hogan. [*For a number of years, while Felek Scharf and my mother were still alive and James Hogan lived in London, I had a Sunday routine: around five I would drive to Felek in Willifield Way for a shmooz, then go on to my mother for supper (sometimes bringing a takeaway of Blooms salt beef or Folmans fish), ending up in Hendon for a nightcap with James, his wife Margaret – wit, reader and editor extraordinaire – having retired early as usual or, on occasion, waving as she emerged from the bathroom, a towel turban round her head. James, who is as organised as I am disorganised, as tidy as I am untidy, would have 'everything prepared for the feast', in the phrase of the Talmud: the drink – red wine or whisky – and the music he thought I would like to hear that evening – we share a taste for solo classical piano music and jazz vocals – and a written list of things to ask me or tell me. Sometimes our discussion would be professional. Once he helped me solve a Gordian-knotty structural problem that was driving me crazy. (The book containing that problem will never be published, only quarried for short stories. A section has been thrown way). The deeper issue was how to construct a meta-fiction for a state of mind that itself 'in real life' had been constructing a fiction for the state of affairs it found itself partly responsible for. But that is another story.*

At 9 pm precisely, James' brother Father Edmund phones from Ireland for a brief chat, leaving me to pull on my small cigar (James had his pipe) and sometimes fall asleep to the mesmerising lilt of my friend's soft-toned cork-lined (ha ha) Irish accent. Felek is now at rest in the Jewish cemetery in

Hoop Lane, and James now has his routines in Port-Vendres. Emails whiz back and forth. His latest contains an attachment and a request that I comment on the extract from a recent manuscript. He is in a prose phase at the moment. But the poems will return, as befits a man who had five poetry books published by Menard Press. I miss those Sundays. He took the trouble to copy many cassettes for me, including personalised compilations. That's what a kind person with a tidy mind can do. Two weeks later: I have read the extract. It is not one of his best, and as a licensed buddy-critic I have a responsibility to tell him and explain why. I suspect he did not show it to Margaret before sending it to me. Later: Margaret has died: the mother of all one-offs or ones off.]

Item: The Best of Amalia, fado compilation.[79] [I fantasise that Paula has made a portrait of Amalia Rodrigues. It would have equalled her versions of Germaine Greer and David Hare. President Jorge Sampaio invited her to paint his portrait to mark the end of his term of office. A younger Dame than her, Marina Warner would be a perfect subject. Paula and Lila listen to operas in the mornings but later in the day change to Lisbon fado (as distinct from Coimbra fado), especially as sung by Amalia, the supreme genius. There were suspicions that Amalia had leanings towards Salazar but, according to Saramago, all along she was giving money in secret to the Communist Party. The Portuguese revolution in 1974 dismissed fado as old hat, reactionary. A complex figure in a painful situation, Amalia was no saint, but she was a great interpretative artist in a traditional music of the heart that rivals the blues, even if one does not understand the words. Flamenco and balalaika, klezmer and tango, all these sing to me. A Buenos Aires Jew, for example, could create a fusion to die for, assuming we approve of fusion. I should discuss these histories with Anthony Howell, old friend and Menard poet, who is an authority on tango. A more recent friend, Evi Fishburn, grande dame of Borges studies in Britain, tells me that there are quite a few references to tango and milonga in Borges but nothing on flamenco or fado, and she reminds me that Borges alludes to Xavier de Maistre's Voyage autour de ma chambre which Yves Bonnefoy assumed was the inspiration for the present work. Not so. That was the first time I heard mention of my precursor. De Maistre wrote a sequel: Expédition nocturne autour de ma chambre.]

Item: The Klezmer Festival Band: Echoes of the Shtetl (led by Gregori Schechter) and several other Klezmer cassettes. [*When I started seeing Paula in 1996 I asked myself where I could introduce her to my mother. I hit on the idea of the Yiddish film festival at the Barbican. There were two films I particularly wanted to see,* Yiddl with a Fiddle *(made in 1936) and, for the third time,* The Dybbuk, *an expressionist masterpiece and probably the last Polish Yiddish film; it was made in 1937 shortly before darkness embraced the land. I arranged to take my mother to the first and Paula to the second. That my mother would enjoy a film about a klezmer group set in the world of her family was certain but I was sure too that Paula would be fascinated by the story of the dybbuk – a folk story of the kind she relished in other literatures – and indeed she was; later she made two works out of it. In between the two films I introduced Esther to Paula, my mother smaller than Paula, but bigger than Paula's mother, Maria, who lived long enough for me to get to know her. The last few times I met Maria she was in a nursing home by Archway Bridge. This bridge, as Jonathan Miller said, is the only place in London where you can commit suicide by moving from one postal district to another. Maria was struggling to keep her show on the road – something she had been expert at when younger – and succeeded in retaining her old-world elegance almost till the end. On one memorable occasion she was speaking to to me in French, to Paula in Portuguese and to the nurse in English, her tone as if in a hotel: 'Please bring my guest a cup of tea.'*]

Item: Songs by Ra'hel. [*Ra'hel was a celebrated Hebrew poet from Russia whom I published in the translations of the late Robert Friend. Many of her poems were set to music after her death, thanks to their intrinsic song-like quality. Ra'hel, as the poet Gabriel Levin says, was mythologised as the kibbutz pioneer and poet who died young. One of her poems, 'Sad Song', not in Robert's translation, was recited in outer space by the Israeli astronaut who died when the American spacecraft he was in failed. I have the Menard book on my desk by chance, for I am giving it to my niece Rebecca as a twenty-first birthday present. As stated earlier, Rebecca and family now live in Israel. At a time when the policies of the present Israeli government are regularly excoriated – deservedly in my opinion – not everyone understands that Jewish diaspora links with Israel are often intimately based on family ties. Solidarity with the country is instinctive and support for the idea of a Jewish state virtually universal, at least until recently. Many diaspora Jews are less supportive of Israeli government policies than their secular and religious leaders, who have a vested interest in identifying with the Israeli establishment. But it is essential to separate one's emotions from an intellectual assessment of disastrous government policies. The countries I know best and which mean the most to me – France, the USA, Israel and above all my own country – are the ones that anger me most. How could it be otherwise?*

Portugal is something else. Much as I have enjoyed my regular but short visits to the country, I have 1) come to it too late to have the intimate relationship I have with the other four countries, and 2) my experience is inevitably coloured by Paula's complex and complicated attitude to her native land, which is not dissimilar to James Joyce's vis-à-vis Ireland. They certainly do things differently there. When, for example, Paula had a show at the Serralves Museum in Oporto, we experienced again the way everything is done at the last minute – catalogue proofs, guest-lists and so on – in contrast to the Protestant efficiency of Tate Britain or Old Tate as taxi drivers say). The other side of the escudo is that Portuguese people are cool, relaxed and friendly, and they have had at least one president whose demeanour and attitude have confirmed my intellectual and instinctive view that the UK should become a republic. This is Paula's friend and former lawyer, former President Jorge Sampaio, whom I have been privileged to meet a few times and with whom I had a conversation on the subject of republics at a Guildhall dinner Paula was too ill to attend. He was standing alone so I went up to him – as one could not to the Queen – and reintroduced myself. When I expressed my doubts about monarchies he said he could not comment, but he smiled and I like to think he was pleased rather than merely being diplomatical. We then briefly discussed the EU and the UN before turning to art. The chapel in the Presidential Palace at Beleym has Paula's Life of the Virgin *suite, eight devotional and beautiful pastel paintings, done specifically for this site at his request and drawn from the matrix of the same imaginaire that made the abortion pictures.*[80] *'It is all one,' as the Talmud says.*]

Item: Tape of my Radio 3 interview with Yehuda Amichai, 19 September 1979; *Dreamstreets:* Robert Friend poems. [*The label on the cassette is in my father's handwriting which, as usual, moves me – as recordings of his voice do – more than photographs: hardly surprising, since they emanate from the person. The interview was the first or second of the ten or so broadcasts I have made. It was recorded under the aegis of the producer Fraser Steel – later head* of BBC Editorial Complaints Unit, where he still presides at the time of writing – at the house of Olwen Hughes in Chetwynd Road. I had been introduced to Yehuda at Poetry International quite a few years earlier and we would meet in London and Jerusalem. Yehuda secreted poems. He was a metaphor generator of genius, a teller of miniature stories full of tears and smiles, and sometimes both at once, as in Pushkin's comment on Gogol. Yehuda bypassed the self-censorship, the auto-radar, that some poets require in order to generate their truth; apparently effortlessly, he produced hundreds of poems: these poems speak of war and love, Jerusalem and family, Bible and Palestine. In his polymorphous prodigality, he resembles Bob Dylan, who astonished Leonard Cohen with his sheer quantity and speed. Yehuda in his pomp was like the young Neruda, or the older Ted Hughes (his close friend).

Once, at Ben-Gurion Airport, a young security guard asked me whom I knew in Israel: I named (all right, name-dropped) Appelfeld, the late Shlonsky, Oz, Amichai, Carmi, Megged, Gilboa, Zach, shall I continue, I said? Silence, then she replied: 'I studied them all at high school', and waved me through. Security at the airport was always a slow business and doubtless it has got worse since 1995, when I made the latest of my many visits. I would like to show Paula around the Bauhaus quarter of Tel-Aviv and take her to old Safed. In Jerusalem, we would stroll to the bench commemorating the spot where Holman Hunt painted his views, walk the Stations of the Cross as I once did with Claude Vigée,, have lunch in my favourite Jerusalem haunt, Anna Tikho house, with Aharon Appelfeld; I would introduce her to Dov Noy. But Dov Noy is now dead and it is no longer possible to go to his apartment –previously the home of the former Prime Minister Moshe Sharett – in Rehavia, 19 Balfour Street, on a Monday evening, to participate in the salon of the man with the largest address book in the world, the ex-Kolomyia scholar who was the undisputed 'zeida' of Jewish folklore studies and who taught all the experts on the subject, now themselves retired professors around the world. So many of my Israeli (and other) friends have died: Yehiel Denur (better known as Katsetnik 135633, which tells us he arrived in Auschwitz earlier than Katsetnik 174517 (aka Primo Levi) and later than Piotr Rawicz, Katsetnik 102679 (albeit under a false name), Yehoshua Bar-Yosef, Robert Friend, Avraham Yaffe and all the names dropped at the airport.]

Item: Songs of the Soul, Radio 4 poetry feature; Remember, Jewish cantorial music sung by Simon Hass (I return the lately unplayed cassette to its container, blowing the dust off); *The Art of the Cantor:* Jan Peerce. [*Some years ago I was interviewed at home by Rosemary Hartill for Radio 4's programme,* Songs of the Soul. *There were three interviewees: a Christian, a Muslim and myself. I spoke about Jewish poetry and literature and lent them my cassette containing the rendering by Simon Hass – a famous London cantor – of Psalm 121, 'I shall lift up mine eyes unto the hills', the tune a famous one from the Ashkenazi liturgy. The music in Ashkenazi synagogues – apart from ancient Torah keenings – is often less than two hundred years old, and in the West has been influenced by Christian, especially German Christian, church music that Jewish composers would be familiar with in Berlin or Vienna. In ancient days, the Torah chant influenced the muezzin's wail and other Muslim chants. Overall, I am struck by how much more familiar Islam – apart from specific Christian iconography that Western art from the Renaissance to Chagall and Kitaj draws on – is to me, in terms of law, education, land, emotion, than the Christianity I grew up surrounded by. Jewish fundamentalism in Israel has sadly come home to roost; when not aping the American Wild West, it shows signs of Muslim influence, whereas, in the eighteenth century, radical movements like Hasidism bore Christian influence.*]

Item: Andrew Rosenblum: Schumann *Kinderszenen.* [*I have had the pleasure of working with visual artists and have always wanted to work with a composer or singer. A more recent project concerned a visual idea involving music which I put to the printmaker and painter Jane Joseph, whose Folio Society edition of Primo Levi's* If This is a Man *I had reviewed. The rule of the game was that we both react to one of my favourite compositions, Schumann's* Scenes from Childhood, *but not to each other's work as triggered by it. We listened privately to recordings of these small marvels of the keyboard and went to a performance at Wigmore Hall by Alan Schilling, armed with the score – something I haven't done for years. After the performance, we had supper at a pleasant Turkish restaurant, Sofra, off Wigmore Street and discussed the project.*

In the versions of Scenes from Childhood *I have here, the pianists allow only two or three seconds between each scene, as you would expect. So I hit upon the idea of commissioning an unknown and previously unrecorded young pianist to record them for us with a whole minute's gap each time. Lori Laitmann is a composer who entered the picture some years ago when she needed copyright permission to set poems by Jerzy Ficowski in Keith Bosley's translation. Her emails had revealed that her pianist son Andrew Rosenblum was about to enter Yale on an undergraduate music scholarship. I asked her if he would consider doing a recording for us, and if a hundred dollars would be an appropriate fee. Yes and yes were the answers. He duly sent cassettes and CDs of his performance, in which he allows the required gap and announces the titles. This made our own reactions to each scene more amenable to reflection. These scenes are popularly thought to be an example of programme music, but it is known that Schumann gave them titles after writing the music. Music invoked subject, rather than subject evoking music. I played the music several times in all my recordings and then settled down with Andrew's version. Eventually I wrote thirteen short texts, telling myself I was reacting to the music, but how could I not be reacting to the titles? Jane in turn made linocuts, which were later exhibited with my texts.[81]]*

Item: Charlie Haden and Carlos Paredes: dialogues. [*This cassette was copied for me by Z. Kotowicz, who is the greatest jazz aficionado among my friends, and also a guitarist of near professional quality. When he lived in England, I would meet Z. Kotowicz from time to time to see a film – typically an Iranian or Algerian one and usually at our favourite cinema the Renoir – followed by a meal at Caprini in Waterloo, where there is a photograph of Alberto de Lacerda on the wall . Z. Kotowicz, like Augustus Young, travels light. He has been a nomad but (or and) also written books, including a remarkable study of Pessoa for Menard Press. This has even been translated into Portuguese, a signal compliment. Jose Blanco, an authority on Pessoa as well as a source of subsidy at the Gulbenkian Foundation – the mother of all combinations from a publisher's point of view – was deeply impressed and said it was the first time anyone had analysed and explained the links between Camoes and Pessoa. Z had a three-year scholarship from the Wellcome Foundation to write a history of frontal lobotomies. Antonio Damasio – whose books I have read and whom I met through Paula – is not going to like the book (mainly the part on Egas Moniz) which has emerged from Kotowicz's research, since Z is going to show that the brain is no place for surgery or drugs, and that almost all invasions of that organ are based on ignorance or wilful misunderstanding of the mind and the psyche. I am an amateur in this field, and I place on record here that aspects of Damasio's work have helped me conceptualise my thoughts on autobiography, but Z. Kotowicz is highly persuasive in, for example, his revisionist reflection* on previous accounts of the celebrated case of Phineas Gage, including Damasio's. Later: Z. has since died.]

Having 'completed' the tops of the two cupboards, I move along the hall. To the left is the long radiator on which I hang towels after washing them; over the radiator are bookshelves. Facing these shelves is the airing cupboard, which comes between the toilet and the bathroom. In front of it is the gramophone on which I play my 78s and on which I used to play my 33⅓s and 45s until my mother gave me a hi-fi system for my fiftieth birthday. Behind the gramophone is the plug where I recharge my mobile phone and my electric razor. The hall is a bit wider in this middle section, so this is where I hang my shirts and jackets and trousers from high bookshelves, instead of the cupboard that serves as a wardrobe in the bedroom.

I see that one of the screws fixing these high bookshelves to the wall is beginning to work loose. If the shelf lands on me it could break my neck. Misadventures are possible at home, oh yes. Never mind other men's lives, which Coleridge said were the poet's chaos, one's own life is chaos enough. There are small walls jutting out by the bathroom and the toilet, smaller rooms than the kitchen and Naomi's former bedroom up from the bathroom. These walls on the right and the space around the airing cupboard are covered with pictures. Some of the doors have images hung from or stuck on them. It is time to embark on a round tour of the pictures in the hall. A few at the front door are awaiting a re-hang on the existing space in the flat. But, for the time being, I can look at these floor-bound pictures more easily in the hall than anywhere else in the flat.

Item: Axe, lithograph by Victor Willing.[82]

Item: Means of Escape, lithograph by Paul Coldwell.[83] [Paul gave me this lithograph as a fee or, better, as a thank you for the catalogue text I wrote to accompany a show of his work at the Print Centre in Harrow Road. I have already written about him in the Kitchen chapter of this book. Writers of catalogues can build up good collections of artworks. Yves Bonnefoy's was a good example. André Breton had a fabulous collection, now sadly broken up and sold off. The relationship between writers and painters goes back to antiquity.]

Item: Shipwreck and Window, Blizzard and Condensation, two etchings by Jane Joseph. [*I went to Jane's about-to be-vacated studio off Ladbroke Grove, having told her on the phone I wanted to buy an etching. She said she would like to give me a print, so we compromised: I would buy one and also be given one. Once again I experienced the thrill of an artist's studio: we went through her available etchings. Finally I settled on one from her Primo Levi series and one from another series. Later on I showed Paula the Levi etching, 'Shipwreck', and she immediately identified the Goya allusion.*]

Item: drawing of a heron by Fran Burdon. [*This was one of the illustrations I commissioned from Fran, who – like Charlotte Hodes and Tracey Emin (the latter on the strength of one tutorial at the Royal College) – is a former student of Paula's. These were for a book of poems by Fred Beake.*[84] *Fred and Fran and I met for coffee at the Royal Festival Hall to discuss the project. In the old days I enjoyed being a publisher, not least for this kind of connection. Now Menard is on the back-burner, and will soon be off the stove. Fran used to be so shy that when Paula first met her she was hiding under a table at the Slade. Paula bought a strange picture by her, an image of a cat with green snotties coming from – where else – the nose. Later I gave Paula a drawing by Fran of an anthropomorphic sausage.*]

The Walls in the Hall

Above the doorway into the lounge is an etching of three Beckettian figures, drunken sailors judging by the Popeye hats and pipes, by Gyula Zilzer, a Hungarian Jewish graphic artist, who had studied with Hans Hofmann. This is one of three Zilzers in the hall. I met his late widow Mary on several occasions in Jerusalem. She was the companion and translator of one of the Hebrew poets I published in the seventies and eighties, Manfred Winkler. He himself was Celan's main Hebrew translator. I visited the Nora Gallery on Ben-Maimon Street in the early 1990s, where there was a show of Zilzer, whose expressionistic work I admire. I said I would buy a print because I could not afford a painting. Mary immediately announced she would give me one since I had offered to buy one: if I had asked to be given one, maybe she would have said they were for sale... Well, that's a lesson. [*fig. 118*]. She also gave me a folio of Zilzer's powerful expressionist prints, published by Labor Arts at 6 East 17th street, New York City – with an Introduction by the once world-famous Nobel Prize-winning writer Romain Rolland – on the subject of gas warfare. I told her I would explore the possibility of finding a publisher to reissue it, perhaps even producing it at Menard Press. Mission not accomplished. The folio contains a publicity leaflet, where we find a letter from Einstein, dated 26 March, on the letterhead of the liner *Belgenland*. [*Later: I have presented the Zilzer folio to Peter Redman for good reasons.*[85]]

On the side of the wall jutting out by my lounge doorway, at right angles to the cupboard with the answerphone on it, are five pictures:

Item: one of four wood engravings by Willow Winston dotted around the hall. [*These wood engravings were among those later reproduced for the Menard edition of Kim Chernin's poems* The Hunger Song. *Willow Winston, painter and print maker, also did a cover for Jeremy Reed's* A Long Shot to Heaven. *For years Willow lived and worked – Radio 4 permanently on – in an L-shaped room in Leather Lane: the naughty lady of Leather Lane, as she was known to her friends. Before that she had a room in Tottenham Street, in the house where Michael Rowan Robinson lived premaritally. She is now creating 'soft' sculptures and I have written a poem for one of them.*]

Item: Moment, one of two small paintings in the hall by Paula's close friend, Natalie Dower.[86]

Item: etching by Carol Wheeldon for Richard Berengarten's *Tree*

Item: etching: *Jane's Cottage* by Sophie Mason. [*Jane was Sophie Mason's aunt, Jane Carrington, a member of the famous family. Jane ran the rotas in the Bush House newsroom for many years. A legendary character, she knew all the secrets of those with double lives who needed to change a shift in order to betray their spouse or lover or both; or, more mundanely, go on holiday a day earlier. In return for helping people with their private shenanigans, she would call in the favour when, for example, she needed someone to come in on Christmas morning because a colleague had genuinely gone sick. If you didn't cooperate...*]

On the narrow front of this jutting-out wall, before we reach the radiator, are two reproductions of Jewish astrological prints I bought from John Trotter's bookshop at the Sternberg Centre in Finchley. These attractive images, now seemingly unobtainable, cost about two pounds each, and framed made nice presents. Over the years I must have bought about thirty to give to friends and relatives. Here are my own, Virgo (*mazal betulah*), and my daughter's, Leo (*mazal arieh*). On this wall, too, are woodcuts by Peter Paul Piech I bought in the Englands Lane bookshop back in the 1970s. One is of Isaac Rosenberg, [*fig. 119*] the other of John Donne. There is too a nice pen-and-ink drawing by Aldous Eveleigh, who illustrated Z. Kotowicz's Pessoa book. Aldous was to have an exhibition at a gallery in Covent Garden, opening on 11 September, 2001. The central image, as seen on the invitation several days earlier, was the destruction of the towers... The exhibition was cancelled.

Pass the radiator on the left, pass the doorway to Nathaniel's former bedroom, and you will see four pictures on the wall between Nathaniel's room and my bedroom. At the top is a tiny painting of two figures in Walpole Park, Ealing, by my aunt Margaret, the wife of my mother's youngest brother Leonard, who are the only survivors among my uncles and aunts.[87] Margaret is a naïve, an untrained artist of mood with a quirky eye, perhaps marginally influenced by Lowry. [*Later: Margaret has died and Leonard, now ninety-five, is the last living person who, then a teenager, knew me when I was a baby.*] There are three other pictures on this narrow stretch of wall:

Item: brass rubbing by Irene Gunston [*Irene ran the foundry of the Royal College of Art for several years.*]

Item: Two Manet etchings of Baudelaire [*This famous image is thrice treasured: Manet is one of my favourite artists, Baudelaire one of my favourite poets (here top-hatted, in dandy mode), and Jonathan and Kathy Griffin, whose present it was, were two of my dearest friends. The embossed studio print is dated 1862.*] [*fig. 120*]

Item: David Jones, wood engraving: *Politicians with Map.* [*There can be no doubt that, like his contemporaries and peers D.H. Lawrence and Isaac Rosenberg, David Jones's primary medium was words. I don't like his watercolours but I admire his prints and went with Alan Wall to a centenary exhibition at the Wolseley Gallery, where we each bought a print. Alan chose an* Ancient Mariner *copper engraving. My wood engraving is dated 1922 – soon after Jones met Eric Gill– and set in the Great War, with politicians being briefed by a general. David Jones, a private, suffered greatly from life in the trenches, but unlike Isaac Rosenberg, he survived, though he was afflicted for the rest of his life. But if ever suffering bore fruit in art, David Jones supplies the proof text. It is significant that it took him several years even to begin work on his epic* In Parenthesis, *one of the rare book-length English-language masterpieces inspired by the war. It was published, by his champion, T.S. Eliot at Faber, in 1937. John Montague took me to meet Jones in 1972. He signed a book I brought in different coloured inks. Recently Wall and I discussed our treasured purchases but we soon moved on to the poetry of the common soldier, the songs – often disrespectful of authority, often funny, sometimes heartbreaking, sometimes proud – gathered later in* O What a Lovely War. *In her studio, Paula has a CD of French soldiers' songs of the Second World War which I sometimes ask her to put on when I'm sitting for her: these engender similar reactions.*]

Blue-Tacked to the hallside of my bedroom door are a small reproduction of a Balthus picture of a girl on a horse and a 'Tony' nameplate. To the right, on the door of the hall cupboard, is a beautiful unframed poster – that has survived thirty years undamaged – published by Penguin to promote Jon Silkin's anthology of First World War poetry: it shows Rosenberg's 'What in our lives is burnt' and flaming poppies. To the right of this door is an extremely narrow strip of wall, but not too narrow for me to hang small pictures there, including a tiny etching from the late sixties by Julia Ball, a Leicester friend of Peter Hoy's and Rigby Graham's. The three friends produced the smallest of all small magazines, *Fishpaste*, each issue being a postcard. Turning right, I now face Naomi's room, the beginning of the home straight. Here, Blue-Tacked to the door, is a treasure: a card of Raymond Briggs's characters, Snowman, Father Christmas and Fungus the Bogeyman, which he sends to children. He has drawn balloon spaces for rude messages. Ours says: 'Blooming Nathaniel! Blooming Naomi!' and, 'Are they both smelly?' It is signed, 'Worst wishes from Raymond Briggs, Christmas 1983'. At that point the children were sleeping in bunk beds,

fig. 119

fig. 120

Drawn for END (European Nuclear Disarmament) by Josef Herman OBE
Hebrew script by the artist
Verse from Southern Black folk song (USA)
Proceeds on card to
JONAH (Jews Organised for a Nuclear Arms Halt)
and to AND (Artists for Nuclear Disarmament)
Published in 1982/5743 by The Menard Press
8 The Oaks, Woodside Avenue, London N12 8AR
Telephone 01-446 5571
Printed by Skelton's Press, Wellingborough

fig. 121

God gave Noah
The Rainbow Sign:
No more water –
The fire next time!

Wishing you a year of peace

fig. 122

fig. 123

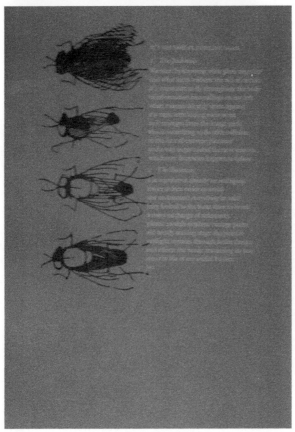

fig. 124

Nathaniel upstairs. Nathaniel moved across the hall a year or two later, and I moved my office into the lounge.

Above and around Naomi's door are several pictures, including:

Item: linocut of an owl by Zykmunt Frankel. [*Zygmunt Frankel, better known as a writer, gave me this simple and stark image in Tel-Aviv. Years later in New York I met a composer called Ari Frankel at the apartment of Mike Heller and Jane Augustine. Frankel was the composer of an opera on Primo Levi so we had plenty to talk about. It turned out Zygmunt was his father. 'It's a small world!' is nonsense as an expression of surprise when you meet someone's son in another country. 'Small world' in my experience is normal. Indeed, I'm surprised when there is no connection, but that might be the experience of one who has always been a go-between. Besides, the real test is when you find a connection with a stranger in a public place. These are versions of the 'six handshakes'. I shook hands with Brian Coffey, who was six handshakes from Marie-Antoinette via an old man in Ireland whose father as a boy had worked for a landowner who had shaken hands with, etc.*]

Item: Josef Herman pastel: artwork for a Jewish New Year card [*fig. 121 & 122*] [*This is in a two-sided frame. On the reverse, with a message typed in blue ink, is Herman's letterhead from Edith Road in West London, where I visited him two or three times to see new work and marvel always at his collection of African art and artefacts. During my final visit, he showed me the only picture he had ever bought back from a client (who made a hefty profit) and also a small picture which was not behaving well: Joseph had decided to do a larger version of the small one and had wrongly persuaded himself it would be identical, allowing for scale. Impossible, even to the same scale, since you are not the same person second time round and therefore find new problems to solve. All the more so when the copy is not to scale. 'I should have known.' And now he was hard at work on it, a new picture. I was pleased when David Elliott at Elliott and Thompson wanted to use a Herman painting as the cover illustration for my revised edition of Piotr Rawicz's* Blood from the Sky.

Herman's blue-ink letter reads: 'My dear Tony, I am glad that you would like to keep the original drawing. Please do keep it. As for the payement [sic]*, you can pay whatever you can afford to the Artists for Peace, c/o Michael Tilley. My best wishes to you, Josef.' Below the message are pasted other* *elements of the card: the verse from the southern spiritual, earlier made famous by James Baldwin, which I chose for the card:*

God gave Noah
The rainbow sign:
No more water –
The fire next time.

and the traditional New Year greeting in Hebrew: 'Leshana tova', in the artist's own script (translated on the card as 'Wishing you a year of peace') as well as the colophon information that the card was drawn for END, European Nuclear Disarmament, and that proceeds would go to JONAH (Jews Organised for a Nuclear Arms Halt) and AND (Artists for Nuclear Disarmament) plus details of Menard as the publisher. This was the last of seven New Year cards Menard published, the first one being in 1969.[88] I was a founding member of JONAH, along with Colin Shindler and other concerned friends. When we turned up on the scene, Bruce Kent commented that he had been wondering when members of the Jewish community would make an appearance. The affable monsignor had been right to wonder. We sought and found proof texts for our position (such as the environmental principle of baal tashchit) and even a statement by the Israeli government that they would support a nuclear-free zone in the Middle East along the lines of the Latin American Treaty of Tlatelolco. But basically our concern was the situation in Europe. JONAH eventually divided into two factions: one said you could demonstrate on the Sabbath, on the traditional grounds that the saving of life permits the breaking of the law, and in any case if you were later seen on TV News why should people not think you had walked from north-west London to Hyde Park, Jewish law is supposed to give you the benefit of the doubt. The other faction said you could not demonstrate. It was a curious way to leave the stage, and perhaps unconsciously stage-managed by both factions... but for a few years JONAH had fulfilled what, realistically, was its primary task: to educate the Jewish community within, and to represent a Jewish religious perspective without.]

Item: Carol Farrow painting on metal.
Item: Arnold Daghani painting.

Item: Painting by Youval Yariv. [*A few years ago Lionel and Sheila King Lassmann – friends from the days when I was a member of Finchley Progressive Synagogue – invited me to their house: they wanted to show me a whole bunch of works by Youval Yariv that the artist had left there thirty years earlier when he returned home to Israel. I can't remember if Lionel knew that I had known Youval, and indeed had written a catalogue introduction for his first exhibition (held in Brussels), my own first published writing on visual art. Lionel wanted to dispose of the works since every effort to track Youval down had failed. I chose one that I liked, as a belated reward to myself for writing the catalogue intro and arranging its French translation. On the subject of tracking people down: my rule of thumb is that if you hear nothing, they are alive. Word filters back when people die. I wondered for a long time what had happened to Abdullah al-Udhari, author of three early Menard books long ago.*[89] *This sweet and gentle Yemeni poet, married to an Italian woman, Lara, was said to have upped and gone from London. But no, he is here.*]

Item: four watercolours and two hand-coloured postcards by Miriam Neiger. [*Elsewhere in these pages I discuss my ongoing email collaboration with Miriam Neiger, working towards an eventual book of her poems in translation, just as Ifigenija Simonovic and I worked with fax drafts a few years ago. Ifigenija and the Slovak-born Jerusalemite Miriam are unusual in that their gifts as verbal and visual artists are equal. I think most artists with two gifts – whether two genres of writing or two completely different arts – tend to have a dominant one and that people sometimes overestimate the quality of the secondary one. William Blake and, as already discussed, Isaac Rosenberg and David Jones, are more significant as poets than as visual artists. William Faulkner and Muriel Spark are incomparably better as novelists than as poets. Lawrence and Hardy, however, are great poets and great novelists. Pound said of Hardy, who had a second life as a poet after writing his novels: 'There is the harvest of having written twenty novels first.'*]

Item: Yves Bonnefoy poster [Poems on the Underground]

Let a place be made for the one who draws near,
the one who is cold, deprived of any home,

tempted by the sound of a lamp, by the lit
threshold of a solitary house.

And if he is still exhausted, full of anguish,
I say again for him those words that heal.

What does this heart which once was silence need
if not those words which are both sign and prayer,

like a fire caught sight of in the sudden night,
like the table glimpsed in a poor house.

Around the bathroom door and between that door and the airing-
cupboard and then between the airing cupboard and the toilet and finally
between the toilet and the wall jutting out where the kitchen begins, we
find more pictures, up and down the narrow strips of wall. This is closer
to the Victorian approach than to the spare, sometimes minimal, style of
hanging beloved of or dictated by modern taste. Think of Ruskin's Lake
District house filled with Turners and not an inch of wall space to be
seen, or pictures of the old Royal Academy shows in Somerset House,
where the Courtauld Gallery now is. Among these are:

Item: cover artwork for the *New Statesman* by Will Hill. [*This is on a
nuclear theme I can no longer decipher – probably something to do with cruise
missiles –but no matter, it is a typically dark and small work of the kind I
favour.*]

Item: etching of Baudelaire by Anthony Dorrell.

Item: collage by Amber Jacobs. [*A birthday card/present from the former
chief baby sitter, already mentioned.*]

All on their own, down one narrow strip of wall, are four small acrylic
paintings by Anne Davies, three of which I bought from her. They are
apparently abstract but closer inspection reveals delicate landscapes, my
favourite being a shoreline, painted with a tiny brush. I bought the first
one at an artists' fair in Battersea Town Hall. I remember telling a painter
that I liked his work and would return. But a few minutes later I found

Anne Davies's stall and fell in love with her work. I paid twenty pounds for the painting. She put me on her mailing list and I left with the picture hidden under my coat so as not to embarrass the other painter or myself. I bought two more of Anne's pictures in later years, and she very sweetly gave me another for being a good customer.

There is a lesson to be learned from these purchases. Some people think that buying prints or paintings involves spending a great deal of money, having special, perhaps inside, knowledge about the art world, and being knowledgeable about the history of contemporary art. The first is not true, the second minimally true, but all the information you need is easily acquired from open sources, while the third is a bonus, an optional extra. What such purchasing does involve is love of pictures, and trusting your eye, even before you have educated it by going to exhibitions or shops or open days in studios and art colleges. Thanks to my work and other factors already obvious in this book, I am in a privileged position and sometimes get given things. But I do buy what I love and can afford. To go to a studio or a print fair and spend a hundred pounds or less on something I know I will cherish is one of the greatest pleasures known to me. I hope for the sake of the artists that their prices go up but I am not in the investment business and even if they strike lucky I have no desire to sell work I have bought. What I might need to sell are my first edition books and my publishing archive. Final point about the pictures: I get my frames from a very well-run small business, the Picture Factory, which is in a picturesque old courtyard you would not expect to have survived in North Finchley.

The next narrow strip of wall has a number of tiny works, including the smallest one of all, a painting by Ifigenija Simonovic, about two inches square, using colours familiar to fans of her pottery and those who have seen my poetry tie. [*fig. 123*] Here too is Professor Raphael Loewe's Latin translation of the Sabbath hymn *Adon Olam*, although what you can see is the original Hebrew and a small woodcut of a large hand (God's) protecting a young woman. Underneath it there is a tiny surrealist etching, provenance forgotten. On the toilet door hangs a woven scroll with Egyptian-style figures that Jean Goldman sent me from Israel. Jean and her sister were daughters of a widowed mother who lived near us in the Suburb when I was a boy. Then, within a short period of time, Mrs Goldman and the sister died, leaving Jean alone in the world. She visited

Israel, and married a local boy. She might even be a grandmother now. Stranger things have happened to school friends or synagogue friends from childhood. Thus, I sometimes wonder what became of John Coberman. He lived in Church Mount, near Hilary Sefton.[90] The last time I was at Bushey Cemetery, I saw by chance what I am guessing was his parents' tombstone and noticed that they had died within two weeks of each other, and that he is not mentioned among the family on the tombstone, but it could of course have been his uncle and aunt. A vague sensation stirs like a worm in the compost of my amygdala cells. 'In the grave all, all shall be renewed', as Yeats says in his poem 'Broken Dreams', about a woman 'more beautiful than anyone' who yet had one flaw, her hands were not beautiful, which oddly enough is also true about a classical beauty I knew. Yes, a vague sensation stirs, call it a memory: something about a synagogue friend, possibly John Coberman, dying young. 'Vague memories, nothing but memories', writes Yeats in the same poem, and my summoning up a remembrance of this poem was, of course, triggered in the first place by the phrase 'vague sensation'. Later: I was wrong, thank goodness, about his early death, thanks to a Google search, since many people have an internet footprint: lo and behold, a photo of him, immediately recognisable, living not all that far from me.

Now, to the inside of the jutting wall between the toilet and kitchen:

Item: number 21 out of an edition of 75: a letterpress poster printed by Asa Benveniste and others on 'January 31, the Year of the Ox' at Trigram Press, 15 Southwark Street. [*fig. 124*] [*This is a beautiful image, sombre and severe: it consists of a poem by Asa with four insects alongside. At the house in Upper Holloway, back in the mid-seventies, Yves Bonnefoy gestured in its direction, and I sensed it was the artwork he liked best. Asa was an American Sephardi with celebrated ancestors, including great rabbinical scholars and printers, one of whom printed a Venice Talmud in the sixteenth or seventeenth century. The family originated from Narbonne, where there had been a Jewish kingdom in the eighth century. He could be a difficult poet and, indeed, a difficult man, but he was a central figure on the small-press scene, exceptional in that, like a fellow Sephardi Guy Lévis-Mano in Paris, he was a printer as well as a publisher and poet. After Asa's divorce from Pip, he married the Swedish poet Agneta Falk but sadly spent his last years afflicted with severe diabetes that eventually involved amputation, Latterly he lived,* and died, in Hebden Bridge, a well-known centre for poetry and art. I have great affection for and good memories of the small- press world, which Menard was part of, but small presses have a natural life. As I said earlier, I no longer get a buzz from being a publisher. Without the buzz, the adrenalin doesn't flow, and without the adrenalin there is not the commitment to the work, much of which is tedious but without which the interesting side – editing the books, meeting writers and artists, etc. – could not happen.

Recently I went with Z. Kotowicz to a book launch near Trigram's old premises. A fine new small press, Waywiser, run by Philip Hoy, was bringing out the posthumous memoir of Richard Wollheim, a brilliant philosopher, whose writing on art is essential reading, along with that of Berger, John Golding, Arikha and others. Kotowicz and I pushed off for dinner and ended up not in our regular haunt Caprini opposite Waterloo Station but in a small Italian restaurant near Drury Lane called San Francesco. The Sicilian patron delivered himself of a rant – we were the only people there – about education, how his own baptismal certificate was required before his daughter could go to a Catholic secondary school in London but the church back in Sicily was bombed during the war, the papers lost, etc. As he left he told the waiter to give us a drink on the house.]

Item: letterpress poster from Skelton's Press: *The Practice of Printing.* [*By accident rather than design, this poster sits next to Asa Benveniste's. Hand printed by Chris Skelton, it is a beautiful text by the distinguished American printer Daniel Berkeley Updike.*]

Item: collage and painting dated 1970 and entitled *Moroc* [*sic*], Brian Williams. [*I bought this painting from the artist himself, whom I met when I was working in the Covent Garden Bookshop. The poet Elaine Randell worked there too and, through me, met her first husband, the late Barry Macsweeney, whose pamphlet on Thomas Chatterton Menard Press published. Did Brian perhaps work in the print department or was he one of the many characters who wandered in – people with all kinds of agendas and business to conduct with one of the principals, Dr or Mrs Nothmann, or their equally idiosyncratic sidekick John Wantoch? That was one strange place, one strange set-up, a perfect nexus for Iain Sinclair or Alan Wall to fictionalise. Change the names and location and no one would know the place had not been invented by a London biblio-mythographer.*]

The last wall has an etching by Brian Coffey, a drawing by Martin Wiener and two pressed and framed botanical specimens, a gift from Michel Couturier. One of them is inscribed 'Polysiphonia elongella', which is a kind of seaweed and looks like human hair. The other is an unidentified leaf. Michel's grandmother made these in Orleans when she was a girl, at some point in the period between the end of the Paris Commune and the early years of the Belle Epoque. I accept that this is a picturesque rather than scientific way of identifying her generation, but even to type the words gives me a buzz; all the same I resist the temptation to riff a solo about Rimbaud or Proust. Michel grew up in Orleans, where he knew Georges Bataille around 1951 when the latter was working there as a librarian.

And so we have reached the end of the walls. But there remain the kitchen door and a few more visual items hanging from the bookcases that continue along the wall between the kitchen door and the front door of the flat. On the kitchen door is a 3000-year calendar I bought in Ukraine and another poster poem by Asa Benveniste. Beneath these is a hook Nathaniel made at school on which hang my anorak, my raincoat and my leather jacket.

Hanging from shelf brackets are several small and flimsy tin cutouts of Mexican folk figures sent as presents by Homero and Betty Aridjis, friends from the 1960s with whom I remain in contact. Although Homero has a classic Mexican face – far more Indian than Octavio Paz's – the younger poet is half Greek. Like Octavio, Pablo Neruda, Pablo Armando Fernandez, George Seferis and others, Aridjis served as ambassador, in his case to Holland and other countries and, latterly, to UNESCO in Paris. Betty is a Jewish New Yorker. Theirs, like that of Octavio and Marie-Jose Paz, is a classic complementary union. Close by these Mexican cutouts are two attractive egg-shaped sculptures, again provenance forgotten.

On the shelves in front of the books are two small collages by the late Michael Thorp, artist and publisher in Durham. He ran Cloud, the smallest of small presses, so small that when things went wrong, as they do sometimes, between publisher and author, between idea and reality, there was not even the minimal space to regather his forces, so he had to close the press down: fell the shadow, indeed. But Cloud left its mark, a good and truthful deed in a world of number. A tiny engraving of a Strasbourg street scene completes the works. I picked this up in a secondhand bookshop in Strasbourg, while in the city for the launch of

Yves Bonnefoy's eightieth birthday book published by the university press. Its charismatic head until recently, the former President of the University, is a compelling and forceful personality Professor Lucien Braun, who spends every evening playing harpsichord. He is a philosopher and art historian. I tried and failed to find an English publisher for a translation of his fascinating illustrated work on the figure of the philosopher in art, *Iconographie et philosophie*. [*Later: he died in 2020.*]

Before we reach the end of this journey around the hall, I list bits and pieces that live on a bookshelf by the front door, where we began:

Item: keys to my neighbour's flat.
Item: Blu-Tack.
Item: visiting cards for local taxi firms.
Item: Parker propelling pencil that belonged to my father.

Many years ago, I Blu-Tacked two posters to the front door, after removing the dartboard on which Nathaniel and I used to exercise our skill: plenty of pinpricks in the door suggest our aim could have been improved. One poster is from Jerusalem: 'In London it is Charles Dickens House. In Paris it is Victor Hugo House. In Jerusalem you visit Agnon's House.' Agnon was a great writer even though Victor Gollancz, according to his quondam employee the late Giles Gordon, groaned when the novelist received the Nobel Prize, for it meant he could not drop him: 'Each title sold two hundred copies. Now they will sell three hundred.' There were rumours that Amichai would share the prize with the Syrian-born poet Adonis, but I suspect Israel will not receive another Nobel literature prize until there is peace. Lastly, we find Menard's certificate of business registration, although I do not have the faintest idea what privileges or responsibilities this confers. I do remember my father pressing on me the fact that any debts run up by Menard were my own personal debts since Menard was not a limited company. Menard has reached the end of the road, and I have reached the end of the hall. Soon it will be time to embark on the lounge.

Lounge

Lounge **was mainly written when my working desk was still in the lounge itself and my books had not yet been terminally disturbed by hands-on research for** *Silent Conversations* **(see note at the beginning of the present work). Several years on, the mess throughout the flat remains, although there has been some moving around of deckchairs on the future** *Titanic*.

You have now visited all my rooms, except the first one on the left as you walk along the hall from the front door. Treading softly, and carefully avoiding the obstacles, you doubtless remain astonished that anyone can live in this mess. Surely, you tell yourself, the lounge is a sanctuary, a sacred grove, a place to receive visitors. But *hôte* means guest and host in French and sadly I feel like an uninvited guest. Yes, the lounge, like the rest of the flat, is a mess, a *balagan*, to use the expressive Polish/Yiddish word that entered the Hebrew language at some point.

The flat's state undoubtedly reflects, but also feeds back to, my chaotic mind. Collage or montage is what I generate in writing, given this mindset, and I have to make the best, or the most, of it. I wish I knew why I put obstacles in my own way – the work is difficult enough without that – and the state of mind has nothing to do with 'the fascination of what's difficult', to quote Yeats. When I was young, my father told me to keep notes loose-leaf rather than in a notebook. I think he got this bad idea from academic friends, one in particular, whose research was recorded on index cards, appropriately enough for their kind of work, but not for a writer. Ever since, for well over half a century, in pathetic obedience to what was never a command in the first place, I have failed to keep proper notebooks, and yet some of the writers I particularly cherish depend upon the habit more than most, or so I suspect: Barthes, Perec. If you throw into the pot the fact that one's brain moves faster than one's touch-typing fingers, you have a meta-mess. Maybe I should take up mind-mapping and hyper-texts. One form of invention resides in editing a pre-existing text. Collage rather than readymade is what I am talking about. I tape-recorded my paternal grandfather back in 1975, and could therefore write the poem, constructed from his own words, which will be the centrepiece of my eventual book about him. Nearly twenty-five years after he died at ninety-nine in 1980, I began the process of transcribing the tapes, spurred on by an invitation from Iain Sinclair to submit work to a London anthology, *City of Disappearances*, in which an extract appeared.[91] The poet John Seed is a master of this kind of writing: see his 'Reznikoff /Benjamin book of the London Blitz', *Smoke Rising*. Svetlana Alexievich, born in my ancestral Stanisławów in western Ukraine, writes wonderful polyphonic books based on hundreds of interviews, such as *Secondhand Time*.

Right-Hand Wall

On entering the room, you will see that the entire right hand wall is covered with books: there must be a couple of thousand, like pretty maids or toy soldiers, all in rows. After the one and only occasion the flat was repainted, I sorted the books into categories. These just about survive: books taken down are rarely put back in the proper place, but sadly as a 'connoisseur of chaos' I have no 'idea of order' and the books that remain where they should be are the ones I have not consulted since the repainting or, possibly, took the trouble to replace correctly, on a rare good day. Whatever, enough original order survives for me to name the categories found on these particular shelves.

Item: books on music, cinema, theatre and art
Item: French books in their series
Item: Russian books
Item: social anthropology and sociology
Item: poetry books

One of the poetry books on the right-hand wall is the *Collected Poems* of John Masefield, a book I have rarely opened. On 2 September 2, 2020, I heard Jeffrey Wainwright launch his fine new book of poems, *As Best We Can*, online. This contains references to the Festival of Britain in 1951, an important celebration on the South Bank, funded and promoted by the post-war Labour government in order to generate national pride. The implied social(ist) vision was much disapproved of by Churchill, and his government demolished the Dome and Skylon after returning to power in 1951. ('Churchill's vengeful barge', writes Wainwright). I emailed Jeffrey and our fellow Carcanet poet Jon Glover immediately after the launch to tell them that I had gone with my father to the South Bank during the Festival, and that he had bought me a book in the Royal Festival Hall, namely the Masefield. We certainly went to the Festival because I remember the Skylon and Dome and Royal Festival Hall, but inside the book is the receipt, which is very revealing: it proves I have a false memory about the date of purchase, which was 1955, November 16. This was two weeks after my bar mitzvah and it was a Wednesday. During all these years, I conflated the two visits to the Royal Festival Hall, and did not open the book. [*fig. 125*]

Did we go in the evening after I came home from school and he came home from work? Perhaps we arranged to meet at the RFH, which was a few hundred yards from my school and a short drive from his office. Note that the book was paid for with a book token: 12/6: twelve shillings and sixpence in old money. About fifteen pounds in today's money. 12/6 was surely an odd amount to give as a present. I imagine a couple, invited guests (or the parents of a friend) arguing whether to give me ten or fifteen shillings, and splitting the difference. I note too that the price of the book was twenty-five shillings. So either the book was half price or, more likely, my father paid the balance. Why Masefield? Certainly because he was Poet Laureate. Years later my father would become Ted Hughes's accountant, financial adviser and friend. Another book we bought on the same occasion was Louis Untermeyer's once ubiquitous *Albatross Book of Living Verse*, which is falling apart from over-use, the opposite of the Masefield book, although when I read poetry to Paula over the phone I always, at her request, include 'Sea Fever', which we both learned by heart at school. The end of the collected poems has an 'Index of Beginnings', surely a lovelier phrase than 'Index of First Lines'.

Against these shelves leans the loft pole, which enables me to open the trap door to the loft – shared with my friendly downstairs neighbour Elena – outside my front door, and pull down the stair ladder. The loft, as I wrote in another chapter, is a third repository room, and the only one with a good excuse: it was never intended for any other purpose. [*fig. 126*]

Hi-Fi and Furniture (with a Deathbed Fantasy)

Here, by the right-hand wall is my hi-fi, with the radio section set permanently to Radio 3. (The small radio in the kitchen moves between Radio 4 and Radio 3, depending on whether I want to listen to a talk or music or while doing my exercises or cooking. Today, for example, Boxing Day, I shall listen at 4 o'clock, on the exercise bike, to an interview with Ruth Rendell. Later: a new digital radio is set to Radio 4 Extra, for the *Goon Show* and *Take it from Here*, etc.) The lounge hi-fi has a gramophone and a cassette section, naturally; but strongly competing with Radio 3 are my CDs. Even as I type, I am listening to my favourite music – Beethoven piano sonatas – first Svyatoslav Richter and then Daniel Barenboim.

The music brings on a deathbed fantasy: I slip in and out of the personal, the professional and the political: I pray that that my family – children and grandchildren and siblings – and friends, are safe and living peaceful and productive lives. I think of Paula in her studio, working her pastels or drawing Lila; I think of loved ones who have predeceased me; I contemplate the books I have written and those I have failed to write; I want to believe that the world will turn its back on complacency, denial, stupidity, fanaticism and evil by setting in train an international and collective response to the horrendous problems that face us, rather than dumping the work on unborn generations who will curse our incorrigible leaders.

The USA, along with China, sets the agenda. Untamed and unregulated markets (otherwise known as socialism for the rich and powerful) are already proving to be the death of those living in the wrong parts of the world, and this will spread until we are all engulfed, even without natural disasters. Radical social democracy remains my creed and some version of that is our only hope, even if it is hope in the dark, the title of Rebecca Solnit's essential book (2016). The battle for scarce resources in a worsening physical and security environment is the matrix of the USA's political economy as currently envisaged by the military-industrial complex responsible for the country's energy and defence policies, a nexus warned against by Eisenhower in his eloquent farewell speech of January 1961, whose sixtieth anniversary will doubtless be commemorated by that vital resource, the Bulletin of Atomic Scientists: their doomsday clock is currently at one hundred seconds to midnight, the closest it has ever been (see website).

Governments sometimes get their act together when the crisis is of the magnitude or at least of the nature of the 2004 tsunami in South Asia, a crisis generated by a phenomenon apparently unconnected to the political economy. The world rallies to mitigate the worst effects of natural catastrophes. And if the richest countries, the ones who sell arms and intervene militarily, had spent even one per cent of their budgets on warning systems if not prevention, much more could have been done in advance. The crises that will face us in the years ahead need to be addressed as if they are happening *now* (which they are), but such a radical approach requires leadership that is not on offer. Governing elites and corporations in the USA, China and elsewhere, have created a virtual imperialism.

The restructuring of the Russian economy, under American guidance, was not done in the interests of ordinary people. Will China succeed in reconstructing its economy – with a green tinge – during its present governance? The industrialisation of the third world means that the climate will get worse and worse, since traditional industrialisation, we are told, requires fossil fuels. The problem is that while charity is appropriate and on offer when there is natural catastrophe, a solution to the man-made problems of the world requires taxing the incomes and moderating the life-style of the *haves*, and that requires a socialist or genuinely social-democratic leadership, not a triangulating ratcheting of conservative policies.

Enough of politics. I am slipping away – caught between my living and my dead – to the sound of piano music. Debussy? Beethoven? No, it has to be Schubert's final sonata. Paula's husband Victor Willing in his last months listened to Beethoven's late string quartets. Vic knew about deathbeds without fantasy. His life and work and death are close to the centre of Paula's story. By extension, they are part of mine, but I never met him and must be careful not to take the idea of extension to the extreme, lest I dilute the real presence at the heart of light and darkness. And, lying there on the deathbed, perhaps I shall have sufficient awareness to reread for the last time *Psalms* and *Koheleth*. Yes, if I have cancer, hopefully pain-free; no, if I have Alzheimer's. What follows from this fantasy? Simple: do not waste time. Before it is too late, learn from Paula and others to concentrate on the essentials.

The hi-fi equipment stands on a beautifully designed 1930s trolley, a wedding present to my parents in 1938. My sister Annie has the desk my father was given as a bar mitzvah present in 1927 by his cabinetmaker uncle and cousin Ike Flashtig, but this trolley is something else, West End rather than East End. On top of the speakers and the hi-fi itself are CDs, documents, books and other bits and pieces. One of the CDs is '1935' which I bought copies of in Winterthur next door to Zurich, during one of our holidays,[92] as a seventieth birthday present for Paula herself, Dan Weissbort, Eddie Linden, Moris Farhi, Stephen Cang and Tom Rosenthal. 2005 is a vintage year. [*Later: Tom and Dan and Moris have now left the conversation.*] Other friends of mine, in their forties when I first knew them, are now dead or in their late eighties. As of now, the latest old timers are from the generation of my 'older sibling figures' rather than the quasi-parental ones. Of my objectively old friends, the poet Carl Rakosi died in 2004 aged a hundred, and the painter Fermin Rocker in the same year aged ninety-five. But thanks to the biblical three score and ten there is a particular resonance about reaching seventy.

An LP is on the turntable, Lipatti playing Chopin's first piano concerto, which works beautifully, although the composer's particular and peculiar genius was for short forms. Would a novel by Borges, among the greatest short-story writers, work? Not on the evidence of the stories. And his Introduction to *Fictions* suggests that he knew his *imaginaire* required the short haul. His stories are compressed novels. Bruno Schulz's only novel went missing. He too was a great short story-writer. Would the novel have proved to be a disappointment? Would that we could pass judgement!

I shall not itemise the stuff perched on the speakers and hi-fi since, unlike the books in the surviving categories on the shelves, it has no particular reason to be there and one of my rules is that inventory is taken only of things that do have a reason to be where they are. Let's take a look at other aspects and vistas in this room. There are two rugs on the floor, placed where they are to cover stains on the light-beige carpet I chose with Audrey at Jones Brothers in Holloway Road around 1986. The first rug, also beige and brown, I bought in Crete during a holiday tour with her of the island in the late 1980s. The other rug is from a wonderful shop in Edinburgh called Rani. This was towards the end of my month as a fellow at Hawthornden Castle, south of Edinburgh, in 1993. I bought all my Chanukah presents at Rani, and went to far more trouble than I have ever gone, before or since. I chose carefully for my children and mother and sisters and their children and for Ana, a Polish student and family cleaning lady, who was flat-sitting for me while I was away. I wonder what became of Ana. She once saw my aunt lighting Sabbath candles and remarked that her Catholic grandmother did that too. It turned out that the maternal great-grandmother had been Jewish and hidden during the war and Ana had no idea that technically she was Jewish, even though her parents were practising Catholics. She got very excited by this. I advised her to handle her discovery carefully and to treat it as an adventure rather than an existential commitment, lest possible pain for her parents and herself ensue.

Other items in the room include three leather armchairs, the two unbroken ones being virtually the only good furniture in the entire flat, a television and video machine and a piano which has real ivory keys but which is beyond repair. I tell myself I play the piano. Well then, if I'm not fooling myself, it's time to buy one that works. Mr Fairey, the cockney piano tuner, is too ill to help. Get your act together, dude. You need to find a non-verbal hobby, even if it means spending yet more time in this room. Let this lounge become a real lounge where you can relax, eat dinner in front of the television unencumbered by piles of books and papers across the floor. One day there will have to be a reckoning, lest I break my neck.

[NB This was written before I moved my computer to Naomi's old room.] The computer table, which once belonged to Claude Royet-Journoud, is full of papers, files, books, postcards, remotes. To the right of the table is my black Anglepoise lamp, which belongs with Routemaster Buses and Parker 51 pens as design icons. Not that I live in a retropolis of the mind, perish the thought. The computer is the second one to be installed by Ivor, my computer wizard, who is always available on the end of a phone with his free helpline when a techno-twit is in trouble. Occasionally he comes round to sort out the machine, advise on expanding its memory, teach its master new tricks. Ivor is also a saloon-bar pianist and occasional pharmacist. I found him through an advertisement he placed in a newspaper when I was in a state of distress after my first two computers gave up the ghost without hope of redemption. He set me up again and eventually introduced me to the Internet and, six months later, to email.

I shall not dwell on these two revolutions, save to say that not only have they changed my life, I believe they have affected the very fabric of my mind and my imagination, and, if mine, then surely that of others, and if enough others, then there is critical mass, indeed critical-mass conversion. Provided that the Internet and email are our servants and not our masters, obsessional surfing and correspondence indulged in to sidetrack oneself from real work need not occur. One's day begins with overnight emails, not with the post. If I could master even a small percentage of the computer's possibilities, I suspect that I would find myself creating hyper-texts, a modality of cybernetic communication that my collage-based rather than narrative-based literary mind could adopt or adapt for its own purposes and that I am beginning to explore, encouraged by the thoughts of Hillis Miller on this topic.

Paula, on the other hand, would rather I wrote more like Henry Miller than Hillis Miller. Besides, my distinction between narrative and collage or indeed montage simplifies a complex argument about the spectrum of artistic communication. How ashamed I am of the younger me, 'my conscience or my vanity appalled': Yeats understood. No longer shall I go about parroting simplistic oppositions (doubtless stolen from an article or book) such as: Antonioni's films are prose, whereas Fellini's are poetry. Now I know that it is a question of emphasis, rather than either/or.

What happens now, at this moment in time, is that, having heard the post drop through the letter box and the phone ring, I realise I need my second cup of coffee and, needless to say, I check the computer – but there are no new emails. Aharon Komem in Israel, the Shakespeare translator and poet with whom I worked on translations of his own poems, has not yet replied to my early-morning copy-editing comments about his scholarly essay on Jacques's monologue in *As You Like It*: he has noticed that in 'they have their exits and their entrances' the translators into French, German, Russian and Hebrew *all* turn the phrase round, as if *not* to begin with 'entrances' were counter-intuitive and Shakespeare did not know what he was doing. I check Yves Bonnefoy's more recent translation: he too does the same! I have offered to email Komem's text to Yves, who might well comment and indeed offer a *mea culpa* for not noticing the reversal which Komem tells us is a figure of speech called hyperbaton, and I shall email writer or academic friends in Portugal (Paula's scholar cousin Ana Morais), Spain (John Butt at the Spanish Faculty of King's College London) and Slovenia (Ifigenija Simonovic) to advise me whether translators have done the same thing in their languages. Aharon is on to something, although Christopher Middleton, in a reply to a recent letter, and Alan Wall reckon that Shakespeare's reason for the reversal was simply metrical. Even so, the unanimity among translators is eloquent. I shall not reply immediately to other substantive emails sitting in the inbox. Manousha Lisboa will have to wait for my thoughts on her essay about Paula's *Life of the Virgin* series commissioned by President Jorge Sampaio for the chapel in his official palace. And I want to give some thought to Richard Berengarten's current reflection – influenced by Levinas and Derrida – on the nature of 'gift' before replying to him. [*Portugal, Spain and Slovenia have come through: all the translators perpetrate the same reversal. Yves Bonnefoy tells me he is intrigued and will certainly comment on this remarkable phenomenon once Aharon Komem's article is published.*]

I am about to go into the kitchen to fix the coffee but, of course, the phone rings again. It is Alan Wall, to tell me what I already knew from Paula, namely that Susan Sontag has died, and so in addition to the *Guardian* I shall buy the other papers today for their obituaries of this woman. She was a first-rate non-fiction writer, a distinguished mind, and a public intellectual of quality. She succumbed to her cells. Harold Pinter quoted his nurse as saying: 'Cancer cells are cells that have forgotten how to die.'

Balcony and Rotating Bookcases

It requires great skills of navigation to manoeuvre one's way to an important feature in the room's landscape: the door which opens on to my balcony. Paula always heads for the balcony, courtesy of the weather, when she comes round. It is her favourite corner of the flat. In the late afternoon, seated at the little table, enjoying the ancient listed tree in the garden and surrounded by the flowers in the rotating boxes Chalkie constructed during one of his many minor but important interventions in the flat (and which Chris, then in number 6 – whose balcony is as close to mine as an adjacent theatre box, – would stock for me on his annual trip to the garden centre), she sips a glass of champagne. Later, when Chris's sister-in-law inherited the house of her old aunt, Paula acquired a tiger's-head rug which she put in a couple of pictures, including *Life of the Virgin*.

Paula wastes nothing.[93] She sees an object; she senses that one day she will use it; if it is for sale she buys it and it sits in the studio until, lo and behold, it generates a story or is generated by an already started story. Little by little, you are drawn in, metaphorically speaking, and sometimes literally. When my beloved Phoenix Cinema (ex-Rex) in East Finchley was being refurbished, they were selling off the old red plush seats and I bought two for Paula as a present. I patiently await their arrival in a picture. But they won't get into the lithograph she's working on at the moment, involving a man, yours truly, laying eggs... Paula herself made the mannikins that ended up in her *Pillowman* triptych, inspired by Martin McDonagh's superb eponymous play, which we saw at the Cottesloe. It's not so much that they keep still, rather that they can be manipulated into positions human models can't maintain, and possess a different kind of expressivity.

Perched on the floor by the French windows are two rotating bookcases. I bought one of them very cheaply in the late 1960s in a shop off Prince of Wales Road, opposite the swimming baths where I interviewed a young cross-channel swimmer for a children's magazine which I briefly edited for the educational publisher Mary Glasgow and Baker. The pieces are attractive, although they take up a lot of room, as do my Globe Wernicke bookcases. Neither kind of bookcase was intended for a lounge in a flat. They presuppose hardbacks, a house, and another age. Globe Wernickes, now collectors' items, are described on Internet sites as stackable lawyers' bookcases; they fit together and look solid and reassuring. Mine are against the wall by the French windows, facing the door as you come into the room.

As you face the French windows, the wall to the left used to contain the fireplace, now out of commission and hidden behind my piano. Above the piano is a painting I shall return to. On both sides of the jutting-out part of the wall, appear the two almost symmetrical remaining sections of the wall, covered by bookshelves from ceiling to floor. As with the right-hand wall photographed above, something of the categorisation of the books survives today. Certain configurations and shapes remain identical or virtually the same. But the photographed pile of books by Charles Reznikoff – regularly consulted during a certain phase of my work – is no longer on the right of the top shelf. This has created a typical problem. Long ago I had an idea for a one-woman recital by Paula's actress daughter Victoria Willing involving a particular book by Reznikoff, but where tell me where is that good idea now? Ah, the obstacles I create, the rubbish I shall have to *work through* before I sort out my mind.

Treasure Shelf

Three of the shelves on the right-hand side of the piano contain not books but 'treasures' [*fig. 127*] – bits and pieces, bric-a-brac, I acquired over the years. I select:

Item: scimitar and knobkerry

Item: silver sovereigns for the wedding of Charles and Diana and the death of the Duke of Windsor. [*I do not have the faintest idea where these come from. They are not the kind of thing I buy. They are not the kind of thing people give me.*]

Item: broken ceramic ashtray from the old city of Jerusalem

fig. 125

fig. 126

fig. 127

fig. 128

Item: Roman coin. [*I found this on the beach at Ashkelon where Claude Vigée and his family took me for a barbecue in 1969 during my first visit to Israel. Claude told me on the phone that we must wait for a rainy day and go next morning. After rain, you find interesting things, even valuable antiques. I wrote a long poem – dedicated to the Vigées – about these two visits, which was published in a magazine edited by Maurice Carr, who was, he told me in his office, the nephew of Isaac Bashevis Singer.*]

(*extract*)[94]
I stumble on a coin
shaken to the surface

by rain and wind. We polish it
until reliefs and contours show.
....

Ah, the season of
the dying of the oranges
is the season of
the budding on the wild vines.

Item: Moss Hall Junior School chess and soccer champions' badges. [*It's time to give these to Nathaniel, now ensconced in his own house.*]

Item: non-Fabergé eggs of various descriptions. [*I am three handshakes from Fabergé: my relative in Phoenix, Arizona, the late Alexander Kower, a jeweller of distinction, was the grandson of a jeweller trained by Fabergé. This forebear was that rare specimen, a Jew at the court of the Czar in Petersburg. When I was in Los Angeles on a visit to Zygfryd Rudolf in 1964, he gave me the money for a ticket and ordered me to fly to Phoenix for twenty-four hours. There I talked with Alex, who gave me a brooch Zygfryd had commissioned for my mother, who was always a great favourite of his from his wartime days in London when my parents were the only members of the family who appreciated the qualities disguised by a difficult personality. Alex had made jewellery for Elizabeth Taylor, who spent some of her early years in Wildwood Road, Hampstead Garden Suburb. If you know it's there, you can spot a blue plaque right at the top of the house.*]

Added in August 2020: After Zygfryd died, his family sent me his possessions, including his Omega fobwatch dating back to World War I, in which Zygfryd saw service under Emperor Franz-Josef. During lockdown, something strange happened. Four of my watches – Ralph Leigh's gift and my bar mitzvah watch, both discussed earlier in this book, plus my father's watch and one that Paula gave me – all stopped working. The fifth, Zygfryd's, was never used. When I picked it up, the stopped watch registered precisely the right time which, in normal circumstances, happens twice every twenty-four hours, regular as clockwork. I wound it up. It works perfectly. [fig. 128]

Item: nickel silver memorial coin for Lord Mountbatten. [*Stardust trigger of memory: In 1979, when Lord Mountbatten was assassinated, Sir Martin Ryle and Enoch Powell both believed that this had been perpetrated not by the IRA as reported but by British Intelligence – because of a speech Mountbatten gave to the Stockholm Peace Research Institute (SIPRI), written or drafted for him by Solly Zuckerman. Mountbatten argued sophisticatedly against official attitudes to nuclear weapons; coming from him, this could not be dismissed as CND propaganda. It is my greatest regret as a political publisher[95] that, a few years later, I did not publish Enoch Powell's writings on defence when I could have done so, partly because of his views on immigrants, partly because I was running out of steam and almost burned out as an obsessed publisher on the nuclear issue. Martin Ryle wrote to me about Mountbatten and said Fleet Street had a huge unpublished dossier on the matter and warned me not to discuss it with him on the phone, which he believed was tapped. I raised it with Solly but he dismissed it all as conspiracy theory. The tapping business bothered me. It reminded me of the occasion when I picked up the phone and found myself speaking to the military police at an MOD centre near Mill Hill, not far from where I live. As I recall, the conversation made me feel that it was not a coincidental misrouting but a knock-on effect involving a more important person than me. I became a touch paranoid, which is always a good thing, and checked my telephone points and leads for what one could call tell-tale signs, and contacted my only MP friend, a privy councillor, the late Reg Freeson, who had been Minister of Housing until James Callaghan fired him on becoming Prime Minister in 1976. Reg contacted MI5 (he did not ask me first) and they invited me to come in for a chat. I agreed; I was intrigued, and I had nothing to hide. Doubtless they were aware of my association with senior establishment figures at odds with* the received wisdom, and they surely knew about my long correspondence with a civil servant at the MOD which began after Martin Ryle wrote to Michael Heseltine, the Minister of Defence. Heseltine replied to Ryle, an establishment VIP. Ryle, being Ryle, answered him. Heseltine in turn replied, this time via the civil servant and from then on I continued the good-natured correspondence with the latter, all about the famous concept of deterrence.

I heard the then high priest of deterrence and guardian of the grail, Michael Quinlan of the MOD, debate with Bruce Kent of CND at an off the record meeting organised by Donald Reeve at St James's, Piccadilly. The two had a lot in common, despite opposing views: they were brilliant intellectual Catholics, perhaps even Jesuits. In retirement, like so many decision makers including Robert Macnamara, Michael Quinlan went on to write articles at odds with his former public stance. Tony Blair's position, although he appeared to be intellectually persuaded concerning climate change, was well to the right even of the old pro-nuclear right-wing of the Labour Party when it came to nuclear weapons (at least in public): his position was a deep affront to educated intelligence and clear thought. I had an interesting conversation with the young MI5 woman in a nondescript building near the British Council in Trafalgar Square, and explained that I was part of establishment opposition to the madness of our policies. I am ashamed to say I forget if I raised the question of phone-tapping, but why would they invite me in for a chat if something was not going on? You don't have to be paranoid to know that something is always going on. The world is heading for disaster. Watch the rich and powerful head for New Zealand, but this time there will be no escape, except technically, for there is no life in de luxe lockdown, whether in New Zealand or in space.]

Item: Ifigenija Simonovic pottery: a mug. [I wrote about this poet and potter elsewhere in the flat, I commissioned a coffee set from her for my son and daughter-in-law as a wedding present. This mug is in permanent non-use on the treasure shelf. It has one of her famous spelling mistakes in the design: among all the words inside and outside the mug, we find 'Persuation'.]

Item: Paula Rego mug. [One of many such items produced in Portugal, some in hand-painted limited editions, others mass-produced. This particular one, of a cat and grasshopper, is from Paula's Lisbon gallery, Galeria 111.]

Item: Ship in a bottle

Item: A found sculpture. [*I combined a pebble that looks like a pair of testicles with an antique schnozzle from an old jug. Together they form a perfect uncircumcised cock and balls, a subject on which my grandfather waxed eloquent as he recalled watching operations for syphilis on unfortunate colleagues during his period as a messenger in the Austro-Hungarian army.*][96]

Item: JNF Centenary (2001) Collecting Box. [*Time was, every diaspora Jewish house had a collecting box for Erets Yisroel, the land of Israel. Ours was kept in the hall cupboard, on the shelf above the coats, the tennis rackets and the Jokari set. This one is grey, but traditionally they were blue and white, and the money went to the Yishuv, the pre-state Jewish collectivity in what later became Israel. Recent Israeli historians such as Benny Morris have shown that the version of history we defended in our Hashomer Hatzair (socialist Zionist) days was not accurate and that Israel's foundation was far crueller to the Palestinians than we knew or believed or wanted to believe. But I still adhere to the view that the pass we have arrived at today was not inevitable, and that if both sides had had better and braver leaders, things could have been different. Rabin bit the bullet and that, very simply, was why he was murdered – bit the bullet indeed a second time – by clerical fascists on his own side. Yes, Rabin was slowly and painfully (see his face in the famous photograph with Arafat and Clinton)) moving towards an understanding with the Palestinians and a serious attitude to peacemaking: he understood that Israel was the stronger party and that it was therefore in its own interest to be magnanimous. Even Anthony Julius in a remarkable pamphlet, which in his customarily and lawyerly brilliant way makes conceptual clarifications concerning things that tend to get conflated, has had to concede that this is truly a conflict between two rights, although he does not go far enough in assigning greater responsibility to the stronger party. An earlier generation of secular progressives was in denial (Golda Meir) about the reality, whereas secular conservatives, including Begin and Sharon, understood the reality and wanted to deny statehood to the Palestinians, falsely claiming it was them or us and treating the problem, in short, as a zero-sum game. They used and were used by religious Zionists (a vociferous minority even in the Orthodox community) and later came up against demographic and other realities, the fruits of their own irresponsibility and short-sightedness. Ben-Gurion was a* leader in the mould of Roosevelt, Churchill and de Gaulle – except for his failure to treat with the Palestinians, which is a huge 'except'. But he did say after the 1967 Six-Day War, when he was no longer in office: 'Give back everything except Jerusalem'. By not putting pressure on Israel, America is not doing what is essential: to save Israel from itself – unlike the time when the first George Bush threatened the cessation of subsidies if Shamir did not go to the Madrid Peace Conference. So much good comes out of Israel, in medicine, science, agriculture and the arts for example, that we never hear about in public. I hope I live to see the day when the good makes the news. Add that to the wish list in my deathbed fantasy earlier.]

Item: pair of gold cufflinks and single sterling-silver cufflink, present from Paula. [*The second one went AWOL. I have two other single cufflinks. What is it with cufflinks, or with me? Perhaps they were stolen by a one-armed bandit. I could set a trend by wearing odd couples. The pair was given to me by my father. How did people fasten them in the old days? They are very small with a very short chain between the two parts of each link. Perhaps shirts and fingers were thinner. Perhaps I am kack-handed.*]

Item: Megillah or scroll. [*This is the Scroll of Esther, one of the five Megilloth (the others being Song of Songs, Ruth, Ecclesiastes and Lamentations). It belonged to my maternal grandfather Meyer Rosenberg, and is read on the festival of Purim, when children stamp their feet and wave rattles every time the name of wicked Haman is mentioned. My brother-in-law Mike Krom has Meyer's tallis (prayer shawl), rightly given to him as someone more likely than me to wear it.*]

Item: Remains of a candle. [*The candle, from an elaborate mould, was given to me by the Czechoslovak students I was teaching English in London in 1968 (see earlier). They supported Dubček and I promised them I would not light the candle until Czechoslovakia was free. I remember our slogan: 'Neither Moscow nor Washington'. This was one of the three major shaping events of my young adult life, as I have written elsewhere in this book: The Six Day War in 1967, the May Events in Paris in 1968 and the Prague Invasion in 1968. Later shaping events: fast forward to Cruise Missiles and fears of Nuclear Winter, and then to 9/11. Later still: Shaping events have become the default setting and Ubu-Johnson is in 10 Downing Street.*]

Item: pastel crayon. [*I took this from Paula's studio, as a souvenir, after she finished a picture for which I had posed: the right-hand panel of the triptych* After Hogarth. *Perhaps it was the very one she handed me so that, at my request, I could fill in a bit of undercoat background. That was a thrill! The studio world is a child of Paula's mind, a real place yet one that doubles with the productions of her spirit. She continually invents it, and is continually invented by it. Upstairs, a tiny bedroom has been created. In the huge double-roomed studio are a small kitchen, bathroom facilities, and an office. The large studio space hosts or indeed is a matrix of invention and discovery, projected from this most fertile of imaginations, and fed back to it in a creative dialectic, wondrous and inspiring.*][97]

Item: locket. [*A precious family heirloom given to me by my cousin, Irit, the sister of my cousin Jerzyk, about whom I wrote a book. He is the only recorded child suicide of the Holocaust. This locket contains a lock of his hair.*][98]

My piano, my poor old upright piano, long unplayed, and now indeed unplayable, is more than an item.. These days it serves as a second treasure shelf, both on top and on the cover that protects the keys. The piano stool contains what passes for my library of music scores. There are a number of pieces I can manage, and in the days when I tinkled the ivories I would play these pieces, over and over. This was a real hobby, concentrated relaxation, since reading books that are not professionally obligatory – one of my greatest pleasures – is too close to what I do all the time to count as a hobby. Visiting museums and listening to music are not hobbies, defined as gratuitous activity (acte gratuit, quoi), pursued purely for pleasure: the reason they are not hobbies is that, while involving primary feeling and emotion, they also feed into my ongoing reflection and meditation on what it is to feel, and to be human. The same might be said of sex, and even red wine. And then there were the years, before my cross-trainer exercise machine took over, when I enjoyed running, especially if the endorphins kicked in. But running was always utilitarian, as was swimming. And so, if I no longer play the piano, what hobbies do I have? And if none, why not? Well, I have been known to watch television programmes other than news and documentaries (utilitarian) or plays and films (art)… Aha, my other hobby: watching test or county cricket – but never the one-day version – on television (followed a long way behind by tennis and soccer), with my son on the other end of the phone, both of us groaning when England perform badly. Sadly one can no longer watch cricket on a terrestrial channel. This is a disaster. So: no cricket, no piano, no nothing.

The solutions stare me in the face, like the late Horace who sat in my local High Street outside W.H. Smiths and looked up from his suitcase full of crayons and other possessions and, when he felt like it, eyeballed-passers by with his trademark words: 'And the best of British luck': yes, subscribe to Sky and buy a replacement piano. Neither is beyond my means, though at the moment both require mending my ways, for inertia and conservatism rule OK. 'What does not change/ is the will to change,' wrote Charles Olson. I wish. But, meanwhile, I shall list my repertoire, and one day, who knows, I may return to the piano – unless my downstairs neighbour Elena knocks on her ceiling, poor thing, to beg relief from the cacophony. The main repertoire seems always to have been there. I have no recollection of buying the sheet music, and yet I am certain nobody gave it to me.

Repertoire

Item: 'Yellow Bird'
Item: 'La Vie en rose'
Item: 'Where have all the flowers gone?'
Item: 'Sucu Sucu'
Item: *It's Easy to Play the Blues*

Item: Chopin *Waltzes.* [*This final item in the list has a dedication: '27/12/60/ To Tony / with affection from Aunt Freda and Uncle Leon/ on the occasion of your going to the Sorbonne'. Technically I was not going to the Sorbonne but to the British Institute in Paris, which was part of the University of London, but it felt like going to the Sorbonne; in those days the Institute was in the Quartier latin, rue de la Sorbonne. I wrote about my Paris stay[99] and mentioned that Leon gave me a book by Leonard Bernstein,* The Joy of Music, *as a present for that trip, but I overlooked the Chopin. Clearly I had been asked what I wanted, and was in a music phase. I had already bought my treasured*

LP of Lipatti playing the waltzes. Opus 34 Number 2 is the only one with fingerings pencilled in, in the hand of my piano teacher, Douglas Zanders, but dated the month after I returned from Paris, the summer of 1961, when I was also trying to polish up my rusty knowledge of Russian, in preparation for my ill-fated time, academically speaking, as a Cambridge undergraduate.]

Future Repertoire

Item: anthologies: *East-West Songs* (UNESCO), Community Song Tunes, Golden Hour of Melodies from the Overtures, Cole Porter made easy for the Accordeon, MicroJazz, Popular Jewish Songs, Twenty Jazz Piano Hits

Item: sheet music: 'Little white lies', 'Lullaby of Broadway', 'Exodus', 'Down town'

I turn now to the things that are on the piano, but not the accidental ones, put there in a typical moment of disorder by a SNAFU (situation normal all fucked up, army acronym spelled out for younger readers) mind engaged in an SAS obstacle exercise: SOS more likely, designed to make its owner's working life as difficult as possible. No, I turn to the things that I placed there with aesthetic intent. On the movable wooden frame, where you put the music you read from while playing the piano, are two tiles by Paula, one hand-painted, the other mass produced. *Azulejos* or painted tiles are a great Portuguese tradition.[100] Paula has resisted following the artists who have created tiles for Lisbon's underground tube system. At the Lisbon palace of the Marquis of Fronteira, there are celebrated and wonderful-seventeenth century tiles of animals dotted around the fabulous gardens. To his great credit, the eccentric and talented Marquis, when he came to restore his ancestral heritage, rather than make copies of historic old tiles, agreed to a suggestion that Paula make new ones for a bench that was beyond repair. The first of the two tiles I have here is of a hunter with a hare and scythe, the other, inspired by *The Dybbuk*, which we saw together, is of a pelican with his beak down the throat of a frog, a classic Rego use of animals to portray people, in this instance kissing and more.

The top of the piano is covered with CDs and books placed there by a preternaturally untidy person, but still visible are artworks and a huge and tottering unsorted pile of catalogues and papers, cuttings and leaflets about art, mainly but not exclusively Paula's. One picture has a jutting-out and painted-on frame protecting the canvas, and was posted to me from the East Village in Manhattan by the New York artist Linda Goldfine in 1966 when I was living in Notting Hill. Somewhere in this flat is 'The Linda Poem' in which I mistyped 'Do you know what time it is?' as 'Do you know what time is?' Next to Linda's painting are two I bought from Merlin James, part of a series of works on paper framed in glass-fronted boxes, and alongside them are four medallions by Irene Gunston commissioned by the British Museum. There is an etching sent to me by Mary Oppen, depicting six versions of the same bird. Lastly there is a fiftieth- birthday gift from Audrey – a fascinating painted empty wooden box (of tricks) that opens up, the images symbolising something I never figured out, just as it took several years for me to realise that three cassette compilations she gave me contained didactic intent in the juxtaposition of songs. [*Later: Audrey died on Christmas Day, 2020.*]

Paintings

Among Paula's works in the lounge are five on the wall to your left as you enter, and two leaning against the radiator below them. Here too are lithographs, *Ruth* and *Abraham*, by R. B. Kitaj, a reward for writing the catalogue essay of his 2001 show at the National Gallery. Colin Wiggins the Gallery's brilliant and engaging educationalist did an interview with him for the same catalogue, and also received two prints. After the private view, we phoned the painter from Trafalgar Square on the mobile of his assistant Tracy Bartley who had come from Los Angeles, with her new baby, to represent him.

For some years Kitaj and I corresponded sporadically. I had tea with him before he left England in 1997, having a few years earlier reviewed his *First Diasporist Manifesto* in the *Jerusalem Post*. On some level we understood each other, and I visited him in Los Angeles in 1998. I was struck by his book collection: I doubt that any other visual artist has had a library of non-art books of that extent and importance, but I might be talking through my hat. Just because others don't go public in the way K did, it does not mean they are not great readers. One whole room contained books on Judaic themes including anti-Semitism, and there was a photo of Ezra Pound, K's 'favourite antisemite'. We came to an agreement that I could edit K's letters and postcards to me and publish them in a small book: the deal was that I would not change a single word; however, I could move things round, which was what David Sylvester did with Francis Bacon, as revealed in the introduction to the third and best edition of their conversations. The correspondence eventually tailed off, mainly because K began writing his autobiography (published many years later) and also doing a book-length interview with Andrew Lambirth. These took up a lot of the *extra-studio* psychic energy he deployed in the early mornings when he strolled down to Westwood village high street near UCLA for breakfast and a period of writing on yellow legal notepads. The character named Craig in my novella *Pedraterra* is based on him.

Paula and K liked and respected each other. From time to time one of them asked a question of the other via me. After experiencing delight and pleasure and pride in being asked by K to write his catalogue essay, I panicked and said to Paula in the studio that I couldn't do it. She simply took out a sheet of paper and a pencil and told me to start talking, and thus began the first draft.[101]

Among Paula's pictures[102] here are the following:

Item: etchings, proofs and as editioned, including: *Ba-Ba Black Sheep.* [*Judging by gallery sales of the edition, this is the public's favourite among Paula's nursery rhymes, which were also reproduced for a Folio Society book.*]

Item: Perch. [*This is a large pastel from* The Crime of Father Amaro *series, shown at Dulwich Picture Gallery. It is a kind of portrait, even though most often when posing for Paula one is an actor playing a part. However, in this picture, my likeness is a primary datum unlike the ones where the likeness appears less important than the overall structure and environment and psychology, in short what Paula calls story. However, by definition very few people who look at* Perch – *it has left my wall from time to time, on loan to museums, and I have bequeathed it to the Fitzwilliam – know it is 'me', and so it works in the same way the other pictures do, just as a composer might write a piece for this or that friendly virtuoso but it is played by other people.]*

On the narrow stretch of wall between the Globe Wernickes and next to the window with the wine flask is one of Aldous Eveleigh's fine drawings of Pessoa, done to illustrate Zbigniew Kotowicz's book on the poet. The book was launched in a building next door to the artist's studio in Charing Cross Road, now demolished. Susannah York had to drop out at short notice and another friend John Shrapnel stepped in to replace her as reader of Pessoa's poem 'The Tobacconist', translated by Suzette Macedo. Suzette and her husband Helder were close friends of Sylvia Plath and Ted Hughes's. Ruth Fainlight and Suzette were involved in the worry about the children after Plath died. I find Frieda Hughes's devotion to her wrongly maligned dad deeply moving and her defence of his actions well argued given that she cannot be objective. More important than objectivity is truthfulness. Any light thrown by that remark on the work of an artist who works from life is another matter, and one that raises philosophical, spiritual and artistic questions I shall pursue elsewhere. Above the piano is my Fermin Rocker painting. This picture is an idealised and simplified image of the main streets at his local tube station, Tufnell Park, or rather the image forms the backdrop to his three figures, painted in the familiar restricted palette. He died in 2007 on the eve of his final exhibition, held at the Chambers Gallery, where Paula bought a small watercolour.

[from an occasional diary] January 1, 2005: it is time to get on the exercise bike and then drive to the studio. After inspecting Paula's work in progress, I will give Lila a lift to her place and then drive Paula home, where we will watch *Finding Neverland*, thanks to her son Nick, who as a BAFTA juror gets advance copies of new movies. Last week we watched Mike Leigh's powerful *Vera Drake*; one could not fail to think of Paula's etching suite on the subject of abortions. [*Fifteen years later:* Portrait of a Woman on Fire: *I am certain the director, Céline Sciamma, has studied Paula's comments on her work as a figurative painter.*] The phone rings: it is my niece Rebecca, who has to write an essay for her Wimbledon School of Art degree course on any artist excluded from Martin Kemp's canon of innovative artists. She would like to write about Paula, and I suggest she choose *After Hogarth*. I also suggest she visit the Degas exhibition at the National Gallery because Paula has been looking closely at the way he did his pastels. Paula invited her to the studio and we visited her graduation show. She has since switched to architecture.

Conclusion

If home is where the heart is
And my home is in New Orleans
Well, take me to that land of dreams

KEN COLYER, 'Goin' Home'

Wherever I have been, however warmly I have been received, I return to this flat with a sigh of relief that I am behind closed doors once more, alone with my toys and my rubbish and my mess. Home is where the heart is. This is my very own playpen, my very own Neverland, my very own land of dreams. We learn at the beginning of *David Copperfield* that Betsey Trotwood was 'forever in the land of dreams and shadows'. Forty years spent (saved) living in this flat sometimes feels like that.

I have been wondering if Matthew Arnold picked up the phrase 'land of dreams' from *David Copperfield*, published in 1850, a year before 'Dover Beach' appeared, but no, he did not read it until 1880. I also wondered if he and/or Dickens knew Blake's poem 'The Land of Dreams', written in 1803 or 4. At the suggestion of Deryn Rees-Jones, I consulted our mutual friend John Lucas, who told me it was not impossible that Carlyle had a copy of the poem courtesy of James Montgomery and showed it to his friend Dickens in time for the phrase to register and end up in his novel. But the poem was not published until 1866 in the Pickering Manuscript, too late for either Arnold or Dickens to quote from in their texts. In any case, perhaps I am pushing the connection a little too hard, since 'land of dreams' out of context could well be invented independently by three writers. John Lucas also reminded me of Ken Colyer's classic song 'Goin' Home', quoted as the epigraph to this conclusion, which John himself used to play on the cornet with his Nottingham quintet, the Burgundy Street Jazzmen.

The time has come to grow up, but I would prefer not to, in the phrase of one of my favourite fictional figures. Maybe I shall wait until I myself have become an old-timer, or at least until I have finished writing the books I want to write. I referred earlier to my deathbed fantasy. Provided it is not too late, I ought to have a shot at maturation before that day arrives, before I move to the place of no sun, 'north of the future' (Paul Celan), 'on the other side of mankind' (Celan again). The fact that I would prefer not to is not the point, and not the point with a vengeance, if not divine vengeance.

With those thoughts in mind, I shall now make a token attempt to clean the kitchen, tidy the flat and, generalising the activity, get my act together – before the dustmen in their white coats put me in a plastic bag, and crunch me up in their garbage cart. What a fate, to be reduced to negative essence in a Barnet Council (a pox on the majority party) out-sourced dustcart: 'The onward tendency of human things' (*The Mill on the Floss*) comes to mind.

What an example to set to loved ones. Meanwhile, with the easing of lockdown, Paula is drawing me again at home, and then, during the second lockdown, at the studio. This does both of us good. A bonus is that it takes my mind off the *balagan*… And so, as in one of my favourite paintings, the music of time goes round and round, an eternal present warding off the sorrows and the dreads, a magic circle, a sacred grove, a dance of hopeless esperance in a place of longing, whose only end is darkness. I see a troika waiting in the snow: Chekhov prepares to go to the station after visiting Tolstoy. The younger writer looks up to the stars, repeats joyously what the grand old man said to him: 'Your stories aren't bad, Chekhov, but your plays, your plays, they are even worse than Shakespeare's.' As for me, all proportions guarded, 'the classification of the constituents of a chaos, nothing less is here essayed': a sentence from *Moby Dick* my Venice friend Giacomo Donis, singular author of a singular book *The Empty Shield*, likes to quote.

Reverie on a winter evening: I step out of the black cab of my nephew, Nick Bell. I enter a Mayfair casino. The Lord of Hosts (and guests) is the croupier. *Les jeux sont faits. Rien ne va plus.* All night a discreet figure quietly noses around, indistinguishable from the clients. His job is to ensure that no one is cheating. Love may be careless, but the stakes are high. Koheleth the Preacher (Ecclesiastes), translated by Robert Alter: 'Through sloth the roof-beam sags, and through slack hands the house leaks.'

APPENDICES

Pereciana

1: Places lived in[103]

For Michael Sheringham

There is the enchantment of accuracy, which seems
more imperative than the personal
MARIANNE MOORE, letter to Wallace Stevens

Figures of the everyday
MICHAEL SHERINGHAM, *Everyday Life*

In December 2005, I embarked on some research for a project which did
not take off. My research notes 'languished' in a computer folder, until
this excellent opportunity arose to resuscitate one of the topics, an exercise
in what Georges Perec called 'endotic anthropology'. I wrote to – or, more
relevantly, received answers from – seventy-five persons (writers, painters,
etc,) in my address book, asking them three questions. The most
interesting question in terms of endotic anthropology was the third one
and that is the one I go into on this occasion.

i) Do you listen to music while working?
The answers ranged from more than one indignant 'never' to
several enthusiastic 'always'.
ii) Are the rooms in your present house/flat named differently
from when you were a child?
The answers revealed that only the lounge and the WC had

changed their names over the years.

iii) How many places have you lived in?

I circulated blind copy ('BCC') the following group email:

> How many places have you lived in? Please exclude holiday hotels, etc., unless you return or returned to the same one for many years. Please include college residences if you stayed there for at least one academic year.
>
> Please exclude any residences where you have lived for a very short time – use your judgement.
>
> Your reply can be one word – i.e. the number – or a list or even a more detailed inventory, as in mine below. How typical is my experience? We shall find out.

I then listed in the email the following residences but without the detailed locations:

Parental house 1942–1966: 41 Middleway, Hampstead Garden Suburb, London NW11 6SH) [*including break to countryside near High Wycombe during the war, but length of stay now unknowable: probably very short – and therefore ineligible – since I recall being told later that we returned to London quickly: it was 'too quiet' in the country.*]

Jewish students' hostel in France, 1961: Le Toit familial, 9 rue Guy Patin, 75010 Paris)

Three rooms in Cambridge while at Trinity College, 1961–1964: K7, New Court, Trinity; 25 Jesus Lane; and E4, Angel Court, Trinity

Flat in USA, 1966: Apartment 311, 5465 South Everett, Chicago, Illinois 60615)

Two bedsitting rooms in London, 1966–8: 2 Powis Square, Notting Hill, London W11 2AY; 26 Granville Park, Lewisham, London SE13 7EA

Flat in London, 1968–1974: 1 Primrose Gardens, London NW3 4UJ

House in London, 1974–1981: 23 Fitzwarren Gardens, London N19 3TR

Flat in London, 1981–

Excluding the wartime evacuation, my personal total is 11. The 75 replies I received averaged 17 and ranged from 7 to 37. A detailed analysis must await another occasion, if ever. Among the respondents, Julian Barnes numbered 11 residences, John Forrester 17, Ruth Rosengarten 18, Lisa Appignanesi 25, Marina Warner 25, Stephen Romer 14, Michèle Roberts 20, Deryn Rees-Jones 14, Gabriel Josipovici 19, Susan Saffer 18.

2: Arnold House School names 1951 and 1953

I have left it too late to dig deep in the Internet in order to see who has a digital imprint, although an essay on the future of these boys would be an interesting exercise in endotic anthropology. The school uniform entailed short trousers, grey shirt, long grey socks and red/green blazer. In those days, Arnold House was a feeder for various public schools, especially Westminster, and indeed still is.[104]

Photograph of Arnold House Juniors, July 1951
(Reading from left to right: XX = can't remember the name; ? = not sure)

> *Back Row:* Webber (?), Richard Scoular (?), XX, Myers, Elton, XX, Colin Rayne, Anthony Rudolf, David Assersohn, Bernard Mocatta (?), Stephen Hunt, XX

> *Second Row:* XX, Robin Morton-Gill, De Vere-Green, Robert MacLeod, XX, XX, XX, Mark Wilson, XX, XX, XX, Nigel Pollitzer, Edmonds

Third Row: Alistair MaCrae, Whitely (?), Stephen Potter, William Falk, XX, XX, Michael Hoare (?), XX, Robert Atkin, David Kleeman, Paul Raingold, XX

Front Row: Broderick, Whitcomb, Michael Pennington, James Loudon, Macaulay, Alan Lorenz, Colin MacLeod, Anthony Champion, Peter Scorer (?), Robin Hirsch

Future career known to me: Robert MacLeod (bookseller and co-proprietor of the Owl Bookshop), Nigel Pollitzer (playboy), Michael Pennington (actor), the late Colin MacLeod (scholar), Robin Hirsch (theatre). Anthony Champion died of polio and we all gave a small sum towards a wreath.

Photograph of Arnold House pupils, 1953
Second photo (two years later?)

Back row: XX, Whitcombe, Stephen Potter, Adler, XX, XX, XX, Quintin Livingstone

Second row: Peskin, Levy (?), Paul Raingold, XX, XX, Richard Elias, XX, Lass, Richard Scoular

*Third Row:*David Assersohn, XX, Webber, Sylvester, XX, XX, William Falk, XX, Anthony Rudolf

Front Row: Nigel Pollitzer, Mark Wilson, XX, XX, Lorenz, Colin Campbell Golding

(See Figures 22 and 23 on Page 58)

Further reading about particular episodes – and a few notes

[1] *The Arithmetic of Memory*, London, Bellew, 1999

[2] *Silent Conversations*, London and Calcutta, Seagull Books, 2013

[3] One of about 180 cards published over fifty years: many languages, many translations

[4] Included in *European Hours: Collected Poems*, Manchester, Carcanet, 2017. The title is taken from a phrase which might be from a catalogue essay by the painter (although he does not recall it and was perhaps quoting a third party), which I included in an earlier version of the poem: 'The true inflections of the masses in space…'

[5] *Silent Conversations* and a book in progress on being Paula's model, *In the Picture*

[6] I discussed my unscientific concept in a memorial note on Michael O'Brien in *PNReview* 238, 2017, and on the cover of Anne Beresford's pamphlet, *14 Poems*, Nottingham, Shoestring Press, 2019

[7] *The Same River Twice*, 1976, *Zigzag*, 2010, and *European Hour*s

[8] *After the Dream*, St Louis, Cauldron Press, 1979

[9] Yves Bonnefoy: I have published my translations of Bonnefoy at Cape Editions, Delos Press, MPT Books and Menard Press and in many journals since 1966. Carcanet published an anthology *Yves Bonnefoy: Poems*, which I co-edited with John Naughton and Stephen Romer (2017) and which included many of my translations of the earlier poems. A second anthology, *Yves Bonnefoy: Prose*, co-edited ditto (and with one essay translated by me), was published in 2020. Claude Vigée: *Flow Tide; Selected Poems*, London: Kings College/ Menard, 1991, and *Songs of Absence*, London/Paris, Menard/Temporel, 2007. Edmond Jabès, *A Share of Ink*, London, Menard, 1979. Michel Deguy: I have translated enough poems – published in journals and unpublished – for a book. This is one of several books that I do not know if I have the time and energy to publish. Michel Deguy – half

a generation younger than his friends and mine, Bonnefoy and Vigée, and a generation younger than Jabès – is a philosopher/poet of great distinction and influence, a sovereign intelligence. Evgeny Vinokurov. *The War is Over*, Carcanet, 1976. Alexander Tvardovsky, *Tyorkin and the Stovemakers*, Carcanet, 1974. Ifigenija Simonovic, *Striking Root*, Menard, 1997. Miriam Neiger-Fleischmann, *Death of the King and Other Poems*, Shoestring Press, 2017

[10] Much of my book *Silent Conversations* deals with the themes in this paragraph

[11] See *Silent Conversations*

[12] See *Menard Press 1969–2009: Keepsake Catalogue*, London, Menard Press, 2010

[13] See *European Hours*

[14] *Zigzag* contains a section about my grandfather. I hope to expand it one day

[15] See *The Arithmetic of Memory*

[16] *Voices within the Ark*, New York, Avon Books, 1980

[17] *After the Dream*

[18] For more on Edward Hopper, see *Silent Conversations*.

[19] See the *Keepsake Catalogue* on Menard's printers, etc.

[20] I was very pleased that Ilan Kelman of University College London placed the entire pamphlet series online: www.ilankelman.org/menard.html

[21] For Cathie Pilkington and much else about Paula and other artists: see one day *In the Picture*. Specific Pilkington websites: cathiepilkington.com and redbreasteditions.com

[22] *Gillette* or *The Unknown Masterpiece*, London, Menard Press, 1988, reprinted 1999

[23] On Musa, you can find my short obituary on the website of the Royal Society of Literature and my long celebration in *Fortnightly Review* online

[24] See my Chicago poem in *European Hours*

[25] See *European Hours*

[26] *A Vanished Hand*, Bristol, Shearsman Books, 2013

[27] *The Death of Hektor* (1982), *Advent* (1986) and Mallarmé (1990)

[28] For more on Davie, see *Silent Conversations*

[29] The poem is collected in *European Hours*

[30] For more on Baldwin, see *Silent Conversations*

[31] See *The War is Over*

[32] See *In the Picture*

[33] Earlier book: *The Arithmetic of Memory*, see above

[34] For more on Pinter, see *A Vanished Hand*

[35] See the final paragraph of *Silent Conversations*. The campfire mentioned

there was in North Carolina after the Palatine Illinois group dispersed to various parts of the country as part of the Quaker programme. We were taken to meet Professor J. B. Rhine – at Duke University in Durham NC – the pioneering parapsychologist. Some would say he was on the cusp of science and metaphysics

36 For more on Johnny Leach, see *A Vanished Hand*, as above

37 I have a poem on her in *European Hours*

38 *The Arithmetic of Memory* (see above) and *Zigzag* (ditto)

39 *The Arithmetic of Memory*

40 See poem 'For All We Know' in *European Hours*

41 I have checked this as best I can and find that I did not write or, at any rate, publish a poem about the Route 66 episode but a line about the motel bed vibrating for a quarter appears in a different context in a poem 'Late Night' written some years later. See *European Hours*

42 *The Same River Twice*

43 See *Silent Conversations* for more on the Objectivists

44 See *Keepsake Catalogue* as above, note 12

45 See *Silent Conversations* for more on the Kaufmans as well Louis's memoir, accompanied by a CD: *A Fiddler's Tale: How Hollywood and Vivaldi Discovered Me*

46 See *Keepsake Catalogue*

47 See *The Arithmetic of Memory*

48 See *Voices within the Ark* as above, note 16

49 In unpublished volume of stories: *The Mermaid from the Azores*

50 See *The Arithmetic of Memory*

51 For Eça, in *In the Picture*. Jake Auerbach has made an excellent film about Celia, following his films about Freud, Auerbach, Paula and others

52 ibid.

53 For more on Hopper and Reznikoff, see *Silent Conversations*

54 This poem and a note on it can be found in *European Hours*

55 See Bosley's *The Wedding-Guest: Selected Poems*, which I co-edited with Owen Lowery

56 *Modern Poetry in Translation*, Autumn 1971

57 Neiger-Fleischmann: *Death of the King*, see note 9

58 See *In the Picture*

59 See *In the Picture* and the title poem in *European Hours*

60 See note 22

61 From a poem in *European Hours*

62 More on Lorca's *duende* in *Silent Conversations*

63 See *The Arithmetic of Memory*

64 New Year cards: see *Keepsake Catalogue*
65 See note 20 above: Menard's pamphlet series
66 *Jerzyk*, Bristol, Shearsman, 2017
67 From *Striking Root*, Menard, 1997
68 More on the casino in *In the Picture*
69 *Sheriff and Outlaws in the Global Village*. See note 20
70 See *In the Picture*
71 There is a long essay on Robert Ford in *Silent Conversations*
72 New Year Cards as in note 64
73 *Broccoli*, Culford Press, 1989
74 *Mandorla*, Birmingham: Delos Press, 1999
75 *Mandorla*, Ki Press, 2020
76 See note 49
77 See *Keepsake Catalogue*
78 Balzac: see note 22 above
79 For more, see the forthcoming *In the Picture*
80 ibid.
81 My prose/verse sequence Kinderszenen is published in full in *Zigzag*
82 See *In the Picture*
83 ibid.
84 See *Keepsake Catalogue*
85 For more on this, see *In the Picture*
86 See *In the Picture*
87 For more on family, see *The Arithmetic of Memory*
88 See *Keepsake Catalogue*
89 ibid.
90 See *The Arithmetic of Memory* for more on Hilary Sefton
91 Later reprinted in my book *Zigzag*
92 I write about our annual holidays in the title poem of *European Hours*
93 See *In the Picture*
94 Later reprinted in *European Hours*
95 See *Keepsake Catalogue* and note 20 re online reprint of the pamphlets
96 See my grandfather text in *Zigzag* where there is also material on Zygfryd
    Rudolf mentioned a few paragraphs earlier in the present work
97 I discuss Paula's studio and being her model at length in *In the Picture*
98 See note 66
99 In *The Arithmetic of Memory* (note 1 above)
100 I write more on Portuguese tiles in *In the Picture*
101 R.B. Kitaj in the Aura of Cezanne, London, National Gallery, 2001
102 All discussed in *In the Picture*

103 *Pereciana* was first published in a volume of essays, prose and poetry by friends and colleagues of Professor Michael Sheringham, *The Made and the Found*, Oxford, Legenda, 2018. The book was originally intended to mark his retirement (2015) from teaching but he died in 2016; sadly and appropriately, the book ended up being dedicated to his memory. His own books taught me a lot, in particular *Everyday Life: Theories and Practices from Surrealism to the Present*. Among our many common interests was the work of Yves Bonnefoy, whom we were both privileged to count as a friend

104 For more on Arnold House, see *The Arithmetic of Memory* (note 1 above)

Lightning Source UK Ltd.
Milton Keynes UK
UKHW041224270421
382710UK00001B/6

9 781848 617698